rosa's
new mexican table

rosa's new mexican table

ROBERTO SANTIBAÑEZ WITH CHRISTOPHER STYLER

PHOTOGRAPHS BY CHRISTOPHER HIRSHEIMER

ARTISAN ■ NEW YORK

Published by Artisan
A Division of Workman Publishing Company, Inc.
225 Varick Street
New York, NY 10014-4381
www.artisanbooks.com

Library of Congress Cataloging-in-Publication Data
Santibañez, Roberto.
Rosa's new Mexican table/Roberto Santibañez.
p. cm.
ISBN-13: 978-1-57965-324-8
ISBN-10: 1-57965-324-3
1. Cookery, Mexican. 2. Rosa Mexicano (Restaurant)I. Title

TX716.M4S27 2007
641.5972—dc22   2006046916

Design by Jan Derevjanik
Photography styling by Melissa Hamilton

Printed in Singapore
First printing, April 2007

10 9 8 7 6 5 4 3 2 1

CONTENTS

INTRODUCTION · VII

1 INGREDIENTS, EQUIPMENT, AND TECHNIQUES · 1

2 TO START · 25

3 TACOS · 87

4 ENCHILADAS · 109

5 QUESADILLAS AND TORTAS · 129

6 ENSALADAS · 141

7 MAIN COURSES · 161

8 ON THE SIDE · 213

9 DESSERTS · 237

SOURCES · 268

ACKNOWLEDGMENTS · 269

INDEX · 270

INTRODUCTION

If you enjoy Mexican food in restaurants but are reluctant to cook it at home, this book is for you. The recipes are designed for people with busy lives and precious little time for kitchen duty, especially during the week. Many of the dishes can be executed in thirty to sixty minutes—or less, if you have on hand a few Mexican staples like zesty homemade salsas that you put together in minutes, as well as condiments and spices. And many can be made ahead and are in fact *better* made ahead. Once you get into the rhythm of Mexican cooking, you may find yourself showing off your newfound skills by preparing some of the more elaborate recipes for dinner parties that would surely impress even the most jaded gastronome.

In the United States, the common perception of Mexican cooking is that it calls for a lot of heavy lifting—labor-intensive preparations, complicated techniques, and all kinds of exotic ingredients. As you will see in this book, that is hardly the case. This style of cooking is no more work than other more familiar cuisines. As for kitchen skills, you don't have to be a knife-twirling Iron Chef to pull it off. Often the blades of your blender will do the work for you. There may be a few new ingredients and techniques for you to learn about, but we give you alternatives and shortcuts.

It goes without saying that high-quality ingredients make the difference between a good dish and great dish. Ten years ago, it was difficult to find a variety of chile peppers and vegetables like jicama. Today, many Mexican ingredients can be found in American supermarkets as well as in Latin American and Mexican groceries. And if you can't locate the ingredients in stores, online sources like mexgrocer.com, among others, carry virtually everything. (See Ingredients, Equipment, and Techniques, pages 2–23, and Sources, pages 268–69.)

There is one thing you can count on in a Mexican kitchen—just about everything is laced with chiles, but the dishes are not always necessarily hot. On pages 2–11, you'll find a brief primer. Aside from contributing heat, different chiles add distinct and pronounced flavors to dishes—smoky, sweet, even floral. Before long, you will understand how important it is to add chiles to a dish incrementally, not all at once. Individuals have different tolerances to hot and spicy—and a bonfire is easier to build than extinguish.

You might be surprised to discover that Mexican food is exceptionally healthy. The cuisine uses little butter, very little cream, and no flour-based sauces; almost all sauces are based on thickened vegetables purees. The dried beans served with almost every meal are excellent sources of fiber and minerals. (I say "almost" because *frijoles negros* are traditionally cooked in lard. If that is a scary prospect, use vegetable oil, as we do at Rosa Mexicano.)

Mexican cooking is as varied as the regions of the country: the seafood of Veracruz, the moles and pipianes of the central high plains, the spice mixtures of the Yucatán Peninsula, and the flour tortillas of the north reflect each region's specialized cooking. When the original Rosa Mexicano opened in New York City in 1984, it was nothing short of revolutionary. At the time, the Mexican restaurants in the city were characterized by mountains of shredded iceberg lettuce, viscous sauces, indigestible fried tacos, and more starch than a Chinese laundry. Rosa Mexicano broke the mold by serving lighter, inventive yet authentic regional fare. Among the early offerings were sliced duck with pumpkin seed sauce, grilled red snapper with warm cilantro vinaigrette, dishes made with cuitlacoche (see page 15), soft tacos filled with pulled pork, and, for dessert, sweet pink-fleshed cactus pears. As the company's culinary director, I strive to preserve the soul of Rosa while helping the restaurants evolve in a manner that is both exciting to our guests and respectful of Mexico's culinary heritage.

My road to Rosa Mexicano involved many exciting detours. The journey began in my hometown of Mexico City, where I was inspired by both my mother and grandmother (doesn't every chef say that?). My grandmother, in particular, was a superb and well-traveled cook who held informal cooking classes in our home incorporating techniques and seasonings from around the world. From my earliest years, there was never a second thought about my career path. At nineteen, I went off to Paris and the Cordon Bleu, where I learned classical French techniques and a great respect for European foods of all kinds.

While at school, I was fortunate enough to secure apprenticeships at several first-rate Paris restaurants, including the celebrated La Bourgogne, followed by study at the famed pâtisserie Lenôtre, and finally, two cooking stints in England. Having sampled the best of European cuisine, I started to look at Mexican food through a more global prism upon returning home. I began researching every aspect of Mexican cuisine and attempted to raise the bar in both the sophistication and presentation of my cooking. Within several months, I was hired as chef of El Olivo, one of the better restaurants in downtown Mexico City. My dream of owning my own restaurant was realized in 1990 when I opened La Circunstancia. Once diners understood what I was doing, they took to it enthusiastically, and the restaurant was a great success. It was at La Circunstancia that I met Josefina Howard, one of Rosa Mexicano's founders.

Next stop was the United States—specifically, Austin, Texas. I took over the kitchen of a restaurant called Fonda San Miguel and continued my experimentation with Mexican ingredients. The cooking of Fonda San Miguel garnered much praise.

Shortly after leaving Fonda San Miguel, I met one of the principals of the growing restaurant community called Rosa Mexicano. He described their dream of developing Rosa nationwide. I was thrilled to join as culinary director, to oversee an ever expanding family of restaurants. So that is where I am today. This book is a reflection of what we have accomplished so far. I often say that the food at Rosa Mexicano, and in this book, is authentic but not orthodox. As you will see, from time to time we have a little fun with a recipe, by imparting a new flavor fillip, or playing around to make it look really great on the plate. And, for professional and home cooks alike, isn't fun the whole point of cooking?

LOS INDISPENSABLES

Throughout this book you will find recipes that are titled "Uno de los Indispensables." Most are sparkling and versatile condiments, pickles, and salsas that you can assemble well in advance and store for anywhere from several days to a week or more. While the majority are savory, I've also included some sweets that are tasty and versatile. As elementary as they are, they pack a big punch of bold and festive flavors. I recommend that you become familiar with at least some of these "indispensables" and that you always have one available, since they are cornerstones of the Mexican table. If you have them on hand, you can use them to energize any simple home-cooked meal. For example, blow your friends away at a Sunday barbecue by simply adding a couple of easy-to-make salsas from the list below to your menu.

Green Salsa	47	Fresh Corn Tortillas	92
Quick Pickled Poblano Strips	43	Pickled Red Onions	101
Pico de Gallo	57	Adobo-Marinated Chicken	133
Chicken Broth	66	Tomatillo and Chile de Arbol Salsa	149
Tortilla Chips	76	Salsa Mexicana	183
Cooked Green Salsa	114	Rajas con Crema	195
Spicy Habanero Escabeche	117	Cinnamon Custard Sauce	263
Ranchera Sauce	122	Mexican Caramel Sauce	266
Rosa's Pickled Jalapeños	125		

RIGHT: Epazote

1
INGREDIENTS, EQUIPMENT, AND TECHNIQUES

CHILES

They are found in all shapes, sizes, and colors, from dull green to bright red, yellow, or orange when fresh and from near black or tan to vivid red or chocolate brown when dried. What follows are brief descriptions of the chiles used in the recipes in this book and how to prepare them. If you want to learn more about all kinds of chiles—and there is a lot to know—there are many good sources out there. My favorites include Jean Anderson's *Red Hot Peppers* (Macmillan, 1993) and any (or all!) of Diana Kennedy's books, which include *My Mexico* (Potter, 1998), *From My Mexican Kitchen: Techniques and Ingredients* (Potter, 2003), and a compilation, *The Essential Cuisines of Mexico* (Potter, 2000).

dried chiles

Buying dried chiles is like buying dried fruit. Although they have been dried, there should be some life left in them. Dried chiles should be healthy looking, smell wonderful, and, except for some varieties, as noted below, have a somewhat pliable texture.

to toast dried chiles

Dried chiles are always toasted for the recipes in this book. Toasting does two important things: it starts the process of breaking down the skin, which is completed with soaking, blending, and cooking, and it adds different layers of flavor, depending on to what degree the chiles have been toasted. (That's why we tell you how to toast the chiles in each recipe.)

Regardless of the type of chile, the process is similar. First, it is very important to wipe the chiles clean with a damp towel. This removes any dust they may have picked up during drying and storage. Second, pull the stems off (unless the dried chiles will be stuffed) and cut a slit down the length of each chile. Open up the chile and scrape and tap all the seeds out. (Chiles de árbol and other small chiles are the exception: always leave their seeds inside when toasting.) Save the seeds, if you like, in an airtight container to use as a seasoning. (See notes on pure chile powders on page 7 and Rack of Lamb with Pistachio, page 210.) Once they are cleaned, there are three methods I suggest for toasting chiles, described on the next page.

When a recipe in this book calls for *lightly toasted chiles,* toast them until they soften a little, just begin to change color without browning, and blister in a couple of spots.

When a recipe calls for *well-toasted chiles,* toast them until they blister, take on some color outside, and turn a tobacco color inside. Once dried chiles heat up, this can happen very quickly, so be careful. Overroasted chiles will make any dish they end up in taste bitter.

DRY SKILLET/COMAL METHOD ▪ Heat a dry skillet or comal (see page 17) over low heat. Lay the chiles in the skillet and, using tongs, press the chiles lightly and turn them often until they are toasted to the desired doneness, about 30 to 45 seconds per side.

BROILER METHOD ▪ Position a rack about 8 inches from the broiler and preheat the broiler, to low, if possible. Arrange the chiles in a single layer on the broiler pan or a baking sheet and broil, turning once, until toasted on both sides to the desired level. This can take as little as 15 seconds for lightly toasted large chiles or as long as 30 seconds for well-toasted chiles de árbol.

TOASTER OVEN METHOD ▪ Toasting one or a few chiles works well in a toaster oven. Preheat the oven to 350°F. Place the chiles on the broiler pan and toast, turning them once, to the desired doneness.

to soak toasted dried chiles

Depending on what they will be used for, toasted dried chiles should be soaked in either hot or cold water. Unless a recipe states otherwise, soak chiles in cold water. Although a lot of cooks in Mexico use hot water for all chiles, I think that using very hot water gives the chiles a slightly "boiled" flavor, which I don't particularly like. There are exceptions, however—mostly in recipes for stuffed ancho chiles in which the chiles are cooked alone or in a sauce. Regardless of the type or number of toasted chiles you are soaking, or the temperature of the water, put the chiles in a container large enough to hold them comfortably but snugly and pour in enough water to cover them completely. If necessary, weight them lightly (an overturned saucer works well) to keep them completely submerged. Let them soak until they are completely softened but not mushy or falling apart. The time will vary depending on the chiles and the temperature of the water, but generally speaking, chiles will be soaked properly in anywhere from 20 minutes to an hour or two. As soon as they are softened, drain them and discard the liquid. There are a lot of cooks who use the soaking liquid. I don't, since I find that it imparts a funky flavor and, in some preparations, it interferes with the clean flavor of sauces.

ancho

Ancho chiles (pictured on page 4) are a variety of poblano chile that have been ripened to red and then dried. *Ancho* means "wide," a reference to the chile's broad shoulders that taper down to a point, giving it a triangular shape. The perfect ancho is pliable, a deep brownish red color, and somewhat shiny, with

wrinkled skin. Anchos have an aroma and flavor that reminds me of dried fruit—which is, of course, what they are. They are one of the milder chiles, but every once in a while, you can get some with a real kick.

ANCHO CHILE PASTE ▪ Ancho chile paste is nice to have on hand to add color and chile flavor to soups, stews, and marinades without using much heat. Wipe, clean, and lightly toast 2 large ancho chiles using one of the methods on page 2. Soak them in cold water until completely softened and drain them well; discard the liquid. Put the chiles in a blender jar and blend to a thick puree, adding water a tablespoon at a time (approximately ¼ cup) to help the blades of the blender turn easily. The idea is to use as little water as necessary to yield a very thick puree. Scrape into a small container with a tight-fitting lid and store in the refrigerator for up to 1 week. The paste can also be frozen in small containers.

RECONSTITUTING ANCHO CHILES FOR STUFFING

Stuffed anchos can be filled with salady fillings and served at room temperature, as we do with the Ancho Chiles Stuffed with Tuna and Potato Salad on page 154. Or they can be stuffed with meat or seafood and served hot, as we do with the Ancho Chiles Stuffed with Beef Tenderloin, Shiitakes, and Cremini on page 207. Regardless of whether you fill ancho chiles with one of our stuffings or create one of your own, soaking them in this sweet-sour mixture gives them a head start on flavor. For stuffed anchos, choose the largest, most pliable chiles you can find. They will be easier to stuff and will hold their shape better after stuffing.

8 pliable, brick-red, large
   (about 6 inches long) ancho chiles
⅔ cup cider vinegar
¼ pound piloncillo (see page 16) or
   3 tablespoons dark brown sugar plus
   2 tablespoons molasses

A 2-inch piece of Mexican cinnamon
   stick
½ teaspoon salt

Cut a slit down each ancho from the "shoulder" of the chile to the tip. Carefully remove as many of the seeds and as much of the core as you can without tearing the chile or pulling out the stem.

   Combine 4 cups water, the vinegar, piloncillo, cinnamon, and salt in a nonaluminum saucepan and bring to a simmer, stirring until the piloncillo is dissolved. Add the chiles and remove the pan from the heat. Weight the chiles with a plate to keep them submerged, and soak until they are very soft, about 1 hour.

   Drain the chiles thoroughly and blot them dry with paper towels. They are now ready to fill.

CLOCKWISE FROM TOP: Chiles de árbol, chipotle, guajillo, pasilla, pasilla de Oaxaca, ancho, and cascabel

cascabel

The word *cascabel* means "rattle," as in baby's rattle, and the name refers to both the round shape of the chile and the fact that the seeds rattle around when the chile is shaken. Cascabels (pictured on page 4) have smooth, glossy, deep red skin and measure about an inch across or slightly more. They are quite spicy. Although cascabels should be cleaned and toasted like most other dried chiles (see page 2), if you are using just one or two for a salsa or in an adobo, they don't need to be seeded or soaked; in large amounts, they do need to be seeded and soaked.

ADOBOS

The term *adobo* embraces generally two concepts: a pastelike marinade made with dry chiles, garlic, and spices, and a thinner sauce made with the same ingredients, in which meats and poultry are stewed.

Whichever adobo you are making, they all start the same way. Dry chiles—ancho, mulato, pasilla, and guajillo most commonly—are wiped clean, seeded, deveined, then toasted and soaked. When the chiles are soft, they are blended to a fine puree with garlic and spices. The spice mixture as well as the choice of dry chile will depend on the region or family preferences, and sometimes a little vinegar is added to brighten up the flavor of the dry chiles. This scented paste is now used as a rub to marinate chicken, duck, or quail as well as pounded pork, beef, or any other meat. The meat is grilled or just panfried to form part of any given meal (see Adobo-Marinated Chicken, page 133, or Grilled Chile-Marinated Skirt Steak, page 94).

If you are planning to make an "adobo stew," or the thinner sauce, the meat of your choice is panfried—in a deep saucepan, where it will fit comfortably—until golden brown with a little oil. The chile paste, or adobo, is then added along with some water or stock to create a braising liquid in which the meat or poultry is left to slowly cook until tender. The sauce should always have a loose consistency, similar to that of a thin gravy. Maintain the consistency through the cooking process by adding water or stock as needed.

chiles de árbol

Many chiles, such as anchos, are known by one name when fresh and another when dried, but chiles de árbol (pictured on page 4) are known by the same name whether fresh or dried. When fresh, they can be green or ripened to red. Dried chiles de árbol are slim (no more than ½ inch wide), pointy, and long (about 2 to 3 inches), with brick-red, smooth, shiny skin. They are one of the spiciest dried chiles we use—the rule of thumb that "the smaller the variety of chile, the spicier it is," applies to chiles de árbol. Chiles de árbol are generally left whole (seeds intact) for toasting, and they are always well toasted. The stems are discarded after toasting, but the seeds are always used. The seeds take on a rich nutty flavor during toasting.

chipotle

Chipotles (pictured on page 4) are jalapeños that are left on the vine until ripened and then dried and smoked. In addition to intense heat, they add a wonderful smoky flavor to many dishes, as in the short rib sauce on page 201. There are several varieties. Chipotles mecos, which are larger than most other types, have a brown-beige exterior and a very red interior. Chipotles moras, or simply moras, are smaller and are burgundy red. Moras are the type most often found canned in adobo. Regardless of variety, chipotles are cleaned, toasted, and soaked before using. Chipotles en adobo have been cooked in an adobo sauce (see page 6). While they can be prepared at home, most often—even in Mexico—they are bought in cans. The brands I recommend are La Costeña, San Miguel, and Herdez. In Mexico, chipotles en adobo are eaten as is from the can, either whole or cut into pieces, in a torta (sandwich) or taco. Because you may prefer not to bite into a chipotle with its intense heat, you can turn the chiles into a puree (see below) and use the puree to season dishes.

CHIPOTLE ADOBO PUREE ▪ Scrape the contents of a can of chipotles en adobo into a blender and blend at low speed until smooth. Store in a small glass jar in the refrigerator for up to 2 months.

guajillo

Called mirasol when fresh, guajillos (pictured on page 4) are thin-fleshed but thick-skinned chiles with an elongated triangular shape; they run from 6 to 7 inches long. They have smoother skin and a less fruity aroma than anchos, but more heat and a unique earthy flavor. They add flavor and beautiful color to adobos and stewing sauces, like the Lamb Enchiladas with Tomatillo-Pasilla Sauce (page 123) or Guajillo Chile and Pineapple Adobo (page 191). For adobos and sauces, they are lightly toasted; for moles, they are usually well toasted. For certain Oaxacan moles, they may even be toasted until blackened.

mulato

Mulatos are another variety of poblano, one that ripens to purple, so they are close to black when dried. They have a shape similar to an ancho but are fleshier—almost like a raisin or a prune in texture—and more fruity. Generally, mulatos are mild in heat. It can be difficult to find mulatos with all the right characteristics—color, size, fruitiness, and fleshiness—so if you find a good source, stick with it! Mulatos are most often used in moles and adobos; they can be toasted to various degrees, depending on the use.

pasilla (pasilla negro, chile negro, or pasilla de Mexico)

Medium-high on the heat index, pasillas (pictured on page 4) are hotter than anchos or mulatos but not as hot as chipotles or chiles de árbol. When fresh, they are known as chilacas and are similar in fleshiness and color to poblanos, but they are longer—up to 7 or 8 inches—and very thin. Dried, they are slightly wrinkly with a deep black, shiny skin. Pasillas are used in several of the darker moles and many salsas, including a well-known one from central Mexico called *salsa borracha* (drunken salsa) that is made with pasillas, garlic, a touch of cumin, and pulque.

SAVING CHILE SEEDS

If you find yourself toasting dried chiles often for use in these or other recipes, it is a good idea to save the seeds. When you accumulate ¼ cup or more (which will probably happen faster than you might think), toast them in a small pan over low heat and grind them to a powder in a spice mill. The powder can be used in the same way as any chile powder, but in addition to heat, it will add a pleasant nutty flavor. (See the rub used for the Rack of Lamb with Pistachio on page 210.)

pasilla de Oaxaca

Completely different from the pasilla negro, pasillas de Oaxaca (pictured on page 4) are also known as chiles mixes because of their association with the Mixe, an indigenous people from Oaxaca. Like chipotles, they are smoked after drying and lend both heat and a mysterious smoky flavor to any dish they season. They are quite hot. They have wide shoulders and taper to a point. Their wrinkly skin can range from deep red to near black even in the same chile.

fresh chiles

Much of the heat of fresh (and dried) chile peppers is found not in the seeds, but mainly in the ribs and core inside the pepper. When a recipe calls for "chopped fresh chiles," that means everything but the stem. You can play with the heat in the recipes by removing some or all of the seeds, cores, and/or ribs from the chiles before chopping them. Chiles of the same variety, even those that share the same bin in the produce department, can vary greatly in heat, as hotness depends on many factors: how much rain and sun the plant received, where the individual chile was on the plant, and more. One way to determine the heat in a chile without running the risk of burning your tongue is to cut off a piece of the chile and cautiously take a sniff. If you get a good jolt, you've got a fairly hot pepper. A milder jolt means a milder pepper.

For information on roasting fresh chiles (and bell peppers), see page 21.

habanero

Known as the hottest chile in the world, the habanero is a small chile that is shaped liked a delicate Japanese lantern but is anything but delicate in heat. One habanero with seeds and ribs intact can raise the fire level of a pot of soup or stew to three alarms. Habanero chiles range in color from pale green to orangy yellow, sometimes all in the same chile. They are very similar to Scotch bonnet chiles, which can be substituted for them (and vice versa).

DISPOSABLE GLOVES

A package of disposable latex gloves is a wise investment if you work at all frequently with fresh or dried chiles. The oils from the chiles penetrate the skin and stay with you for quite a while: several hours after you have chopped or seeded even a single chile, rubbing your eyes can be a painful experience. Despite popular belief, removing the sting of chiles by washing your hands with milk or with lemon and salt doesn't necessarily work. Nor does plain soap and water. Latex gloves, which keep the oils from penetrating the skin in the first place, are the only sure bet.

jalapeño

One of the most commonly used chiles in the United States, jalapeños can now be found fresh in almost any market. Most often they are green, but they can sometimes be found ripened to red. Maybe one of the reasons for its popularity is that the jalapeño is so easy to deal with—if you are among those who like to clean your chiles of seeds and ribs to reduce their heat, that is very simply done. Their flavor benefits from roasting (see page 21) or pickling (see Rosa's Pickled Jalapeños, page 125).

poblano

Poblanos are milder than other green chiles, such as serranos or jalapeños, so you can eat a lot more of them. Still, it is important to remember that they (like any green fresh chiles) are essentially unripe fruit and, like a green banana or unripe apple, can be a little difficult to digest. For that reason, poblanos are rarely eaten raw. Most often, they are charred to blacken the skin, which is then rubbed off and to soften the chile, as for stuffed poblanos and *rajas* (see page 43).

TO PREPARE ROASTED POBLANOS FOR STUFFING ▪ After roasting and peeling the chiles, make an incision down one side of each chile, and gently reach inside to scrape away the seeds from the core with your fingers and pinch and pull out the ribs. Be careful not to tear the chile.

serrano

Smooth and shiny, with medium to dark green skin, serranos are slimmer than jalapeños and a lot spicier than most jalapeños. But, as with any fresh chile, their spiciness can vary greatly. Serranos can be finely chopped and added raw to salsas or be cooked in dishes like soups or stews. If using them in quantity, it is a good idea to roast and peel them (see pags 21–22).

CHILE HEAT

In Mexican cooking, we do not generally remove the seeds and veins from fresh, small hot peppers such as serranos, jalapeños, and habaneros—this is where the serious heat and much of the flavor come from. However, I most often remove seeds and cores from dried chiles, with chiles de árbol as the exception. (See Saving Chile Seeds, page 8.) You may or may not want to do so, depending on your tolerance of heat. Fresh or dried, I suggest that you add chiles incrementally, tasting as you go along.

LEFT: Poblanos

OTHER INGREDIENTS

THE FOLLOWING INGREDIENTS CAN BE FOUND IN WELL-stocked markets that specialize in the foods of Mexico and Latin America, and in some supermarkets, but we also give Internet sources here.

achiote paste

Achiote is the Mexican name for the seeds of the tropical annatto tree. The seeds lend a pleasantly mild nutty flavor to foods, as well as a brilliant deep yellow to red color. (Some cheddars and other cheeses get their yellow color from annatto.) Achiote paste, made from the ground seeds, contains other seasonings, most often oregano, cumin, cloves, allspice, black pepper, and garlic. (The paste features in the Mayan cooking of the Yucatán, as well as in various Caribbean cuisines. It is integral to Slow-Cooked Achiote-Marinated Pork (page 102) and lends flavor and color to rice with Achiote (page 220), as well as many other dishes. Today many Latin cooks use prepared achiote paste; we recommend El Yucateco brand achiote paste, which is available in 3.5-ounce packages from www.mexgrocer.com.

avocado leaves

Avocado leaves are pale green in color with a pointed oval shape. Their flavor and aroma are delicate, which is why they are usually added toward the end of cooking. (In some of these recipes, I use a little ground anise seed, which is more readily available, to approximate the flavor of avocado leaves.) When lightly toasted, the leaves have a pleasant, anise-y smell. To toast avocado leaves, warm a skillet or comal over medium-low heat. Add the leaves and toast, turning once or twice, just until they change color and are fragrant; this shouldn't take more than 15 to 30 seconds. Before you raid your neighbor's avocado tree, note that not all avocado trees bear fruit that's suitable for cooking. Your best bet is to buy them dried from a Latin market. You can order dried avocado leaves at www.gourmetsleuth.com.

banana leaves

Banana leaves are enormous, with a shiny dark green side and a matte lighter green underside. They are usually sold frozen, folded into neat squares and wrapped in plastic, but you can find them fresh. Banana leaves are used to wrap tamales and to line pits for barbecuing whole pigs, as in the traditional *cochinita pibil;* see our version (which requires no digging) on page 102. Other uses include lining baking dishes and helping keep food from drying out during cooking while imparting a pleasant flavor. Frozen banana leaves are available from www.gourmetsleuth.com.

cheese

MANCHEGO · In Mexico, Manchego cheese is a mild melting cheese—quite different from the sharper and saltier Spanish Manchego. But I happen to love the Spanish Manchego, and we use it in dishes like Rosa Mexicano's Corn Pudding (page 226) and the Serrano Ham and Cheese Quesadilla (page 131). Spanish Manchego is a firm sheep's-milk cheese that is good for grating or cutting into small pieces to snack on or to add to dishes like the corn pudding. Its rind has a distinctive herringbone pattern. Its ivory/off-white interior is mildly assertive and nutty in flavor. Both the color and flavor deepen with aging. Manchego can be found in cheese shops and some supermarkets or ordered online at www.igourmet.com.

QUESO CHIHUAHUA · Queso Chihuahua is a semi-soft, mild cheese that melts and browns well. It is often used to top casseroles. If you cannot find Chihuahua cheese in a Latin grocery or cheese store, substitute mild Monterey Jack or Muenster.

QUESO FRESCO · Queso fresco ("fresh cheese") is a soft-textured, moist cheese with a mild flavor. It is crumbled over soups, salads, tacos, and bean dishes. It has become quite easy to find, even in non-Latin supermarkets, or you can order it at www.cheesesupply.com.

QUESO OAXACA · Queso Oaxaca is a cross between good-quality mozzarella and string cheese. It has a mild bite and melts very well. A slice of queso Oaxaca browned on both sides in a small skillet, then baked in Ranchera Sauce (page 122), makes a simple but delicious lunch, especially served with a salad. You can order it at www.igourmet.com. Also see page 231.

dried corn husks

Most commonly used for tamales, corn husks can be used to wrap all types of food during cooking to keep moisture in and impart a mild grassy flavor. The best corn husks are large and evenly light beige without spots or streaks. Each husk has a wide, straight edge and a shorter, tapered side; this flared shape comes in handy when wrapping food of just about any shape or consistency. (See Trout with Wild Mushrooms Cooked in Foil on page 177 and Brownie Tamales on page 248.)

Corn husks must be soaked before using. Put the husks in a large bowl and pour in enough warm water to cover them completely. Weight with a plate to keep all the husks submerged, and soak until pliable, 30 minutes to an hour. Drain thoroughly and pat dry—or not—before using, depending on the recipe. Corn husks are available in many Latin markets and some gourmet supermarkets, as well as online at www.gourmetsleuth.com and www.mexgrocer.com.

crema

Mexican crema is a slightly acidic dairy product that is not that far removed from crème fraîche, which makes a good substitute. It is usually drizzably thin; if not, simply thin with a little water. In a pinch, full-fat sour cream thinned with water or milk can be used. Crema is drizzled liberally over enchiladas at street vendors' stands and artfully over some entrées at Rosa Mexicano. Canned Nestlé crema is available in Latin groceries, some supermarkets, and online at www.mexgrocer.com.

cuitlacoche

A fungus that grows on corn, cuitlacoche (also spelled huitlacoche) is considered a great delicacy in Mexico. It is very difficult to find fresh, a little less difficult to find frozen, and fairly easy to find canned. The canned version has been cooked and seasoned, usually with onion, chile, and epazote. You can freshen it up by seasoning it with a little more onion, chile, and epazote, as I do in the recipe for Pork Chops with Cuitlacoche and Roquefort Sauce on page 208. Cuitlacoche is delicious in quesadillas or as an omelet filling. Canned cuitlacoche is available online at www.gourmetsleuth.com, www.mexgrocer.com, and www.melissaguerra.com.

epazote

There really is nothing that smells or tastes like fresh epazote (pictured on page 1), a knee-high plant with pungent serrated leaves that add a peppery, almost licorice-y flavor to many foods (especially black beans). Fresh is best; epazote doesn't dry well. As the individual recipes indicate, if you don't have access to fresh epazote, simply omit it. In some cases (again, the recipes will be your guide), cilantro may be used in place of the epazote, not as a substitute—the two are quite different in taste—but for an equally delicious result. Seeds can be ordered from www.seedsofchange.com and are very easy to grow. In fact, epazote grows wild all over Mexico and around areas in the States where Mexicans have made their homes. If you know what you are looking for, you can find it in parks and woodlands from Queens, New York, to northern California.

BIG PLATE, CLOCKWISE FROM TOP: Hibiscus flowers, coriander seeds, cumin, oregano

SMALL PLATE, CLOCKWISE FROM LEFT: Cinnamon, allspice, cloves

fruit purees

Frozen mango, passion fruit, and guanabana (soursop) purees can be found at Latin grocers and some specialty markets. A good source for mango and passion fruit purees is www.lepicerie.com. If necessary, cherimoya pulp (sweetened slightly) can be substituted for guanabana puree, which, to my knowledge, is not available by mail or on the Internet.

mexican cinnamon

Mexican cinnamon, which is actually from Sri Lanka, is flakier, softer, and lighter in color than the more common cassia-type cinnamon. Both are part of the bark of trees. Its softer texture means that Mexican cinnamon, *canela*, can be ground easily in a spice mill or blended more completely into a sauce. (Even so, strain any sauce in which pieces of cinnamon have simmered before serving it.) Do make an effort to track down true Mexican or Sri Lankan cinnamon in specialty or Latin markets, or order it online at www.dvo.com.

piloncillo

A type of unrefined brown sugar with a pronounced flavor of molasses, piloncillo is usually sold in small cones that generally range from under an ounce to about 10 ounces, although it is possible to find much larger or rectangular specimens. You may notice some color variation from lighter to darker brown. Piloncillo is always quite firm, but try to avoid rock-hard pieces—steer toward those that can be shaved with a serrated knife into little shards. Shave the amount specified in the recipe, and store the rest of the cone in a cool, dark place. In most recipes where it is called for, I have suggested a mixture of regular brown sugar and molasses as a substitute. Piloncillo is available at supermarkets and online at www.mexgrocer.com and www.gourmetsleuth.com.

tomatillos

Although tomatillos are not tomatoes, they look very much like unripe (green) tomatoes, but they are covered with a papery husk that must be removed. After husking, wash tomatillos very well under cool water until no trace of stickiness remains. Cooked or raw, tomatillos add a pleasant acidity to sauces and salsas (see the index). Look for tomatillos that have firm, bright green flesh without soft or moldy spots. If very fresh, they keep well for up to 2 weeks in the refrigerator. Tomatillos are becoming more widely available outside Latin groceries, and they are quite easy to grow.

EQUIPMENT

cazuela

It is a wonder that these earthenware casseroles are not found in more non-Mexican households. Usually made from glazed terra cotta, they are attractive, inexpensive, and ready to be called into duty on several fronts, from serving platter and salad bowl to baking dish. Once seasoned, cazuelas can go from direct stovetop heat to the oven or broiler (or table), which means dishes like Slow-baked Haricots Verts on page 235 require only one cooking vessel. Cazuelas come in all sizes, from tiny to enormous.

To season a new cazuela, soak overnight in a mixture of 1 part white vinegar to 2 parts water, then dry completely. Rub the inside with a light, even coating of lard (or vegetable oil) and bake the cazuela in a 350°F oven until smoking, approximately 30 to 45 minutes. Let cool, then rinse and dry. The cazuela is now ready to use, and it will acquire a lovely patina with age. (I do give other baking dish options in all recipes that call for a cazuela.) Various sizes and shapes of cazuelas are available at www.tienda.com.

comal

Essential to the Mexican kitchen, comales are round flat griddles made of clay or tin that are placed over heat and used to make and reheat tortillas, to roast vegetables for sauces, to cook quesadillas, and for a hundred other tasks. Inexpensive thin comales are sold in every market in Mexico, but I suggest investing in a sturdier cast-iron round or oval griddle, available in any kitchenware shop.

molcajete

Another fixture of the Mexican kitchen—not to mention our dining rooms, where *molcajetes* and their companions *tejolotes* (or *manos*) are used to prepare thousands of orders of guacamole a week. A molcajete is like a cast-iron skillet in that it becomes better and better with use. Molcajetes are often compared to mortars, and there are similarities. But generally, molcajetes are wider and shallower than mortars and so better suited to grinding large quantities of dried chiles, garlic, spices, and roasted vegetables—in other words, the basis of so many Mexican sauces and salsas. The best molcajetes (and tejolotes) are made of basalt (volcanic rock), not the mixture of poured concrete and crushed basalt sometimes used. Molcajetes made of basalt are quite heavy and therefore steady on the work surface. They need a little conditioning before they are ready to use. The object is to smooth the surface by grinding it, using the tejolote and raw rice or some other grain. Grind a small handful of rice to a fine powder, then wipe out the molcajete and start over. Continue grinding small batches of rice until the ground rice is white, not gray, indicating that any loose or irregular bits of rock have been removed. The coarse gray- and white-speckled molcajetes make great doorstops, but they remain gritty no matter what you do, so the darker gray (almost black), smoother molcajete is a better bet. An online source, www.gourmetsleuth.com, suggests following the rice grinding procedure by grinding cumin, garlic, salt, and pepper together.

tortilla press

To make perfectly thin round corn tortillas quickly and easily, a tortilla press is essential. This simple tool consists of two round flat metal plates connected by a hinge. You place a ball of dough in the center of the bottom plate and firmly close to form the tortilla.

When buying a press, look for one that is heavy (cast iron or cast aluminum) and well constructed. Check the hinges where the two plates are joined and also where the handle is joined to the bottom plate. There should be some play in the joints, but they should be solidly assembled. The handle will have a flat side and a peaked side. Make sure the flat side faces the top plate (for more even pressing) and the peaked side faces up for a better grip. This little detail will make a big difference.

To prevent the dough from sticking to the plates of the press, cut two circles of plastic (a thin grocery store bag works perfectly). Line the bottom plate with one circle and use the second to top the ball of dough before pressing it.

Most tortilla presses sold in the United States are 6 to 6½ inches in diameter, but in some regions of Mexico, you can find tortillas that are close to 12 inches across. Take a little time to search out a larger 8-inch press (or order online at www.mexgrocer.com or www.gourmetsleuth.com). You can always make smaller tortillas with a larger press, but the reverse is not true.

TECHNIQUES

roasting vegetables

The flavor of dry-roasted vegetables is indispensable to our food. Roasting vegetables, without the customary gloss of oil, until they are browned, sometimes even charred, and softened lends deep flavors to sauces. There are two ways to dry-roast most vegetables and a third one that works very well for bell peppers and chiles. In Mexican kitchens, where there is always a comal on the stove, that would be the way to go. I have found that in restaurant and home kitchens here in the United States, setting the broiler to low (if possible) and placing the vegetables fairly far from the heat for slow, even browning works very well. Note that whether under a broiler or on a comal, several types of vegetables can be roasted together. Simply remove those that cook more quickly as they are done and continue with the others. For examples of this technique, see Coconut Ceviche (page 35) and Seared Duck Breasts with Pecan-Prune Mole (page 172).

fresh chiles and bell peppers

Like the other vegetables listed here, sweet and/or spicy peppers can be roasted to intensify their flavor, to add another dimension of flavor, and to make them easy to peel. Roasting and then peeling makes green chiles, such as poblanos, more digestible too. (Green chiles are in essence an unripe fruit and can therefore be tough on the digestion.) Here are two methods for roasting peppers. Small chiles, like jalapeños and habaneros, are best done under the broiler or on a comal.

UNDER THE BROILER ▪ Position a rack about 8 inches from the broiler for bell peppers and larger chiles like poblanos or about 6 inches from the broiler for smaller chiles such as jalapeños, serranos, and habaneros. Preheat the broiler to high. Place the peppers on the broiler pan and broil until the top side is well blackened and the skin is beginning to separate from the flesh of the peppers. Turn the peppers with tongs and continue broiling, turning as each side blackens, until evenly blackened on all sides.

ON A GAS STOVETOP (OR GRILL) ▪ A gas stovetop is handy for crinkly peppers or for roasting large peppers; it does not work for smaller chiles (which can, however, be roasted in a heavy skillet or a comal on the stovetop following the guidelines for garlic on page 22). Turn the heat to medium-high and balance the peppers on the burner grates. Turn the peppers as each side blackens, angling them as necessary or standing them "on their heads" to get all the crevices. (The same technique can be used on a gas grill set to medium or on a charcoal grill over fairly hot coals.)

For either method, once the peppers are evenly blackened, transfer them to a bowl large enough to hold them comfortably, cover the bowl with plastic wrap, and cool to room temperature. When cool, rub off the blackened skin (rather than rinsing, which would remove some of the flavor along with the skin) with your hands, scraping off any stubborn bits with a paring knife. Wear latex gloves if you are working with chile peppers; touching the seeds and the insides will leave irritating oils on your skin. Pull out the cores (unless you're stuffing the peppers; see page 5) and then turn the peppers upside down to drain them. (Bell peppers will hold a lot of liquid.) Cut the peppers lengthwise in half and scrape away the seeds.

onions

Use thick (about 1 inch) slices of white onions.

ON THE COMAL OR GRIDDLE · Heat the comal or griddle over medium-low heat. Lay the slices in the pan and cook, turning once, until softened and evenly and lightly blackened on both sides, about 15 minutes.

UNDER THE BROILER · Set the broiler rack 8 inches from the broiler and preheat the broiler, to low if possible. Arrange the onion slices in a single layer on the broiler pan and broil, turning once, until softened and evenly and lightly blackened on both sides, about 12 minutes.

garlic

Before roasting, peel the garlic cloves.

ON THE COMAL OR, FOR SMALL QUANTITIES, A SMALL HEAVY SKILLET · Heat the comal (or skillet) over medium-low heat. Add the garlic and cook, turning frequently, until softened and well browned all over and blackened in spots, about 8 minutes.

UNDER THE BROILER · Place the rack about 6 inches from the broiler and preheat the broiler, to low if possible. Place the garlic on a heavy baking sheet and broil, turning a few times, until softened, well browned all over, and blackened in spots, about 5 minutes.

tomatoes

Before roasting, cut the cores from the tomatoes and cut a small X through the skin in the opposite end.

ON THE COMAL OR GRIDDLE · Heat the comal or griddle over medium heat. Add the tomatoes and cook, turning as necessary, until they are evenly softened and their skins are blackened, about 15 to 20 minutes.

UNDER THE BROILER · Place the broiler rack about 8 inches from the broiler, and preheat the broiler, to low if possible. Place the tomatoes on the broiler pan and broil, turning as necessary, until they are softened throughout and the skins are evenly blackened, about 20 minutes.

Either way, cool the tomatoes in a bowl, to capture their juices. It is my preference to remove the skins before using, because peeled tomatoes yield a smoother sauce with a more pleasing texture.

tomatillos

Before roasting, remove the husks and wash the tomatillos thoroughly to remove all traces of stickiness. Leave the cores intact.

ON THE COMAL OR GRIDDLE · Heat the comal or griddle over medium-low heat. Add the tomatillos and cook, turning as necessary, until they are evenly softened and their skins are blackened, about 15 minutes.

UNDER THE BROILER · Position the rack about 8 inches from the broiler and preheat the broiler, to low if possible. Put the tomatillos on the broiler pan and broil, turning as necessary, until the skins are blackened evenly on all sides, about 20 minutes.

Either way, cool the tomatillos in a bowl to capture the juices. It is not necessary to skin or core tomatillos before using them.

rinsing food

Many people wouldn't eat a piece of fruit or a vegetable without washing it first. I feel the same way about poultry, pork, and fish, and I always rinse them thoroughly under cold running water before cooking. Rinsing ensures cleaner flavors and can remove impurities and some bacteria. Rinse any of these before cutting them up—that is, rinse a whole chicken before cutting it into pieces, rinse a whole pork tenderloin before slicing or cubing, or rinse a large piece of fish before cutting it into steaks or fillets.

2 TO START

BOTANAS, ENTRADAS, Y BEBIDAS

THERE ARE A LOT OF WAYS TO START A MEAL IN MEXICO —or at Rosa Mexicano. *Botanas* are a whole group of dishes that are similar to Spanish tapas—food for sharing. Unlike tapas, however, which are little individual plates, botanas are larger bowls or plates for the whole table to share. When you walk into a restaurant in Mexico with a group of people, whether you are seated at a table or at the bar, drinks are ordered first, as are botanas. Maybe a waiter will suggest some, maybe you'll pick them off a menu: chicharrones, guacamole, quesadillas, etc. After botanas and drinks, people move to the table and the meal has its sit-down beginning—sometimes a salad, sometimes a soup, sometimes both.

Some of the recipes in this chapter fit into the category of botanas, some into the category of *entradas,* or appetizers. Some may walk the line between the two. For example, you may go to a seaside restaurant and enjoy a ceviche with a drink as a botana, or you may have a ceviche as part of the meal.

We've adapted a few of the recipes in this chapter slightly to fit this category. Queso fundido would not be traditionally served as an appetizer—it would be part of a *taquiza* (taco party), but I think it makes a terrific dish at a small cocktail party or get-together.

Some of the botanas recipes in this chapter can be served in larger portions as a main course—for example, Garlicky Shrimp and Mushrooms (page 37), Spiced Crab Turnovers (page 40), quesadillas (pages 44–46), various ceviches (pages 29–35), and even Yucatán-Style Baby Back Ribs (page 54).

You can use the recipes however you like: prepare a few of them to serve as botanas, start a sit-down meal with just one of them, or make a whole meal out of several of them. The menus on pages 46, 63, and 69 will give you some ideas, as will the headnotes that come before each recipe. Let's get started.

ABOVE: Ceviche Verde (page 30)

CEVICHE

CEVICHE, WHICH IS ALSO KNOWN AS CEBICHE OR SEVICHE, is, simply put, any type of seafood that is "cooked" (without heat) by marinating it in lime juice or another acidic liquid. The seafood doesn't really cook in the same way as it does with heat, but its texture, color, and flavor change as it absorbs the marinade. After the acidic marinade has permeated the surface of the cut-up seafood, the marinade is discarded.

At Rosa Mexicano, ceviche might include coconut, mango, prickly pear, or mixed herbs as well as seafood. Ceviches can be served fairly dry—that is, removed from the marinade and flavored with salsas like pico de gallo (see page 57)—or wet, with a freshly made citrusy sauce. At Rosa Mexicano we find that our customers prefer the latter, which is light and refreshing.

Our Basic Ceviche demonstrates the crucial balance between acid and salt in a marinade. It is always a good idea to taste the marinade before adding the seafood, adjusting the seasonings as necessary. The individual recipes that follow the basic ceviche each call for a specific type of fish or shellfish, but feel free to wing it with your favorite seafood. (Use your instincts, or see the suggestions on page 31.) Keep in mind, however, that some ingredients, like shrimp, lobster, and octopus, require precooking (grilling or poaching are most common); since these do not get marinated in lime juice, the final ceviche will need a little more acid added to the final sauce.

basic ceviche

1 pound mahimahi, red snapper, grouper, or sea bass fillets, cut as directed in one of the following recipes, and/or other seafood (partially cooked if necessary; see page 31)

¾ cup freshly squeezed lime juice, strained
1½ teaspoons salt
½ teaspoon dried oregano, crumbled

Put the raw fish into a tall narrow glass or stainless steel container. Stir the lime juice, salt, and oregano together in a small bowl and pour over the fish. Refrigerate for 1 hour.

Drain the seafood thoroughly and discard the liquid. Add cooked seafood, if using. Finish the ceviche as directed in one of the recipes that follow.

ceviche verde

You won't find basil in traditional Mexican cooking—however, you may well find it on your plate at Rosa Mexicano, where we like to experiment with new flavor combinations. In Mexico, basil is an ingredient in all kinds of curatives that are stirred up by those who dabble in witchcraft (strange but true!). This recipe works a bit of magic on its own once the basil is blended with typical Mexican ingredients like garlic, cilantro, jalapeño, and mint. This bewitching rendition of green ceviche is inspired by Lila Lomelì, a terrific cook and a longtime friend. ▪ makes 6 servings ▪

photograph on page 28

FOR THE SAUCE

1 cup lightly packed fresh basil leaves

1 cup very lightly packed fresh flat-leaf parsley leaves

15 fresh mint leaves

1 jalapeño, thinly sliced

1 small garlic clove, sliced

1/2 teaspoon sugar

1 cup water

Basic Ceviche (page 29) prepared with mahimahi fillets, trimmed and cut into 1/4-inch slices, then into 1/4-inch strips

TO SERVE

20 green Manzanilla (Spanish) olives, pitted and halved (or quartered if large)

1 red bell pepper, roasted (see page 21), peeled, seeded, and cut into 1/4-inch dice

1/2 small white onion (about 2 ounces), finely chopped

2 tablespoons olive oil

Juice of 1 lime, or as needed, strained

1 jalapeño, finely chopped

Salt if necessary

Thin slices of ripe Hass avocado

6 black olives (optional)

Tortilla Chips (page 76)

While the ceviche is curing, make the sauce: Put the basil, parsley, mint, jalapeño, garlic, sugar, and water in a blender jar. Blend until smooth.

Drain the ceviche and put it in a medium mixing bowl; add any cooked seafood (see opposite), if using. Discard the marinade. Pour the basil sauce over the ceviche. Stir in the olives, roasted pepper, onion, olive oil, lime juice, and chopped jalapeño. Taste and add salt and/or additional lime juice if necessary. Let stand at room temperature for about 30 minutes, but no longer than 1 hour.

Divide the ceviche among six cocktail glasses or small deep serving bowls. Top each serving with 2 or 3 avocado slices and a black olive if you like. Serve with the tortilla chips.

Shrimp, calamari (squid), octopus, mussels, and clams are all fine candidates for ceviche. Because shrimp are denser than fish fillets, they should be very lightly poached—just until pink—and cut into spoon-sized pieces before marinating. Calamari, too, should be very lightly poached until just opaque, then cut into rings or small squares. For the adventurous, octopus can be simmered until tender in salted water seasoned with garlic, oregano, and onion.

Mussels and clams should be just cooked and removed from their shells before adding them to the marinade. (Leave a few in their shells to garnish the finished ceviche if you like.) To cook mussels or clams, pour ½ inch or so of water into a heavy pot large enough to hold the mussels or clams in a single layer, add the shellfish to the pot, and bring to a boil over high heat. Cover the pot and steam just until they open, about 3 minutes for mussels, 6 to 9 minutes for hard-shell clams such as littlenecks or Manilas. (It isn't necessary to season the clams or mussels during cooking; the marinade will take care of that.) Drain well, and pull the clams or mussels from the shell when cool enough to handle.

Any seafood that is cooked before adding to a ceviche should *not* be marinated along with raw fish. Instead, add it to the raw seafood after the latter has been drained and sauced. The sauce used for ceviches that contain cooked seafood may need an extra shot of acidity in the form of lime or other citrus juice.

CEVICHE POINTERS

- If using fish fillets, trim any dark sections of flesh; they would add an unpleasant color and flavor to the ceviche.
- Always strain the lime or other citrus juice before adding it to the fish—the pulp is sloppy looking in a finished ceviche.
- Regardless of how a particular ceviche is to be garnished, the balance of salt and acidity in the marinade is critical. For that reason, follow the recipes precisely.
- A great ceviche should have layers of flavors: sweet, acidic, and salty. Taste the marinade before adding the seafood.
- The dish for marinating ceviche should be deep and narrow so that less liquid is needed to cover the fish than would be needed if using a wide, shallow bowl.
- Once a ceviche is sauced and finished, it will benefit from mellowing for from 30 minutes to 1 hour (any longer could make the seafood, especially fish fillets, mushy).

red snapper ceviche with mango · CEVICHE DE HUACHINANGO CON MANGO

A touch of sweet serves to balance the tartness of the marinade, but too much and it can take over. The mango in this recipe is just enough to add a tropical flavor without bullying the seafood. ▪ makes 6 generous servings

FOR THE SAUCE

1 ripe but not too soft mango (a Mexican Ataulfo mango, if you can find one)

½ cup strained freshly squeezed orange juice

2 tablespoons cider vinegar

½ small garlic clove

½ small chile de árbol (with seeds), wiped clean, well toasted (see page 2), and crumbled

½ small habanero chile

¾ cup water

Basic Ceviche (page 29) prepared with red snapper fillets, trimmed and cut into ½-inch cubes

TO SERVE

½ small jicama (about 6 ounces), peeled and cut into ¼-inch dice (about 1 cup)

1 scallion, white and light green part only, thinly sliced (see Note)

3 tablespoons finely chopped red onion

10 large fresh cilantro sprigs, thick stems removed, the remaining stems and leaves finely chopped (about 3 packed tablespoons)

4 large fresh mint leaves, cut into very thin strips

Juice of 1 lime, or as needed, strained

Salt if necessary

While the ceviche is curing, make the sauce: Cut away the flesh from both flat sides of the mango pit, then trim as much of the flesh from the narrow sides of the pit as possible. Use a large spoon to separate the flesh from the skin of the 2 large pieces of mango. Slice the skin from the smaller pieces. Put the smaller pieces in a blender. Coarsely chop a little less than half of the remaining mango and add that to the blender. Add the orange juice, cider vinegar, garlic, chile de árbol, and habanero and blend until smooth.

Pour the sauce into a mixing bowl. Add the water to the blender jar, swish to rinse it, and add to the bowl. Cut the remaining mango into ¼-inch dice and set aside.

Drain the ceviche and put it in a mixing bowl; discard the marinade. Pour the mango sauce over the ceviche. Add the jicama, scallion, red onion, cilantro, mint, and lime juice. Stir well, then add salt to taste and more lime juice if necessary. Let sit at room temperature for 20 to 30 minutes.

Spoon into large cocktail glasses, stick a strip or two of scallion green into each portion, if desired, and serve.

NOTE: If you like, thinly slice the remaining dark green parts of the scallion lengthwise and use them to decorate the finished ceviche.

coconut ceviche · CEVICHE AL COCO

Often served in a half-coconut or a scooped-out pineapple half or mango shell, coconut ceviche is sweet, smooth, spicy, and crunchy all at once. ■ makes 6 servings

FOR THE SAUCE

2 garlic cloves, peeled

1 habanero chile

1 serrano chile

One 14-ounce can "light" coconut milk

¼ cup water

2 tablespoons strained, freshly squeezed lime juice, or as needed

1 tablespoon sugar, or to taste

Basic Ceviche (page 29) prepared with 1 pound red snapper fillets, trimmed and cut into ½-inch cubes

TO SERVE

½ small red bell pepper, cored, seeded, and finely diced (about ½ cup)

½ small yellow bell pepper, cored, seeded, and finely diced (about ½ cup)

2 small scallions, trimmed and thinly sliced

¼ cup lightly packed chopped fresh cilantro

Salt

Lime juice if necessary

While the ceviche is curing, make the sauce: Place the rack about 6 inches from the broiler and preheat the broiler, to low if possible. Put the garlic, habanero, and serrano in a small ovenproof skillet or heavy baking pan and broil, turning once, until softened and blackened in spots, about 4 minutes. Cool.

Wearing gloves, peel the blackened bits from the chiles. Cut the habanero in half. Put one half in the blender jar, and reserve the other for another use (or add it to the blender if you like your ceviche with a real kick). Add the serrano, garlic, coconut milk, water, lime juice, and sugar to the blender, and blend until smooth.

Drain the ceviche and put it in a mixing bowl; discard the marinade. Pour the coconut sauce over the ceviche, and stir in the bell peppers, scallions, and cilantro. Add salt to taste. Let stand for 20 to 30 minutes at room temperature before serving.

Taste the ceviche and add sugar, salt, and/or lime juice if necessary. Spoon into cocktail glasses and serve.

shrimp with cilantro cream · CAMARONES CON RABOS DE CILANTRO

Here is a terrific way to use the leftover stems from cilantro you'll have on hand when you start cooking from this book. When cooked so quickly, they retain their crunch and so lend texture as well as flavor. If you don't have enough stems to measure 1 cup, you can add some leaves.

Made with small shrimp, this is an attractive first course. Serve it right from the skillet, with toothpicks for spearing the shrimp and a basket of warm tortillas. To turn this into a main course for 3, substitute an equal weight of larger shrimp and cook them a few minutes longer. ▪ makes 6 servings

1¼ pounds peeled and deveined small
  (50 per pound) shrimp (defrosted if frozen)
2 tablespoons vegetable oil
1 cup chopped thick cilantro stems
  (from about 2 bunches; trim root ends
  and wash before chopping)
1 small red onion, finely chopped (about ½ cup)

2 jalapeños, finely chopped
2 garlic cloves, finely chopped
½ teaspoon dried oregano, crumbled
⅛ teaspoon ground cumin
¾ cup heavy cream
Salt
Juice of ½ lime, or to taste

Pat the shrimp very dry with paper towels and set aside.

Heat the vegetable oil in a large skillet over medium-high heat. Add the cilantro stems, red onion, jalapeños, garlic, oregano, and cumin and cook just until the stems and onion are softened, about 2 minutes. Pour in the heavy cream and bring to a boil. Cook until the cream is reduced by about two-thirds and thickened (there should be just enough to lightly coat the vegetables).

Add the shrimp to the pan, season with salt, and toss to coat the shrimp with the sauce. Reduce the heat to low, cover the pan, and cook, stirring, two or three times, until the shrimp are cooked through and there is just enough fairly thick sauce to coat them generously. Remove from the heat and squeeze in lime juice to taste. Add salt if necessary, and serve immediately.

Nearly all of the recipes in this book can by doubled, tripled, or more to suit your needs.

garlicky shrimp and mushrooms · CAMARONES CON HONGOS AL AJILLO

Al ajillo, which simply means "with garlic," is a classic Spanish cooking method that we Mexicans have adopted and stoked up with our arsenal of hot peppers. A Spanish diner would no sooner eat our version than he would take on a fighting bull in his backyard—Spanish cuisine, while wonderful in its own way, is rarely spicy. At Rosa Mexicano we rev up this recipe with a variety of chiles and add some mushrooms for an earthy flavor. Whole chiles de árbol are stirred in the cooking oil to season it. Keep in mind that they are spicy hot, so proceed with caution.

This is one of the few Mexican dishes that contain a lot of garlic. For this reason, you will need considerable frying oil so the garlic "swims" freely. Do not let it cook beyond pale golden, because it turns bitter after that. Have some good bread on hand for soaking up the olive oil. In Mexico, the shrimp are often served with heads and shells still attached—messy but tastier.

Finally, choose a pan large enough to hold all the ingredients comfortably and one that also holds heat well. I like a well-seasoned 12-inch cast-iron skillet. · makes 6 servings

1 pound peeled and deveined medium (about 35 per pound), shrimp or 1¼ pounds shrimp in the shell, peeled and deveined

⅓ to ½ cup light olive oil

6 large garlic cloves, coarsely chopped

1 guajillo chile, wiped clean, stemmed, seeded, and cut into ¼-inch-wide strips

4 chiles de árbol (with seeds), wiped clean, stemmed but left whole

1 pound mixed mushrooms, trimmed (e.g., equal amounts of shiitakes, stemmed, caps cut in half; oyster mushrooms, hard central stems trimmed; and cremini, stems trimmed, caps sliced ¼ inch thick)

2 tablespoons ancho chile paste (see page 5)

1 lime, cut in half

Salt

Crusty bread, cut into pieces or torn (optional)

Pat the shrimp dry with paper towels. Set aside.

Heat the oil in a heavy large skillet over medium heat. Add the garlic and cook, shaking the pan, just until the garlic starts to turn tan. Immediately add the guajillo strips and the árbol chiles and cook for a few seconds, until fragrant. Add the shrimp and mushrooms, increase the heat to high, and cook, tossing, until the shrimp start to change color, 1 to 2 minutes.

Add the ancho paste and toss until the mushrooms and shrimp are lightly coated. Continue cooking, tossing gently, until the shrimp are cooked through, about 3 minutes. Squeeze the juice from the lime halves into the skillet and add salt to taste. Scrape onto a serving platter and serve immediately, passing bread for dipping if you like.

The masa has been colored here with a fine guajillo puree. This gives masa a distinctive brick-red color and a flavor with very little heat. Remember to pinch the edges of the empanadas with gusto—don't be shy about that, or they'll burst open while cooking.

RIGHT: Crab Turnovers (page 40) with Green Salsa with Avocado (page 47)

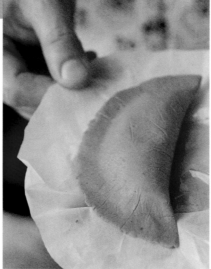

crab turnovers · EMPANADAS DE JAIBA

Empanadas are Mexican turnovers. They can be made with flaky pastry dough or with masa (here, with red masa dough), as they are here, and filled with seafood, meat, or poultry. Empanadas are sometimes known as quesadillas, even though there may not be any cheese in the filling. ▪ photograph on page 39

FOR THE FILLING

½ pound lump crabmeat

2 tablespoons butter

½ cup chopped white onion

1½ tablespoons (or to taste) chopped jalapeño

Salt

¾ teaspoon dried oregano, crumbled

½ teaspoon ground cumin

½ cup crema, crème fraîche, or thinned sour cream (see page 15)

Red Masa (recipe follows), plus additional masa harina (fine corn flour) for sprinkling

Vegetable oil for frying

Peach Pico de Gallo (page 42; optional)

MAKE THE FILLING: Pick over the crabmeat and remove any pieces of shell and cartilage. Blot the crabmeat dry with paper towels.

Heat the butter in a medium heavy skillet over medium heat just until it starts to brown. Stir in the onion and jalapeño, season lightly with salt, and cook, stirring, until the onion is translucent, about 4 minutes. Add the oregano and cumin and cook, stirring, for 1 minute. Add the crema, bring to a boil, and cook until thickened, about 3 minutes. Stir in the crab, leaving the pieces as large as possible, and season to taste with salt. Set aside to cool.

ASSEMBLE THE EMPANADAS: Line a baking pan with a sheet of parchment or waxed paper. Sprinkle the paper lightly with masa harina. Have ready a lightly dampened clean kitchen towel.

Divide the dough into twelve 2-tablespoon (1-ounce) pieces. Roll each into a smooth ball. Cut two circles the size of the plates of your tortilla press (see Note) from a thin plastic bag, such as a grocery store bag. Cover the bottom plate with one circle of plastic, center a dough ball over it, and top with the other sheet of plastic. Press the dough into an even 4½-inch circle. Open the press and peel off the top layer of plastic. With the dough still on the second circle of plastic, center two tablespoons of the crab filling on the dough. Pat the filling to flatten it into an even layer, leaving an inch of dough uncovered around the edges. Fold the dough over to make a half-moon, and press the edges of the dough together to seal tightly. Remove the empanada from the plastic, check to make sure all the edges are pinched closed, and set on the prepared baking sheet. Cover with the damp towel, and repeat with the remaining dough and filling. The empanadas can be made up to several hours in advance. Keep them covered with the damp towel and plastic wrap, and refrigerate.

FRY THE EMPANADAS: Pour ¾ inch of oil into a large deep skillet. Heat over medium heat until a corner of an empanada dipped into the oil gives off a lively sizzle. Carefully lay 6 of the empanadas into the oil. Fry, turning once, until crisp and lightly browned on both sides, about 4 minutes. Adjust the heat as necessary to maintain a lively sizzle without splattering. Drain on paper towels and repeat with the remaining empanadas. Serve hot, with Peach Pico de Gallo if desired.

NOTE: A tortilla press (see page 18) helps to make perfectly round, evenly thick circles for empanadas and tortillas. If one is not available, place each piece of dough between two sheets of waxed paper and roll it out with a rolling pin, keeping it as even and as round as possible.

red masa · MASA ROJA

This very simple dough, used to make the Crab Turnovers, can also be turned into dumplings, or into colorful tortillas following the guidelines for making corn tortillas on page 92. For red dumplings *(chochoyones rojas)*, simply roll the dough into little rounds (about ½ inch) and drop them into a pot of simmering chicken, beef, or vegetable (mushroom is particularly good) broth. When they float to the top, they are done. This type of dumpling is commonly made with regular masa using lard. But when I saw the color of this dough, I thought red chochoyones would be fun to make.

▪ makes enough dough for 12 empanadas

2 guajillo chiles, wiped clean, stemmed, seeded, and soaked (see page 3)
½ small garlic clove

1 cup warm water
1 cup masa harina (fine corn flour), or as needed
1 teaspoon salt

Drain the chiles. Put the chiles, garlic, and warm water in a blender. Blend until smooth.

Stir the masa and salt together in a mixing bowl. Pour in the chile water mixture and beat with a wooden spoon. This is not a delicate dough that should be handled gently; don't be afraid to beat it well to make sure it is well blended. The dough can be made up to several hours in advance. Cover it with plastic wrap or place in an airtight container and refrigerate until needed. (If the dough becomes a little dry as it stands, just moisten your hands and knead lightly to soften it up. If the dough becomes slightly soft as it stands, knead in masa harina a little bit at a time until the dough firms up. Either of these changes are related to humidity in the air.)

peach pico de gallo ▪ PICO DE GALLO DE DURAZNO

The state of Mexico is ringed with mountains that encompass some of the most fertile land of central Mexico. The soil, which has been enriched by volcanic activity, and the relatively cool climate produce beautiful avocados, berries, flowers, and peaches—the last of which are incredibly fragrant but somewhat acidic. They pack quite a flavor punch, and these are the peaches that are used in Mexico for this fruity version of pico de gallo. American peaches sometime slack that punch, so I add a little passion fruit juice for acidity and fruitiness. I also use habanero instead of the manzano chiles that are used in Mexico because manzanos are virtually impossible to find in the States. ▪ makes a scant 2 cups

2 pounds ripe peaches

3 tablespoons finely chopped red onion

1 small habanero chile, finely chopped (about 1 tablespoon)

10 fresh epazote leaves, chopped (optional)

1 cup passion fruit juice

3 tablespoons strained freshly squeezed lime juice, or as needed

2 teaspoons sugar, or as needed

1 teaspoon salt

If your peaches are fairly firm, you can peel them with a vegetable peeler. If too soft, bring a large pot of water to a boil. Half-fill a large bowl with ice and pour in enough cold water to cover the ice. Slip the peaches into the boiling water and leave them just until the skins start to separate from the flesh. Immediately lift them into the ice water, and let stand until cold.

Drain the peaches. Cut them in half along the crease and twist the halves to separate them. Discard the pits and cut the peaches into rough ½-inch pieces. Gently toss the peaches and all the remaining ingredients together in a bowl. Acidity and sweetness will vary depending on the peaches: check for balance—you want the perfume of peaches to be enhanced by a good kick from the habanero, but the sweetness should be similar to that of very ripe fruit; if necessary, add more sugar.

quick pickled poblano strips · RAJAS DE POBLANO

These poblano strips are not pickled in the conventional sense—rather, they are roasted and then soaked in lime juice and salt for a couple of hours. They perk up most any dish, particularly grilled foods, omelets, tacos, and broiled fish. ▪ makes a generous 1 cup

2 poblano chiles, roasted (see page 21), peeled, seeded, and cut into 2 by ¼-inch strips
½ medium white onion, very thinly sliced (about ½ cup)

½ teaspoon dried oregano
2 to 3 tablespoons strained, freshly squeezed lime juice
Salt

In a bowl, toss together the chile strips, onion, oregano, and enough lime juice to give a pleasant acidic note. Add salt to taste. Let stand at room temperature for 1 to 2 hours, tossing occasionally.

Taste the chiles again just before serving and add a little more lime juice and/or salt if you like.

APPETIZER QUESADILLAS

THE NAME *QUESADILLA* COMES FROM THE WORD *QUESO*, which means "cheese." Traditionally the cheese used was a relatively mild cheese that melts well, like queso Chihuahua from the state of the same name or Mexican Manchego. Nowadays in Mexico, many quesadillas are made with Oaxaca string cheese—*queso Oaxaca* (see page 13)—which is more elastic than creamy when it melts (similar to mozzarella), adding a great textural element.

Quesadillas are very much a part of Mexican life. In more urban areas, quesadilla stands dot the streets. Under bright blue canopies strung between streetlights and trees, two women work to prepare quesadillas eaten for lunch or as a snack. One turns masa into tortillas and cooks them on the comal, or griddle; the other turns the fresh hot tortillas into quesadillas, filling them with, perhaps, strips of roasted poblano chiles (see page 43), potatoes and chorizo, cuitlacoche (see page 15), or *chicharron guisado* (stewed pork rind) and cheese, then serves them up. A dousing of salsa—red or green, or both—and your snack is complete. The simple setting is rounded out with milk crates or boxes that can be used as seats if you choose.

At home, quesadillas and soup make a dinner, and a ham and cheese quesadilla can be breakfast. Quesadillas are also a terrific party food, as they are simple to prepare, can be assembled hours in advance, and are always a huge hit. These appetizers are smaller quesadillas. For larger, meal-sized quesadillas made with flour tortillas, see pages 130–31.

QUESADILLA POINTERS

- Just about anything can be turned into a quesadilla, but keep in mind that whatever filling you choose should be fully cooked (there are a few exceptions, such as whole epazote leaves, squash blossoms, or sliced chiles), be cut into bite-sized pieces, and match well with the cheese you have chosen.

- Don't overload quesadillas. For a 6-inch tortilla, start with about ¼ cup packed finely shredded cheese and add about the same amount or less of other ingredients: ham cut into thin strips, roasted chiles or bell peppers, squash blossoms, mushrooms, or chicharrones in sauce.

- Quesadillas can be assembled up to a few hours before serving. Overlap them in a baking dish, cover with damp paper towels and then plastic wrap, and refrigerate.

- Quesadillas are best served warm. For a party, cook them a few at a time and pass them out as they are ready. (Cut them in half for cocktail parties, if you like.) Or prepare them all at once and put them in a napkin-lined basket to keep them warm, much as you would do with warm corn tortillas (see page 92).

- Cook quesadillas over steady medium-low heat. The idea is to slowly crisp up the tortillas while heating the filling through. If the heat is too high, the tortillas will crisp before the cheese is melted.

the basic quesadilla · QUESADILLA BASICA

If you garden or have access to a good farmers' market, a squash blossom tucked into each of these quesadillas is a lovely addition. ▪ makes 6 quesadillas

6 Fresh Corn Tortillas (page 92) or store-bought 6-inch corn tortillas

1½ cups finely shredded queso Chihuahua, Muenster, or cheddar cheese (about 4 ounces)

6 large or 12 smaller fresh epazote leaves (optional)

1 jalapeño, cut lengthwise into very thin slices

About 1 cup Green Salsa (page 47) and/or Pasilla de Oaxaca Tomatillo Salsa (page 53)

Place a cast-iron griddle or comal over medium-low heat or heat an electric griddle to 325°F. If using store-bought tortillas, warm them on the griddle, turning them once, until softened, about 2 minutes.

Spread ¼ cup of the cheese over half of each tortilla, leaving a small border along the edge. Top each with an epazote leaf or two, if using, and a slice of jalapeño. Fold the empty side over the filling and press firmly to close.

Cook the quesadillas in batches on the griddle, turning once, until light golden brown and crisp, about 3 minutes per side. Serve immediately, with one or both of the salsas.

VARIATION · quesadillas with poblanos

Omit the jalapeño. Roast (see page 21), peel, and seed 1 poblano chile. Cut the pepper into ¼-inch-wide strips. Add 5 to 6 strips of poblano to each quesadilla instead of the jalapeño and proceed as above.

mushroom quesadillas · QUESADILLAS CON HONGOS

■ makes 6 quesadillas

¾ pound mixed mushrooms, trimmed and sliced (see Beef Tenderloin with Wild Mushrooms and Tequila, page 202, or Garlicky Shrimp and Mushrooms, page 37, for suggestions and cutting information)

½ small white onion, finely chopped

3 garlic cloves, finely chopped

2 serrano chiles, finely chopped

3 tablespoons olive oil

Salt

1½ cups finely shredded queso Chihuahua, Muenster, or cheddar cheese (about 4 ounces)

6 Fresh Corn Tortillas (page 92) or store-bought 6-inch corn tortillas

6 fresh epazote leaves (optional)

Toss the mushrooms, onion, garlic, and chiles together in a bowl until well mixed.

Heat the oil in a large heavy skillet over medium-high heat until very hot. Add the mushroom mixture all at once, season with salt (lightly—the mushrooms will shrink down quite a bit!), and cook, stirring and tossing, until the mushrooms are browned. The timing depends on the mushrooms, the pan, and the heat—most likely the mushrooms will give off a little liquid first, which must be cooked off before they begin to brown. Scrape the mushrooms into a bowl, taste, and season with more salt if needed.

Spread ¼ cup of the cheese over half of each tortilla, leaving a small border along the edge. Top with 2 heaping tablespoons of the mushroom mixture and an epazote leaf, if using. Fold the empty side over the filling and press firmly to close.

Cook and serve the quesadillas as described in The Basic Quesadilla, (page 45).

GRAZING DINNER FOR 6

A little bit of this and a little bit of that—this is the perfect menu for guests who like to mix it up. You can spread the last-minute work (frying empanadas, reheating the corn soup, and making guacamole) according to how the mood of the party is swinging.

- Crudités (homemade or store-bought) with Guacamole (page 73)

- Fresh Corn in Epazote Broth (page 68)

- Crab Turnovers (page 40) with Peach Pico de Gallo (page 42) or Green Salsa with Avocado (page 45)

- Mushrooms "en Escabeche" with Red Bell Peppers and Chiles (page 70)

UP TO 1 WEEK AHEAD ▪ Make the pickled mushrooms

EARLIER IN THE DAY ▪ Make the empanadas and refrigerate

4 HOURS AHEAD ▪ Make the corn and epazote broth ▪ Make the pico de gallo

AFTER GUESTS ARRIVE ▪ Make guacamole ▪ Reheat the corn broth ▪ Fry the empanadas

green salsa · SALSA VERDE CRUDA

This simple sauce, with its pleasant acidity, is very common throughout the central plains of Mexico. It pairs well with fried or fatty foods, like the flautas on page 50. It is also delicious with steamed fish fillets or grilled poultry, meat, or seafood. With uncooked salsas like this one, it is important to get a good kick from the chile. Without that zing of chile, a salsa cruda seems to me to be only halfway there. ·

makes 2¼ cups

1 pound tomatillos, husked, washed, and coarsely chopped

1 jalapeño or 2 small serranos, sliced, or more to taste

2 small garlic cloves

2 tablespoons chopped white onion

10 fresh cilantro sprigs, torn into rough pieces

2 teaspoons salt

Put the tomatillos into a blender jar and add the remaining ingredients. (Tomatillos contain a lot of water, and when the blender starts, they quickly liquidize, making it easier to blend the other ingredients into the salsa; even if it seems as if nothing is happening in the first few seconds, resist the temptation to add water to the blender.) Blend at high speed until smooth. The salsa can be made up to 8 hours in advance—no longer, or it will begin to lose its fresh taste—and kept, covered, at room temperature.

VARIATION · green salsa with avocado

· photograph on page 93

This salsa is delicious with fried foods, such as the Crab Turnovers on page 40. Put 2 cups Green Salsa in a blender jar. Quarter, pit, and peel a medium Hass avocado and add it to the blender. Blend on low speed until smooth. Add salt to taste.

SALSAS

As you will see in this book, salsas come in as many colors as the Mexican landscape. Their distinctiveness derives from the base ingredients and seasonings. Salsas can be raw or cooked, and they can be chopped, pureed, or left chunky. However a salsa is prepared, it should pack a punch and yield a complexity of flavors—hot, sweet, salty, and sour, sometimes with a lilt from acid (usually vinegar or citrus). I can't imagine Mexican cuisine without salsas—they are the vibrant scarves that set off our culinary raiment.

TIP: Because the heat levels of chiles vary so dramatically, always begin making your salsa by using less than the recipe calls for. If it still comes out too fiery, simply add more of the sweeter elements, like tomatillos and tomatoes.

LEFT: Green Salsa (page 45)

crisp chicken flautas · FLAUTAS DE POLLO

Flauta means "flute" in Spanish. Flautas, essentially rolled tacos, are a somewhat messy snack eaten in little corner stores and other humble locales. They are generally doused with zesty red or green salsa, drizzled with crema, sprinkled with cheese, and sometimes covered with a blizzard of shredded lettuce. At Rosa Mexicano we serve these addictive little munchies as appetizers. At home I often serve them as a main course, accompanied by a salad. This is a great way to use leftover chicken—or, for that matter, any type of meat. Flautas are fantastic filled with lamb barbacoa (see page 123) or shredded beef (see Shredded Flank Steak Salad, page 153).

Unless you grow your own or shop at a farmers' market, your tomatoes will most likely be a little flat. The sugar in the filling helps round out the flavor of less than perfectly ripe tomatoes. ▪ makes 4 to 6 servings

FOR THE FILLING

2 tablespoons vegetable oil or light olive oil

½ cup chopped white onion

1 tablespoon finely chopped jalapeño,
   or more to taste

3 garlic cloves, finely chopped
   (about 1½ teaspoons)

1 large tomato or 2 medium plum tomatoes
   (about 8 ounces), cored and cut into ½-inch
   dice (with seeds and liquid)

Salt

2 bay leaves

1½ teaspoons chipotle adobo puree
   (see page 7)

½ teaspoon sugar, or to taste

¼ teaspoon dried oregano, crumbled

⅛ teaspoon dried thyme, crumbled

1 cup shredded cooked chicken (see Note)

Eight 6-inch corn tortillas
   (the thinner the better)

Vegetable oil for frying

FOR THE TOPPINGS

4 cups shredded romaine lettuce

About 1 cup Green Salsa (page 45), or Pasilla de
   Oaxaca Tomatillo Salsa (recipe follows),
   or ½ cup of each

½ cup crema, crème fraîche, or thinned sour
   cream (see page 15)

¼ cup finely grated queso fresco

MAKE THE FILLING: Heat the oil in a medium skillet over medium heat. Add the onion and cook, stirring, until translucent but not browned, about 4 minutes. Add the jalapeño and garlic and cook for 1 minute. Add the tomato(es), with liquid, and season lightly with salt. Add the bay leaves, chipotle puree, sugar, oregano, and thyme. Bring to a boil and cook until most of the liquid has evaporated and the mixture is lightly thickened, about 10 minutes. Stir in the chicken. The filling should be moist but not wet; if necessary, increase the heat to high and boil off a little of the liquid. Season to taste with salt. Remove from the heat and cool to room temperature, then discard the bay leaves.

[continued]

Crisp Chicken Flautas with Pasilla de Oaxaca Tomatilla Salsa (page 53)

FILL THE TORTILLAS: Wrap the tortillas in a clean kitchen towel and microwave on high power for 1 minute. Let stand for a minute or two.

Place about 2 tablespoons filling in the center of a tortilla. Fold one edge of the tortilla over the filling and then, with your fingertips, pull the edge of the tortilla folded over the filling away from the center, spreading the filling to the edges and making a neat, compact shape of it. Then roll up the tortilla into a tight roll. Fill and roll another flauta, then place the 2 flautas side by side with their loose edges touching in the center. Pass 2 toothpicks through the center of the flautas to hold them together and keep them from coming undone during frying. Repeat with the remaining tortillas and filling. The flautas can be formed up to several hours before cooking. Refrigerate them in a covered container until needed. (The remaining ingredients—lettuce, salsas, and cheese—can be prepared in advance as well.)

COOK THE FLAUTAS: If you want to keep the first round of flautas hot while preparing the second round, preheat the oven to 250°F. Line a shallow bowl with a double thickness of paper towels. Heat ¼ cup oil in a 10-inch skillet over medium heat until the end of one of the flautas dipped into the oil gives off a lively sizzle. Carefully lay 2 pairs of flautas in the oil. Cook until the underside is lightly browned and crisp, about 3 minutes. Carefully turn them and cook the second side. Remove to the paper-towel-lined bowl to drain. (During frying, oil can seep into the center of the flautas; draining them on an angle in a shallow bowl lined with paper towels is a great way to remove excess oil.) Repeat with the remaining flautas, keeping the first batch hot on a baking sheet in the oven if you like.

To serve, line four salad plates with the shredded lettuce. Top each with 2 flautas and remove the toothpicks. Spoon on enough of the salsa of your choice to coat the flautas lightly (or, if using both salsas, spoon one over each flauta on each plate). Drizzle the flautas liberally with crema in a zigzag pattern and sprinkle with the cheese. (If some of the crema and cheese ends up on the lettuce, so much the better.) Serve hot.

NOTES: Flautas are usually made with larger, thin corn tortillas rather than the type used for tacos. This type of tortilla can be hard to find here, but the thicker, smaller type that is available in supermarkets also works well. Using the microwave oven to warm and soften corn tortillas is faster and neater than frying them in oil, the traditional method.

If you do not have leftover chicken from making Chicken Broth (page 66) or from another meal, roast 3 medium (about ¾ pound) boneless, skinless chicken thighs. Season with salt and pepper, place on a greased baking sheet, and roast in a 400°F oven until no trace of pink remains near the bone, about 35 minutes. Cool completely before removing any gristle and/or cartilage and shredding the meat.

pasilla de Oaxaca tomatillo salsa · SALSA DE PASILLA DE OAXACA

Not only does this salsa complement the chicken flautas, it will enliven just about any dish, particularly grilled, broiled, or roasted meat, poultry, or fish. It has quite a kick from the chiles, and that is how it should be. The heat can always be controlled by the number of chiles used and whether some or all of the seeds and ribs are removed from them (the more you remove, the milder the sauce will be). Think of this as a blueprint, not a recipe. Just about any chile with a good kick, like chipotles, chiles de árbol, or piquín, can be substituted for the pasillas de Oaxaca. ▪ makes 1⅓ cups

1 pound tomatillos, husked, washed, and roasted (see page 16)

3 pasilla de Oaxaca chiles, wiped clean, stemmed, most seeds tapped out, and toasted (see page 2)

3 small garlic cloves

Salt

While the tomatillos are cooling, soak the chiles: Put them in a bowl and pour over enough cold water to cover them completely. Soak until pliable but not completely softened, about 20 minutes. Drain.

Combine the drained chiles, garlic, and one-third of the cooled tomatillos in a blender jar and blend until smooth. Add the remaining tomatillos and blend, using quick on/off pulses, just until smooth; don't overblend. Pour into a bowl and season with salt. The salsa can be kept at room temperature for up to 4 hours or refrigerated for up to 12 hours before serving.

Yucatán-style baby back ribs · COSTILLITAS CON ACHIOTE

Nothing, it seems, ignites bonfires of culinary patriotism in America like barbecued pork ribs. Every country claims to serve the best ribs, which, of course is impossible—as these are unsurpassed. The baby back ribs at Rosa Mexicano are incredibly moist and fork-tender. You can simulate our technique at home by first simmering the ribs in seasoned water (see below) to tenderize them, then marinating them in the achiote paste.

These achiote-flavored ribs are as delicious as American ribs, the main difference being that ours contain less sugar, leaving them spicier and less sticky. When separated, individual baby back ribs can be served as an appetizer or as part of a grazing menu that might include guacamole and a couple of good salsas (see pages, 73, 47, and 183). ▪ makes 24 pieces; serves 12 as part of a grazing menu, 6 to 8 as an appetizer, or 3 to 4 as a main course

Two 12-bone racks baby back ribs (about 3¼ pounds), *not* completely trimmed of fat
½ medium white onion
12 garlic cloves, peeled
2 tablespoons salt
10 allspice berries
1½ tablespoons dried oregano, crumbled

FOR THE MARINADE
½ cup white vinegar
2 tablespoons achiote paste (see page 12)
4 garlic cloves
6 allspice berries
1 teaspoon dried oregano
2 teaspoons sugar
1 teaspoon salt
1 teaspoon chile de árbol powder (see page 7), or other pure chile powder
½ teaspoon cumin seeds

Cut each rack in half between the center pair of bones and rinse them well under cold water. Put them in a 5-quart pot and pour enough water over them to cover by about 1 inch. Add the onion, garlic, salt, allspice, and oregano and bring to a boil, then adjust the heat so the liquid is simmering. Cook just until the meat between the bones is tender but not starting to pull away from the ends of the bones, about 1 hour. Remove from the heat and cool the ribs in the cooking liquid.

While the ribs are cooling, make the marinade: Put the vinegar, achiote paste, garlic, allspice, oregano, sugar, salt, chile powder, and cumin in a blender jar. Blend at high speed until the achiote paste is dissolved, then blend at medium speed until completely smooth. Pour the marinade into a shallow baking dish large enough to hold the ribs in a single layer.

Drain the ribs (discard the liquid) and pat dry with paper towels. Add to the marinade and, wearing gloves if you like, rub the marinade into both sides of the ribs. Cover with plastic wrap and let stand at room temperature for 1 hour, or refrigerate for up to 1 day.

TO GRILL THE RIBS: Heat a charcoal or gas grill. Set the ribs bone side up on the grill and grill, turning once, until well browned, even charred in spots, on both sides, about 12 minutes. Rearrange the ribs on the grill as necessary in order for them to cook evenly.

TO BROIL THE RIBS: Set the oven rack about 6 inches from the broiler and preheat the broiler, to low if possible. Set the ribs bone side down on the broiler pan and broil, turning once, until well browned, even charred in spots, on both sides, 8 to 10 minutes.

Transfer the ribs to a cutting board and let rest for 5 minutes. Cut between the bones into individual ribs, pile the ribs on a platter, and serve.

queso fundido

Think of queso fundido as Mexican fondue—creamy, rich, and delicious. Unlike fondue, however, which is thickened lightly with cornstarch or flour, queso fundido will separate and appear oily if it is overcooked or left to cool too long—rarely an issue, as a casserole of this addictive treat disappears minutes after it is put on the table. Also unlike fondue, you don't dip anything in it. Instead, you scoop it onto tortillas. If you like, serve a little Pico de Gallo (opposite) or diced fresh tomatoes on the side. Although you wouldn't be served this as an appetizer at a Mexican meal—it would be most often found as one of the items at a *taquiza* (a meal that features tacos; see page 91)—people do love it served that way or as part of a cocktail spread. ▪ makes 6 servings

½ cup Cooked Green Salsa (page 114)

2 tablespoons crema, crème fraîche, or thinned sour cream (see page 15)

2 poblano chiles, roasted (see page 21), peeled, seeded, and cut into ½-inch-wide strips

6 Fresh Corn Tortillas (page 92) or store-bought 6-inch corn or flour tortillas

1½ cups diced (½-inch) queso Chihuahua, Monterey Jack, or Muenster cheese (about 7 ounces)

2 tablespoons chopped fresh cilantro

Stir together the salsa, crema, and all but a small handful of the pepper strips in a heavy round 8 by 3-inch-deep flameproof casserole or heavy 8-inch pot. Bring to a boil over medium heat and cook until lightly thickened, about 4 minutes.

While the sauce is simmering, warm the tortillas (see page 92).

Add the cheese to the salsa mixture all at once and stir until melted, about 4 minutes. Remove from the heat and stir well until smooth. Scatter the remaining chile strips and the cilantro over the top and serve immediately, letting guests spoon some of the queso fundido onto the warm tortillas and eat them out of hand.

pico de gallo

Like salsa verde, *pico de gallo* (literally, "rooster's beak") is one of the condiments that is found on almost every Mexican table almost every day. It goes onto tacos, grilled foods, and enchiladas, or anything else you'd like to serve it with, such as our "charro" beans on page 221. The seasonings—onion, cilantro, jalapeño, and lime—can be adjusted to suit your taste. Some Mexican cooks add a drizzle of olive oil to this salsa for richness—you can too. ▪ makes about 2 cups

2 ripe medium tomatoes (about 12 ounces)
¼ cup finely chopped white onion, or to taste
12 large fresh cilantro sprigs, thick stems removed, remaining stems and leaves finely chopped (about ¼ cup)

1 medium jalapeño or 1 small serrano, finely chopped (about 1½ tablespoons), or to taste
1 teaspoon salt, or to taste
Juice of 1 lime, or to taste
1 teaspoon olive oil (optional)

Core the tomatoes and cut them in half. Gently squeeze out most of the seeds, and cut the tomatoes into ¼-inch (no larger) dice. Toss the diced tomatoes, onion, cilantro, and jalapeño together in a mixing bowl. Add the salt and lime juice, then stir in the oil, if using. Let sit for a few minutes. The salsa can be made and kept at room temperature for up to 4 hours—no longer—before serving. Stir and taste again before serving.

BELOW: Rosa Mexicano House Salad (page 60).

RIGHT: Pomegranate and Red Onion Dressing (page 61).

Rosa Mexicano house salad · ENSALADA DE LA CASA

We offer several salads at the restaurants. This one with jicama—a root vegetable that's indigenous to Mexico with a slightly sweet flavor and a texture similar to an apple—and toasted pumpkin seeds is refreshing and tasty, with a nice crunch. ▪

makes 6 servings ▪ photograph on page 58

½ small jicama (about 8 ounces)

8 ounces mesclun greens (about 10 cups), washed and dried

2 medium carrots, peeled and coarsely grated

1 pint cherry tomatoes, cut in half if large

½ cup plus 2 tablespoons pumpkin seeds, toasted (see box)

Salt

Pomegranate and Red Onion Dressing (recipe follows)

Peel the jicama and cut into thin (¼-inch-thick or less) slices. Stack the slices a few at a time and cut them into equally thin strips.

Toss the jicama, greens, carrots, cherry tomatoes, and ½ cup of the pumpkin seeds in a large bowl. Season lightly with salt, then pour in the dressing and toss until coated.

Divide among six serving plates and sprinkle some of the remaining 2 tablespoons pumpkin seeds over each. Serve immediately.

TOASTING PUMPKIN SEEDS

Before toasting pumpkin seeds, rub them between your palms in small batches to get rid of any loose skins, which can turn bitter during toasting. Choose a heavy skillet (preferably cast iron) that is large enough to hold the pumpkin seeds in one thick layer. Add the pumpkin seeds and toast over medium-high heat until they begin to swell up and a few of them crackle. When the crackling stops and the seeds are no more than lightly browned in a few spots, they are done. Browning the seeds too much will make them bitter.

pomegranate and red onion dressing · ADEREZO DE GRANADA Y CEBOLLA MORADA

Skillet-roasting chars the onion and garlic in spots, giving them a pleasant bitter edge that nicely balances their natural sweetness. ▪ makes 1 cup; enough for 6 servings

▪ photograph on page 59

1 small red onion (about 4 ounces), cut into 1/2-inch slices

4 large garlic cloves, peeled

1/4 cup lightly packed chopped fresh cilantro

1/4 cup pomegranate juice

1/4 cup freshly squeezed lime juice

1 serrano chile, finely chopped

3/4 teaspoon anise seeds, crushed to a powder in a mortar (see Note)

1 1/2 teaspoons sugar

1/4 teaspoon freshly ground black pepper

1/4 cup olive oil

Salt

Put the onion slices and garlic in a heavy skillet large enough to hold them in a single layer, set over medium heat, and cook, turning once, until charred and blackened in spots, about 12 minutes. Remove the garlic from the pan if it starts to char before the onions are done.

Finely chop the onions and garlic. Scrape them into a mixing bowl and add the cilantro, pomegranate juice, lime juice, chile, anise seeds, sugar, and pepper. Whisk until the sugar is dissolved. Slowly whisk in the olive oil. Add salt to taste. The dressing can be made in advance and kept at room temperature for up to 1 hour or refrigerated for up to 2 days. Whisk well and check for seasoning before serving.

NOTE: If you do not have a mortar and pestle, finely chop the anise seeds. First press firmly on them with the side of a knife or a flat-bottomed saucepan to prevent them from bouncing around. Then chop them, rocking the knife blade back and forth over the seeds until they are finely minced.

tomato, avocado, and red onion salad · ENSALADA DE AGUACATE, TOMATE, Y CEBOLLA

Known simply as *ensalada* throughout Mexico, this simple, pretty, and fresh-tasting dish is found everywhere. It is best if made a little bit (up to 30 minutes) ahead, but any longer and the avocados will darken. If blanching and peeling the tomatoes seems like too much work, leave the skins on.

If you own a mandoline, the sturdy (and expensive) French slicing and cutting tool, use it to cut the onion rings. Becoming more available are smaller plastic versions of the classic mandoline. They are much less expensive and come in very handy.

■ makes 6 servings

½ medium red onion (halved along the equator), cut into ¼-inch rings

3 large ripe tomatoes

2 medium Hass avocados

Salt and freshly ground black pepper

1½ teaspoons olive oil

3 key limes or 1 regular lime, cut in half

Fill a large bowl halfway with ice and pour in enough cold water to cover the ice. Soak the onion rings in the ice water for 4 to 5 minutes. (This will take the bite out of the onion.) Lift them out, shake off excess water, and lay them on paper towels to drain. Do not drain the bowl of ice water.

While the onion is soaking, bring a large saucepan of water to boil. Core the tomatoes and cut an X in the bottom of each. Slip the tomatoes into the boiling water and leave them just until the skin starts to peel away from the X. The time depends on the tomatoes: very ripe tomatoes will need 10 seconds or so, less-ripe tomatoes will take longer. With a slotted spoon, transfer the tomatoes to the ice water. Let them stand until cool enough to handle, then slip off the skins. Drain.

Cut the tomatoes into ½-inch slices and overlap them on a large deep platter to cover the bottom. Cut the avocados in half, working the knife blade around the pit, then twist the halves to separate them. Cut each half lengthwise in half (they'll be easier to peel that way) and strip off the peels. Cut the avocados lengthwise into thin strips and arrange them over the tomatoes. Pile the drained onion rings over the avocado. Season with salt and pepper, then drizzle with the oil and squeeze the lime halves over the top. Cover with plastic wrap and let stand for about 30 minutes before serving.

Bring the salad to the table, toss well, and serve.

COCKTAIL PARTY BUFFET FOR 8

There is very little last-minute work involved in this menu. Use the windfall of time to mingle and schmooze. After all, that's what a party is all about.

- Chile Peanuts (page 77)
- Green Ceviche (page 30) and Tortilla Chips (page 76)
- Queso Fundido (page 56) with Warm Tortillas and Tomatillo and Chile de Arbol Salsa (page 149) or Green Salsa (page 47)
- Garlicky Shrimp and Mushrooms (page 37)
- Toritos (pages 84 to 85)

UP TO 1 WEEK AHEAD ▪ Make the peanuts

EARLIER IN THE DAY ▪ Prep all the ingredients for the shrimp and queso fundido

4 HOURS AHEAD ▪ Make the ceviche

JUST BEFORE GUESTS ARRIVE ▪ Mix the toritos ▪ Sauté the shrimp

AFTER GUESTS ARRIVE ▪ Make the queso fundido ▪ Heat the shrimp

tortilla soup · SOPA DE TORTILLA

In Mexico this soup also goes by the name *sopa Azteca;* it is most popular in the country's central highlands. To thicken the soup, some Mexican cooks place tortilla strips directly into the simmering broth. At Rosa Mexicano, we first bake the tortillas until slightly crispy, then present diners with individual serving bowls holding dried tortilla strips along with cooked chicken and sliced avocado. The steaming broth is poured over everything. ▪ makes 6 servings

3 large ripe tomatoes (about 1½ pounds)

6 cups Chicken Broth (recipe follows) or store-bought chicken broth

3 large pasilla chiles, wiped clean, stemmed, seeded, and toasted (see page 2)

3 medium garlic cloves

3 large epazote stems (optional)

Salt

6 fresh Corn Tortillas (page 92) or store-bought 6-inch corn tortillas

1 tablespoon vegetable oil

1 medium Hass avocado

¼ pound queso fresco, cut into ½-inch cubes or coarsely shredded (about 1 cup)

2 cups shredded cooked chicken (optional)

Place the broiler rack about 8 inches from the broiler and preheat the broiler, to low if possible. Cut the cores from the tomatoes and cut a small X in the skin on the opposite end. Place on the broiler pan and broil, turning as necessary, until the skins are blackened and the tomatoes are softened throughout, about 20 minutes. Remove and let cool. Turn the oven down to 350°F.

While the tomatoes are cooling, heat the chicken broth in a medium pot to simmering. Pour enough of the broth over the chiles in a heatproof bowl to cover, and let stand until softened, about 20 minutes.

When the tomatoes are cool enough to handle, cut them into quarters. Put the tomatoes, chiles and their soaking liquid, and the garlic in a blender jar and blend at low speed until coarsely chopped. Increase the speed to medium and blend until smooth, adding a little more of the remaining broth if necessary.

Strain the mixture into the pot with the broth. Add the epazote and season with salt. Bring to a simmer and cook, uncovered, for 20 minutes.

Meanwhile, make the tortilla strips: Stack the tortillas and cut them into 4 triangles. Cut each stack of triangles into ¼-inch-wide strips. Pile the strips on a baking sheet and drizzle the oil over them. Gently toss and rub the strips until they are lightly coated with oil. Spread them out in an even layer and bake until golden and crisp, about 12 minutes. Stir them once during baking. The tortilla strips can be made up to several hours ahead. Store them uncovered at room temperature.

To serve: Remove the epazote from the soup and season to taste with salt. Cut the avocado in half and remove the pit. Peel each half and cut it into 6 slices (see Note, page 139). Place 2 slices in each of six shallow soup bowls. Divide the tortilla strips, cheese, and chicken, if using, among the bowls, ladle the soup into the bowls, and serve immediately.

chicken broth · CALDO DE POLLO

A good homemade chicken stock is the fuel that energizes so many cuisines. It lends a sturdy underpinning to all kinds of sauces, stocks, and soups. A typical Mexican chicken stock is flavored with onions, mixed herbs, and jalapeño peppers. Store-bought chicken broth will do in a pinch, but it is relatively pale next to this. And homemade stock freezes well for up to three months.

Once you have a good stock on hand, it's easy to throw together all kinds of quick soups and meals. For instance, add some cooked rice, a squeeze of lime, and a spoonful of Pico de Gallo (page 57). If you don't have plans to use the cooked chicken from the broth in a separate recipe, add some of that as well. ▪ makes about 3 quarts broth, with 4 cups shredded cooked chicken

One 4-pound chicken

3 quarts water

1 large white onion, cut into quarters

1 tomatillo, husked, rinsed, and cut in half

1 head garlic, cut in half along the "equator"

2 bay leaves

1 small jalapeño, a small slit cut in the tapered end

1 tablespoon salt

2 fresh mint sprigs

2 fresh thyme sprigs

2 fresh cilantro sprigs

Rinse the chicken thoroughly under cold running water, and put in a 5- to 6-quart pot. (Rinsing the chicken reduces the amount of foam that rises to the surface during cooking, which could make the broth cloudy or bitter.) Pour in the 3 quarts water and add the onion, tomatillo, garlic, bay leaves, jalapeño, and salt. Bring to a boil over high heat, skimming the foam and fat as they form on the surface. Adjust the heat so the broth is simmering, and add the mint, thyme, and cilantro. Partially cover the pot and cook, skimming occasionally, until no trace of pink remains near the joint that connects the thigh to the backbone (the last part of the chicken to cook), about 40 minutes. Remove the pot from the heat and cool the chicken in the broth.

When it is cool enough to handle, carefully transfer the chicken to a large plate. Strain the broth and refrigerate for up to 4 days or freeze for up to 3 months. Pull the skin off the chicken and free the meat from the bones. Shred the meat with your fingers, removing any small pieces of fat, bone, and skin as you go. Refrigerate the chicken until ready to use.

hot avocado soup · SOPA CALIENTE DE AGUACATE

This may sound unusual, but it is delicious, delicate, and a wonderful way to start a meal. Be prepared, though—once the soup is blended, it should be served within minutes in warm soup bowls; you cannot reheat this soup. Any number of toppings can be spooned into each bowl or passed at the table. Consider diced avocado (or even a dollop of Guacamole, page 73), cooked shrimp, Pico de Gallo (page 57), diced tomato, and/or Grilled Corn Relish (page 228). ▪ makes 7 cups; 6 servings

6 cups Chicken Broth (page 66) or store-bought chicken broth
2 medium Hass avocados
1 avocado leaf, toasted (see page 12; optional)
1 thin scallion, trimmed and thinly sliced
8 fresh mint leaves

⅛ teaspoon anise seeds
½ small garlic clove
Juice of ½ orange
Juice of ½ lime
Salt

Bring the broth to a boil in a medium saucepan.

Meanwhile, cut the avocados in half and remove the pits. Scoop the flesh from the avocados with a spoon, dropping it into a blender jar as you go. Add the avocado leaf, if using, the scallion, mint, anise seeds, garlic, and orange and lime juices.

When the broth is boiling, ladle about 1½ cups into the blender. With the lid firmly in place, blend until smooth. Add a little more hot broth if necessary.

Strain the avocado mixture into the broth remaining in the pan and stir over medium-low heat until blended and warmed through. Add salt to taste, ladle into warm soup bowls, and serve.

fresh corn in epazote broth · ESQUITES

At Rosa Mexicano we love to introduce our guests to authentic Mexican street fare that they will not find anywhere else. Here is a great example. Despite its humble origins, when served in small bowls, it makes a tantalizing addition to a cocktail party buffet. It also serves as a bracing appetizer. ▪ makes 6 cups; 6 appetizer servings or up to 12 smaller servings

8 medium ears corn

4 tablespoons butter

1 medium white onion, finely diced (about 1¼ cups)

1 jalapeño, minced

Salt

4 cups water

3 large epazote branches

1 cup coarsely shredded queso fresco (about 3 ounces)

Chile de árbol powder (see page 7) or other pure chile powder

Mayonnaise (optional)

Husk the corn and remove all the silk. Trim the ends of the cobs so they will stand steadily on a cutting board. With a sharp knife, shave the kernels from the cobs (don't cut too deep, or you will include the tough parts of the kernels that attach them to the cob). Then use the back of the knife to scrape any "milk" from what's left of the kernels on the cobs. There will be about 4 cups kernels. Lay the stripped cobs flat and use the heel of the knife blade to cut them in half. Set the cobs aside.

Heat the butter in a large heavy saucepan over medium heat until foaming. Stir in the onion and jalapeño, season lightly with salt, and cook until the onion is translucent, about 5 minutes. Stir in the corn, season lightly with salt, and stir just until the corn is softened, about 3 minutes.

Add the corn cobs to the pan and pour in the water. Bring to a boil, then adjust the heat so the liquid is simmering. Add the epazote and cook until the corn and onions are very tender, about 15 minutes.

Remove the cobs and serve the soup, or let it stand at room temperature for up to 2 hours before reheating to serve. In either case, remove the epazote before serving and add salt to taste. Ladle the soup into warm bowls, or into small cups if serving smaller portions. Top each serving with some of the queso fresco, a sprinkling of chile powder, and a dab of mayonnaise, if you like.

PATIO PARTY FOR 12

Who doesn't want to get involved at an outdoor party? Once you've laid the groundwork for the evening's dinner and your guests arrive, appoint a grillmaster—there is one in every crowd—to handle the ribs, corn, and quesadillas. That will leave you free to handle the cocktail shaker and dispense margarita refills where needed.

- Guacamole with Fruit (page 73)
- Basic Quesadillas (page 45) with (or without) squash blossoms
- Yucatán-Style Baby Back Ribs (page 54)
- Grilled Corn Street Vendor–Style (page 227)
- Pasilla de Oaxaca Tomatillo Salsa (page 53) and/or Green Salsa (page 47)
- Margaritas (pages 78–81)

THE DAY BEFORE ▪ Marinate the ribs ▪ Prepare the seasoned mayo for the corn

EARLIER IN THE DAY ▪ Assemble the quesadillas ▪ Grate the cheese for the corn
▪ Make the margarita mix ▪ Make the salsa(s) ▪ Prepare the fruits for the guacamole

AFTER GUESTS ARRIVE ▪ Finish the guacamole ▪ Grill the quesadillas, ribs, and corn ▪ Shake the margaritas

mushrooms "en escabeche" with red bell peppers and chiles • ESCABECHE DE HONGOS

These marinated vegetables make perfect party food, especially as they only get better after a few days in the refrigerator. In Mexico, some people might pick the garlic cloves out of the escabeche before serving, but I prefer to leave them in. In fact, I spear them with toothpicks and eat them on their own. • makes 6 generous servings

3 tablespoons vegetable oil or mild olive oil, or as needed

¾ pound button mushrooms, stems trimmed, caps cut into eighths

Salt

¾ pound shiitake mushrooms, stemmed

6 ounces oyster mushrooms, thick stem ends trimmed and separated into individual mushrooms

FOR THE ESCABECHE

½ cup olive oil

1 large white onion (about 8 ounces), cut in half and then into thin half-moon slices

3 chiles de árbol (with seeds), wiped clean and well toasted (see page 2)

5 garlic cloves

3 bay leaves

1 tablespoon honey

1½ teaspoons Worcestershire sauce

1 teaspoon Dijon mustard

1 teaspoon dried thyme

¼ teaspoon chile de árbol powder (see page 7) or other pure chile powder

¼ cup white wine vinegar

¼ cup sherry vinegar

1½ cups water

Salt

2 medium red bell peppers, roasted (see page 21), peeled, seeded, and cut into ⅛-inch-wide strips

Heat 1 tablespoon of the oil in a large skillet over medium-high heat. Add as many button mushroom pieces as fit without crowding (overloading the pan will steam, not sauté, the mushrooms), season with salt, and cook, stirring, until tender, about 8 minutes. Transfer to a large bowl. Repeat with the remaining button mushrooms, then the shiitakes, and then the oyster mushrooms, seasoning each batch with salt and adding oil to the pan as needed.

When all the mushrooms are cooked, make the escabeche: Pour the olive oil into the skillet and return it to the heat. Add the onion and cook, stirring, until translucent, about 5 minutes. Add the chiles, garlic, bay leaves, honey, Worcestershire, mustard, thyme, and chile powder and stir until blended. Add the vinegars and water, season generously with salt, and bring to a boil.

Pour the escabeche over the mushrooms, add the red pepper strips, and stir well. Pack into a deep glass or ceramic container and cool to room temperature.

Chill the mushrooms for at least 12 hours before serving. They will keep refrigerated for at least 2 weeks. Bring to room temperature and discard the garlic, if you like, and bay leaves before serving.

ESCABECHES

Think of escabeches as marinades that begin with the slow cooking of onions, gar-lic, bay leaf, and various spices in olive oil and vinegar. This is the platform for countless dishes that carry the name *escabeche*. Main ingredients may include meat, chicken, seafood, vegetables, chiles, shellfish, or even pigs' feet. These ingredients are very often cooked in the marinade and then served in it.

My grandmother used to serve a great chicken in escabeche as well as chiles rellenos en escabeche. You'll find all sorts of great seafood escabeches in Mexico's coastal areas—in earlier times, the technique was used for preservation.

guacamole

Over the years at Rosa Mexicano, we have run through so many avocados for guaca-mole that if you placed them side by side they would stretch from New York to Tierra del Fuego and back—maybe twice! It is our signature dish—nine out of ten guests order it. One of the things that makes guacamole at Rosa Mexicano special is that when we opened in 1984, we were among the first, if not the first, restaurant on either side of the border to serve guacamole prepared tableside in a traditional mol-cajete (see page 75).

We take our guacamole very seriously; in fact, you could say we are obsessed with it, and fanatical about consistency. I am frequently asked what makes our gua-camole so special. For one, we take great care in preparing the chile paste that is the underpinning of the dish—that's where the layered flavors come from. We begin by grinding some onions, chiles, and cilantro together in a molcajete. (The proportions are critical, so follow the recipe.) Then we gently toss in cubed avocado so that every piece is coated evenly. Before one of our waiters is allowed to prepare guacamole tableside, he or she must pass our rigorous training course, which might be called Molcajete 101. For the guest, the guacamole is great theater—and better eating.

■ makes 4 servings

FOR THE CHILE PASTE

1 tablespoon finely chopped white onion

1 firmly packed tablespoon chopped fresh cilantro

2 teaspoons finely chopped jalapeño, or more to taste

1 teaspoon salt, or as needed

3 medium ripe but firm Hass avocados (about 8 ounces each)

3 tablespoons diced tomato

2 firmly packed tablespoons chopped fresh cilantro

1 tablespoon finely chopped white onion

Salt if necessary

Tortilla Chips (page 76)
Fresh Corn Tortillas (page 92)

Make the chile paste: Grind the onion, cilantro, jalapeño, and salt together in a mol-cajete until all the ingredients are very finely ground. Alternatively, use a fork to mash all the ingredients to a paste in a wide hardwood bowl.

Cut each avocado in half, working the knife blade around the pit. Twist the halves to separate them and flick out the pit with the tip of the knife. Fold a kitchen towel in quarters and hold it in the palm of your "non-knife" hand. Rest an avocado half cut side up in your palm and make 3 or 4 evenly spaced lengthwise cuts through the avocado flesh down to the skin, without cutting through it. Make 4 crosswise cuts in the same way. Scoop the diced avocado flesh into the molcajete. Repeat with the remaining avocado halves.

[continued]

Gently fold the avocado into the paste, keeping the avocado in as large pieces as possible. Add the tomato, cilantro, and onion and fold in gently. Check and add salt if necessary. Serve immediately, right from the molcajete (or bowl), with the chips and tortillas.

NOTE: Jalapeños can vary tremendously in hotness, so taste the guacamole just after folding in the avocado and add more if you like.

VARIATION ▪ guacamole with seafood [guacamole con mariscos]

▪ makes 6 servings

¼ pound lump crabmeat (preferably jumbo), picked over for shells and cartilage (about ½ cup)

¼ pound cooked peeled baby shrimp, left whole, or larger shrimp, cut into small pieces

3 tablespoons chopped fresh cilantro

2 tablespoons finely chopped jalapeño

1 tablespoon olive oil

2 teaspoons chipotle adobo puree (see page 7)

Salt to taste

Toss all the ingredients together in a mixing bowl. Let stand at room temperature for 20 to 30 minutes.

Prepare the guacamole, adding the marinated seafood salad at the end along with the tomato, cilantro, and onion.

VARIATION ▪ guacamole with fruit [guacamole con frutas]

▪ makes 6 servings

Diana Kennedy, the Julia Child of Mexican cookbook authors, and Maria Dolores Torres-Izabal, a dear friend and author of *The Mexican Gourmet*, introduced me to guacamole with fruit. This is a specialty of two states in central Mexico—Morelos and Guanajuato. The contrast between the spicy guacamole and the sweet and juicy fruits is delicious. The dish should always look a little over the top—use the most beautiful, ripe fruits you can find and as many of the embellishments as you like.

Prepare the guacamole, omitting the cilantro entirely. Gently fold in 12 black grapes, halved; 12 green grapes, halved; and 1 cup peeled and diced (¼-inch) peaches or mango. Taste the guacamole and add additional chile or salt to balance the sweetness of the fruits.

Pile the guacamole into martini glasses or half-coconut shells and decorate with any or all of these garnishes: sliced peeled peaches, pomegranate seeds, toasted coconut flakes, and/or raspberries.

THE MOLCAJETE

The molcajete is to Mexican cooking what sparkplugs are to a car—an indispensable conduit of energy without which you won't get far. It's great for grinding small quantities of spices, herbs, or garlic and for making any kind of salsa. Fortunately, today molcajetes are more widely available—even Williams-Sonoma features them in its recent catalogues. A good home-size molcajete, which will cost between $30 and $50, should be heavy (as much as 12 pounds) and smooth all around, with a heavy conical pestle (called *mano* or *tejolote* in Mexico). A molcajete needs seasoning before use (see page 17).

tortilla chips · TOTOPOS

Vast quantities of chips are prepared in our restaurants each day to keep pace with the huge demand for our trademark guacamole (and for nibbling in general). The reason our chips are so good is that they are fried fresh just before dinner or lunch service begins. Tortilla chips should have a nice crackle and crunch, a pleasant saltiness, and, most important, a subtle but distinctive taste of corn. Although some of the chips you can buy now are quite good (especially those we sell through our online store), they are easy and fun to make at home. Recently I have been playing with oven-baked chips. They are probably easier, as well as leaner, for home cooks to deal with, but I prefer the texture of a fried chip. Below are both possibilities; try each to see which you think is better. ▪ makes 36 chips; enough for 6 servings of guacamole or salsa

6 day-old Fresh Corn Tortillas (page 92) or six
6-inch store-bought corn tortillas

Vegetable oil for deep-frying or brushing
Salt

TO DEEP-FRY THE CHIPS: Cut the tortillas in half, then cut each half into 3 triangles. Line a baking sheet with a double thickness of paper towels. Pour 3 inches of vegetable oil into a heavy 4- to 5-quart pot. Attach a deep-frying thermometer to the pot and heat the oil to 350°F. Carefully slip half the tortillas into the oil. Using a wire skimmer, stir the chips gently to separate them and keep them submerged in the oil. Cook until the chips are crisp and golden brown, about 1½ minutes. Lift out with the skimmer, letting as much of the oil drain back into the pot as possible, and spread the chips out on the paper towels to drain. Sprinkle with salt. Repeat with the remaining tortillas. Adjust the heat throughout frying to keep the temperature as close to 350°F as possible. Serve the chips warm or at room temperature. Leftover oil can be cooled completely, strained, and then poured into a clean container, tightly sealed, and refrigerated for up to 1 week to fry more chips or other foods.

TO BAKE THE CHIPS: Preheat the oven to 325°F. Using a pastry brush, coat both sides of the tortillas generously with vegetable oil. Season them with salt and cut them as described above. Spread the triangles out evenly on a baking sheet (it is fine if some of them overlap).

Bake until the edges start to curl and the tortillas start to firm up, about 10 minutes. Stir and turn the triangles with a metal spatula, bringing those closest to the edges toward the center and vice versa. Continue baking, turning and stirring twice more, until the chips are golden brown and crisp, about 15 minutes. Serve warm or at room temperature.

chile peanuts · CACAHUATES ENCHILADOS

It is impossible to imagine the bar at any Rosa Mexicano restaurant without a huge glass container of these peanuts—or to imagine anybody resisting them. Bags of peanuts like these (not as good, of course) are sold everywhere in Mexico. Although home cooks prepare these in a pan on the stovetop, I've found that the spice mixture can rub off and the nuts require constant attention if they are not to burn; our oven method is much easier.

The oven is set to a low temperature because, since the peanuts are already roasted, the idea is to crisp them up and toast the spice mixture. Baking them at a higher temperature could overcook them and make them bitter. ▪ makes 4 cups

4 cups unsalted dry-roasted peanuts
2½ tablespoons freshly squeezed lime juice
2 tablespoons olive oil

1 tablespoon sweet paprika
2 teaspoons salt
1½ teaspoons cayenne pepper

Preheat the oven to 250°F.

Toss the peanuts together with the remaining ingredients in a mixing bowl until all the nuts are evenly coated. The peanuts may look wet at this point—that is fine. Spread them out in an even layer on a large rimmed baking sheet (a jelly-roll pan works well). Bake until the coating is dry and the spices are lightly toasted, about 30 minutes.

Let the peanuts cool completely. They can be stored in an airtight container at room temperature for up to 3 weeks. If they lose their crispness after storing, reheat them on a baking sheet in a 250°F oven for 15 minutes before serving.

NOTE: If you have become a chile aficionado and prepare your own chile powder, feel free to substitute some chile de árbol powder or another pure chile powder (see page 7) for the cayenne pepper.

FAVORITE MARGARITAS

BELIEVE IT OR NOT, FEW MEXICANS ROUTINELY DRINK
margaritas. They are really an American phenomenon, found in tourist restaurants and hotels. At Rosa
Mexicano, it seems as if 110 percent of the guests order them. The drink's provenance is unknown,
although there is no shortage of fanciful history and speculation. Margaritas continue to gain momen-
tum with the trend toward boutique aged tequilas. To be sure, you can find some pretty awful examples
of this cocktail, especially those based on bad commercial mixes. However, here are three perennially
popular margaritas from our roster of drinks. Whichever you choose, serve them up or on the
rocks, following the guidelines below. Each can be easily multiplied, and that is why quantities are
given in both ounces (easier to multiply for large batches) and tablespoons (easier for individual
drinks). Remember there are 4 tablespoons in ¼ cup, 8 tablespoons in ½ cup, and so on.

the traditional margarita - LA TRADICIONAL

▪ makes 1 drink

1½ ounces (3 tablespoons) silver tequila
¾ ounce (1½ tablespoons) Cointreau or Triple Sec
¾ ounce (1½ tablespoons) freshly squeezed
  lime juice

1 tablespoon superfine sugar
A lime wedge

Prepare a salt-rimmed glass if you like (see below); use a 10-ounce glass if serving
on the rocks, a 6-ounce cocktail glass if serving up.

Put 6 ice cubes in a tall cocktail shaker. Pour the remaining ingredients (except
the lime wedge) into the shaker and shake vigorously. Pour, ice and all, into the
larger glass or strain into the smaller glass. Garnish with the lime wedge.

SALTING GLASSES FOR MARGARITAS

Oversalting the rim of your glass causes the salt to dissolve into the drink, which can leave your
cocktail tasting like Acapulco Bay on the rocks. To avoid this, follow these simple steps.

1. Roll and press a lime on a hard surface to break down the membranes and yield
   more juice. Halve the lime crosswise.
2. Spread an even layer of fine sea salt on a plate. Lightly rub the lime around the
   outside rim of the glass (just a gloss).
3. Lightly press the rim of the glass into the salt. Lift, and tap off the excess.
4. Allow the salt to air-dry before filling the glass. This is important—you do not want
   too much salt coming off the glass with each sip. In upscale restaurants in
   Mexico—among the few places in the country where margaritas are served—one
   sees salt-rimmed glasses hanging upside down from racks behind the bar.

passion fruit margarita

■ makes 1 drink

2 ounces (¼ cup) silver tequila

1½ ounces (3 tablespoons) passion fruit puree
(see page 16)

½ ounce (1 tablespoon) freshly squeezed
lime juice

¾ ounce (1½ tablespoons) Cointreau
or Triple Sec

1 tablespoon superfine sugar

Prepare a salt-rimmed glass if you like (see page 78); use a 12-ounce glass if serving on the rocks, an 8-ounce cocktail glass if serving up.

Put 6 ice cubes in a tall cocktail shaker. Pour the remaining ingredients into the shaker and shake vigorously. Pour, ice and all, into the larger glass or strain into the smaller glass.

blue margarita · MARGARITA AZUL

■ makes 1 drink

1½ ounces (3 tablespoons) silver tequila

1 ounce (2 tablespoons) blue Curaçao

¾ ounce (1½ tablespoons) freshly squeezed
lime juice

1 ounce (2 tablespoons) pineapple juice

1 teaspoon superfine sugar

Prepare a salt-rimmed glass if you like (see page 78); use a 10-ounce glass if serving on the rocks, a 6-ounce cocktail glass if serving up.

Put 6 ice cubes in a tall cocktail shaker. Pour the remaining ingredients into the shaker and shake vigorously. Pour, ice and all, into the larger glass or strain into the smaller glass.

SALT

Margarita drinkers fall into two distinct camps: those who like salt on the rim of the glass and those who do not. The custom of salt with margaritas probably has something to do with Mexico being, by and large, a hot, semi-tropical country. In Mexico, we use salt liberally in order to restore what we lose during the day through perspiration. Salt helps you absorb and retain water more quickly. No, revelers at the bar of Rosa Mexicano aren't sipping salted margaritas in order to rehydrate their blood—they just taste so good.

TEQUILA

Tequila is produced from the heart of the blue agave plant, which thrives in the dry volcanic soil in the state of Jalisco and many other parts of Mexico. The hearts of this plant are roasted, releasing a sweet sap that is then distilled. The liquor that results can be called tequila only if it is produced in Jalisco—where the town of Tequila is one of the two main centers of production—or in one of four other government-approved regions. Any similar liquor produced elsewhere in Mexico is called mezcal or sotol.

Most tequilas exported to the United States and Canada range from 80 to 86 proof, although you can find some as high as 100 proof. There are two basic types of tequila: 100 percent agave and *mixto*. Only tequilas made from the sap of the agave plant can be labeled "100%"; mixtos can be made with the addition of other alcohols, such as rum, and syrups.

Within the tequila family, there are four sub-categories:

- Silver tequila—or *blanco*, as it is known in Mexico—is clear and mild and has not been aged. These tequilas are used primarily in margaritas and other mixed drinks, not drunk on their own.
- Gold tequila is silver tequila that has been colored and flavored with caramel or another flavoring.
- Reposado ("rested") tequila must, by law, be aged in wooden casks for a minimum of 60 days.
- Añejo ("aged") tequila is aged in wooden barrels for a minimum of 12 months. The best-quality añejos are aged from 18 months to 3 years.

FROM LEFT: Silver tequila, reposado tequila, añejo tequila, and Sangrita de Jalisco (page 85)

toritos

Toritos are brightly colored and refreshing fruit-based drinks that are served as aperitifs. They are typically turbo-charged with aguardiente—sugarcane alcohol—but at Rosa Mexicano we prefer to use tequila. It's fun for a group to order several types for sharing, each presented in its own blue-rimmed glass pitcher. ▪ each recipe makes a pitcherful (about 5 cups), enough for 6 to 8 drinks

mango torito ▪ TORITO DE MANGO

1 large ripe mango
2 cups water
1 cup superfine sugar

1 cup silver tequila
½ cup freshly squeezed lime juice

Cut the flesh from both flat sides of the mango pit and then trim as much of the flesh from the narrow sides of the pit as possible. With a large spoon, separate the flesh from the skin. Chop the flesh, place in a blender jar, and puree. Measure out 1 cup of the puree; reserve any extra for another use.

Fill a pitcher with ice. Pour in the mango puree, water, sugar, tequila, and lime juice. Stir until the sugar is dissolved. Serve over ice.

soursop torito ▪ TORITO DE GUANABANA

"Soursop" may not sound like the most appetizing of fruits, but its sweet, custardy flesh has a delicious flavor and a wonderful perfume. If you cannot find frozen guanabana puree, track down fresh cherimoya—a very close relative of guanabana—and make your own puree from it, after peeling away the skin and removing the large, shiny black seeds.

1 cup guanabana puree
   (see headnote above)
2 cups water
1 cup superfine sugar

1 cup silver tequila
¼ cup freshly squeezed lime juice
6 Mexican cinnamon sticks (see page 16)

Fill a pitcher with ice. Pour in the guanabana puree, water, sugar, tequila, and lime juice. Stir until the sugar is dissolved. Drop in the cinnamon sticks. Serve over ice.

passion fruit torito ▪ TORITO DE MARACUYA

1 cup passion fruit puree (see page 16)
2 cups water
1 cup superfine sugar

1 cup silver tequila
¼ cup freshly squeezed lime juice
4 fresh mint sprigs, coarsely chopped

Fill a pitcher with ice. Pour in the passion fruit puree, water, sugar, tequila, and lime juice. Stir until the sugar is dissolved. Stir in the mint. Serve over ice.

sangrita de Jalisco

Sangrita is not a beverage—it is more of a condiment to be enjoyed when sipping tequila. You taste a little tequila, then sip a little sangrita, and repeat. When they start tasting the same, it's time to go home.

There are many versions of sangrita. One of the more common is made with tomato juice, but I don't like it. Our rendition here, which hails from the state of Jalisco, is closer to the traditional sangrita. It was passed along to me by my friend Maria Dolores Torres-Izabal, a noted cookbook author. ▪ makes about 3 cups; enough for 16 shots ▪ photograph on page 81

2 ancho chiles, wiped clean, stemmed, seeded, lightly toasted, and soaked (see page 2)
2 cups freshly squeezed orange juice
2 tablespoons grenadine

1 tablespoon finely chopped onion
Juice of 1 lime
½ teaspoon salt

Drain the chiles thoroughly. Combine all the ingredients in a blender jar and blend until smooth. Strain through a fine sieve and pour into a jar or other container. Refrigerate for at least 30 minutes (but no longer than 2 days, or the onion flavor will dominate).

3 TACOS

IN SPANISH, *TACO* **REFERS TO A CYLINDRICAL TOOL** used to pack gunpowder into cannons and rifles. Today we call any stuffed and rolled tortilla a taco. It is difficult to overestimate the importance of tacos in Mexican cuisine; in fact, the phrase *"comimos un taquito"* ("we had a little taco") is used to mean that you have eaten. While the common perception of tacos is street food you eat on the run, in fact they can be components of every style of dining, even the most elegant.

Taquerias—places that sell tacos—are of two types: those that sell tacos in which the meat, poultry, vegetables, or seafood is grilled or spit-roasted over a wood fire (*tacos al carbón*), and those that make tacos filled with all kinds of moist and saucy stews (*tacos de guisados*).

Tacos al carbón ("grilled") generally contain beef, pork, chicken, all of which are pounded until thin, or *nopales* (cactus leaves). These ingredients are grilled to order, chopped, and rolled in small (4-inch diameter) tortillas. Dinner at a taqueria al carbón almost always features four to five types of tacos accompanied by grilled spring onions, a small pot of queso fundido (page 56), and Pinto Beans with Bacon and Onion (page 221).

Going for tacos de guisado is, in most cases, an afternoon event; saucy dishes like these are considered slightly too heavy for nighttime dining. The portions of filling tend to be slightly larger, so, in general, two or three different tacos will be sufficient, especially when rounded out with some brothy beans and maybe some overcooked wet rice.

TORTILLAS

TORTILLAS ARE THE MOST ESSENTIAL OF THE ESSENTIALS.
It is not an exaggeration to say that corn tortillas are present at every meal in every Mexican household. Freshly made, they are served warm with meals, as bread is in other cultures, or turned into enchiladas, flautas, and numerous other dishes. Day-old tortillas can be transformed into tostadas or budines (see pages 96 and 170), tortilla chips (page 76), or chilaquiles. If you have never tried freshly made tortillas, you are in for a treat.

making tortillas

Tortillas are made from masa, the pliable corn dough that can be used to make all sorts of other dishes, such as tamales, little dumplings for soup, and small breads that are split and stuffed with a variety of fillings. The traditional way to make masa is to start with water to which slaked (powdered) lime has been added. Dried corn kernels are left to soak overnight in the limed water until the outer skins start to loosen, and the corn is then set aside in the cooking liquid for several hours. When it is fully softened, the corn is rinsed to remove excess lime and as many (or few) of the skins as desired. The softened corn is drained and ground, traditionally at the communal village mill, resulting in the soft masa dough. What type of dried corn is used, whether some of the skins are left on the kernels or all are removed, and how fine or coarse the masa is ground depend on the region and on what the masa will be used for: tortillas, tamales, *antojitos*, etc.

Most likely you will not be slaking your own lime, cooking your own dried corn, or taking your cooked corn to the mill to be ground. There is an excellent and quick alternative: making masa from an instant corn masa mix, commonly labeled *"masa para tortillas,"* which is masa prepared as above and then completely dehydrated to a powder. *Masa para tortillas* is widely available in Latin groceries and gourmet supermarkets—look for Maseca, Minsa, or Quaker brands. (It is also available online at www.dvo.com) All that is needed to restore the powder to masa is water and some mixing. If you have a stand mixer with a hook attachment, use it: it lightens the dough somewhat and makes it easier to shape and press.

warming tortillas

When served on the side as a bread, tortillas are always warmed first. Most people warm tortillas on a comal (the traditional round flat griddle), but some place the tortillas directly over a medium to medium-low flame on a gas range. If you do not have a comal, use a griddle or any large flat-bottomed skillet. Don't be tempted to warm tortillas in a microwave oven—they will emerge limp, which is fine for making flautas (see page 50), but not for eating plain. Tortillas can be warmed over medium heat until just heated through and softened or until toasted and crisp, even charred in places. Toasting rather than simply warming tortillas gives them more flavor. What you use to warm your tortillas and how toasted, or not, you make them is a matter of personal preference. But in any case, warm the tortillas as close to serving time as possible. To serve them Rosa-style, line a basket (there are baskets especially made to hold tortillas and keep them warm) or bowl with a cotton kitchen towel. As the tortillas are warmed, place them in the basket and fold the towel over them to keep them warm.

LA TAQUIZA

To bring the spirit and experience of a taco dinner party, or *taquiza,* into your home is not complicated. But it is a lot of fun, passing the condiments and allowing guests a chance to create whatever type of taco suits their whims. Just as with *taquerias,* there are two types of taco parties you can throw at home. Here is how they work in Mexico.

A TACO PARTY AL CARBÓN, a grilled taco party, always includes at least three salsas for garnishing, as well as a salad of *nopales* (page 234), lettuce salads, sliced avocados, grilled spring onions, pickled jalapeños (page 125), and halved limes.

Your host will greet you and offer you a drink, then he (not to be sexist, but a *taquiza* of this kind is always handled by the men of the household) will ask you to go outside to where the wood-fired grill is going. There a table will be set up with all the garnishes and fillings. When everybody is gathered, the men will start grilling the meats and the women will start warming tortillas. Once off the grill, the meats or chicken are sliced, paired with the warm tortillas, and dressed according to each guest's taste.

(See Grilled Chile-Marinated Skirt Steak, page 94; and Grilled Adobo-Marinated Chicken Tacos, page 96.)

A TAQUIZA DE TACOS DE GUISADO, a saucy-tacos party, is the women's domain. All the women in the household will have worked hard beforehand to prepare the stews, which may include chicken in mole, potatoes with chorizo, pork with tomatillos, chicken stewed with tomatoes, pork cracklings in red guajillo sauce, sautéed mushrooms with epazote, and/or sautéed squash blossoms among many others blossoms, as well as two spicy salsas, one red and one green. Some of the women will warm tortillas and others will help to fill them with the various *guisados.* (Note that while the women pitch in at a "men's" *taquiza,* the reverse is not usually the case!)

(See Seafood Stewed in Tomato Sauce, page 120; Lobster in "Little Adobo," page 106; Chicken in Mole, page 127; and Slow-Cooked Achiote Marinated Pork, page 102.)

As a guest of either type of party, you would lay a warm tortilla on the palm of your left hand and scoop one of the fillings on to the tortilla, then add any salsa you like, squeeze on a little lime, and sprinkle with a little freshly chopped onion, cilantro, and/or any other condiments there may be. Roll it up and enjoy!

fresh corn tortillas

▪ makes about 12 tortillas

2 cups *masa para tortillas* **(instant corn masa mix)**   **1¼ cups warm water, or as needed**

Preheat a cast-iron griddle over medium-high heat or an electric griddle set to 400°F.

Put the masa in the bowl of a stand mixer fitted with the hook attachment. Beat at low speed while gradually adding 1 cup of the water. Add as much of the remaining water 1 tablespoon at a time as needed to make a soft and smooth dough. The dough is the right consistency when a small piece of it can be rolled into a ball between your palms without the dough cracking. Beat for 1 minute more, then use the dough immediately.

Roll 3 level tablespoons (1½ ounces) of the dough between your palms to make a 2-inch ball. Line the bottom plate of a tortilla press with a circle of plastic (cut from a plastic grocery store bag; see page 18 for more on tortilla presses and how to use them). Center the dough over the plastic, top with a second circle of plastic, and press the dough out to a smooth circle, wiggling the handle of the press gently to flatten the dough evenly. Lift the top of the press, rotate the dough circle so the front of the circle is now at the back, and press again. (Most tortilla presses will make tortillas that are slightly thicker on one side than the other. Rotating the tortilla after the first press will make an evenly thick tortilla that will cook evenly.)

As soon as the tortilla is pressed, place it on the griddle. Cook until the underside start to turn light golden brown in spots, about 2 minutes. Turn and cook until the tortilla puffs up. Repeat with the remaining masa, transferring the hot tortillas to a napkin-lined basket if serving them immediately or stacking them on a plate if using them for another recipe. Once you get the hang of it, you'll be able to press more tortillas while those on the griddle continue cooking

TOP ROW FROM LEFT: Pinto Beans with Bacon and Onions (page 221); Tomatillo and Chile de Arbol Salsa (page 149); Green Salsa with Avocado (page 47).
MIDDLE ROW: Serrano chiles, limes; chopped onion and cilantro.
BOTTOM ROW: Grilled spring onions (page 95); Grilled Chile-Marinated Skirt Steak (page 94), tortillas.

FILLINGS FOR TACOS AL CARBON (GRILLED FILLINGS)

HERE ARE RECIPES FOR PREPARING THE FILLINGS FOR your own *tacos al carbón taquiza* party (see page 91). There is last-minute grilling and slicing, but you can prepare just about everything—including the suggested accompaniments that follow each recipe—in advance. The activity adds to the festive spirit. So will a big batch of margaritas (pages 78–81) and a bright, colorful pitcher of toritos (pages 84–85).

grilled chile-marinated skirt steak - CARNE ENCHILADA

The mingling of chiles—guajillos and pasillas for flavor, and cascabels for heat—make this adobo particularly good with skirt steak. I like it with other steaks like T-bones and shell steak and with pork tenderloin. It also does wonders for game like venison and quail. The adobo can be made several days in advance. ▪ makes enough to fill about 15 tacos

▪ photograph on page 93

1¾ to 2 pounds skirt steak

FOR THE ADOBO

3 cascabel chiles, wiped clean, stemmed, seeded, and toasted (see page 2)

2 guajillo chiles, wiped clean, stemmed, seeded, and toasted (see page 2)

2 pasilla chiles, wiped clean, stemmed, seeded, and toasted (see page 2)

½ cup water

1 teaspoon cumin seeds

5 allspice berries

2 cloves

A 1-inch piece of Mexican cinnamon stick (see page 16)

5 garlic cloves

8 black peppercorns

Trim all the fat from the surface of the meat, and remove the silverskin (the thin whitish gray membrane). If the steak is in one piece, cut it crosswise in two, into a thicker and thinner half. Put in a shallow baking pan.

Make the adobo: Drain the chiles, put them in a blender, and add the remaining adobo ingredients. Blend at low speed until fairly smooth.

Wearing gloves if you like, rub the adobo generously all over the skirt steak. Let stand at room temperature for 1 hour, or cover and refrigerate for up to 1 day.

Prepare a charcoal fire or preheat a gas grill to medium-high. Grill the steak, turning once, until charred in places and cooked to medium-rare, about 10 minutes for the thinner half, slightly longer for the thicker half. (Adjust the cooking time as necessary for rarer or more well done steak.) Remove to a carving board, cover with foil, and let stand for 5 minutes.

Cut the steak against the grain into ¼-inch slices, pile them on a platter, and serve immediately.

TO ACCOMPANY BEEF TACOS

Lime wedges

Coarse salt

Sliced radishes

Chopped fresh cilantro

Chopped onions

Pasilla de Oaxaca Tomatillo Salsa
(page 53)

Grilled Spring Onions (recipe follows)

Pinto Beans with Bacon and Onion
(page 221)

Green Salsa with Avocado (page 47)

GRILLED SPRING ONIONS

Just about every *taqueria* in Mexico offers these delicious treats as a snack before and during your taco meal. The onions, which are like a cross between scallions and the large-bulb spring onions we know in the States, are placed without seasoning or oil directly onto a charcoal grill. When they are tender and charred in spots, they are passed out to the diners, who squeeze lime wedges over them and sprinkle them with salt before eating them between bites of taco. Sometimes they are cut into short lengths and added to a taco filling. You can make a perfectly delicious version of this Mexican standard using medium-sized scallions (or spring onions with very small bulbs, if you can find them). Leave the roots intact but peel off any tough outer layers, then rinse and dry them well. Grill, turning once or twice with tongs, until tender and blackened in spots. Right before serving, cut off the roots. Now, all you need is one bowl of lime wedges and another of coarse salt—which should already be on the table if you are hosting a proper *taquiza*!

grilled adobo-marinated chicken tacos · POLLO ADOBADO

- makes enough to fill about 15 tacos

A double recipe of Adobo for Adobo-Marinated
Chicken (page 133)

2 pounds boneless, skinless chicken breasts
Salt

Pound the chicken with a meat mallet to an even thickness of about ¾ inch. Rub the chicken breasts generously with salt and put them in a shallow baking pan.

Pour the adobo over the chicken and (wearing gloves, if you like) rub it into the chicken. Let stand at room temperature for up to 1 hour, or refrigerate for up to 1 day. Bring to room temperature before continuing.

Heat a gas grill to medium-high or prepare a hot charcoal fire.

Grill the chicken, turning once, until charred in places and just cooked through, about 10 minutes. Remove to a carving board, cover with foil, and let stand for 5 minutes.

Cut the chicken into ¼-inch slices, pile them on a platter, and serve immediately.

TO ACCOMPANY CHICKEN TACOS

Lime wedges

Chopped white onion

Chopped fresh cilantro

Traditional Refried Beans (page 224)

Shredded queso Chihuahua

Green Salsa (page 47)

Red Salsa "Molcajete" (page 99)

TOSTADA

Tostada is Spanish for "toasted"; any baked or fried-until-crisp tortilla can be called a tostada. They generally range in size from 1 inch (ideal for bite-sized canapés) to 4 to 6 inches, but they may be as large as 12 inches across, these are called "*totopos*" in Oaxaca. When the tortillas are cut into small triangular wedges, they are sometimes given the diminutive name *tostaditas.* While tostaditas or chips are most often used as a utensil to scoop up salsas or guacamole, larger tostadas may be topped with various hot or cold preparations, like ceviches (pages 29–35), guacamoles (pages 73–74), escabeches (pages 70–71), or chicken, beef, or pork stewed in different sauces.

One of the most popular tostadas, which any Mexican would recognize, is a crispy tortilla spread with a thin layer of refried beans, then topped with shredded lettuce and garnished with shredded chicken, beef, or pork. The top is drizzled with crema, sprinkled with grated queso fresco and cilantro, and topped with either a pickled jalapeño or a chipotle en adobo. These impressive tostadas—which remind me of volcanos because of their shape—are served in sets of three, whether at home or at a traditional restaurant, as a main course. For an appetizer, only one is served.

Corn tortillas constitute the primary diet element for millions of people in Mexico and several countries of Central America.

As wheat was for Mesopotamia and rice for Asia, corn was the foundation upon which our cultures were built, from as far back as the Maya and Aztec civilizations. The pre-Hispanic name for tortilla was *tlaxcala*. The Spanish likened their flat round shape to their egg "tortillas" (omelets) and gave them that name.

HOW WE SERVE TACOS AT ROSA MEXICANO

A cast-iron skillet is a great addition to any cook's kitchen. At Rosa Mexicano we use them by the hundreds! We cook the main ingredients, usually grilled meat or poultry, and transfer them to heated 5-inch-square cast-iron skillets holding melted queso Chihuahua. The sizzling treats are served in the skillets accompanied by salsas and warm fresh tortillas. Garnishes change seasonally: Grilled Corn Relish (page 228), Grilled Spring Onions (page 95), a small salad (see Rosa Mexicano House Salad, page 60), and more.

red salsa "molcajete" · SALSA ROJA DE MOLCAJETE

This easy, flavorful salsa has a wonderful earthy red color. Although it is best prepared in a molcajete (see page 17), you can prepare it in a blender. ▪ makes about 2 cups

3 ripe medium tomatoes (about 1 pound),
  roasted (see page 23)

6 serrano chiles, or more or less to taste,
  roasted along with the tomatoes (see Note)

2 small garlic cloves

1 teaspoon salt, or to taste

Peel the tomatoes and chiles. Cut the cores from the tomatoes and cut the tomatoes into quarters.

Grind the chiles, garlic, and 1 teaspoon salt to a paste in a molcajete. Add the tomatoes, a few pieces at a time, and continue grinding until the salsa is fairly smooth. (Alternatively, combine the chiles, garlic, salt, and about one-third of the tomatoes in a blender jar and blend until the chiles and garlic are finely ground. Add the remaining tomatoes and blend, using quick on/off pulses, just until they are liquified.) Add more salt if you like. The salsa can be made up to 6 hours in advance and refrigerated. Bring to room temperature before serving.

NOTE: If you are making our Simple White Rice (page 216), save the two whole chiles to use in this recipe.

FILLINGS FOR TACOS DE GUISADO

BECAUSE ALL OF THE TACO FILLINGS AND CONDIMENTS are done in advance, there is very little for the cook to do at a *taquiza de tacos de guisado* except relax and enjoy. There is another bonus—because there is no grilling involved, the party goes on rain or shine.

seafood stewed in tomato sauce · GUISADO DE MARISCOS

In northwestern Mexico, people enjoy this filling on a tortilla spread with mayonnaise. It may sound a little odd, but it is truly delicious. This moist, slightly spicy filling would also be delicious used to stuff roasted poblano chiles (see page 11) or reconstituted ancho chiles (see page 5). ▪ makes enough to fill about 15 tacos

Salsa Mexicana (page 183)

$\frac{1}{2}$ cup chopped fresh cilantro

$\frac{1}{2}$ cup chopped fresh flat-leaf parsley

$\frac{1}{4}$ cup chopped fresh mint

12 medium Manzanilla (Spanish) olives, pitted and coarsely chopped

3 tablespoons tiny (nonpareil) capers, drained

2 tablespoons liquid from Rosa's Pickled Jalapeños (page 125) or canned pickled jalapeños

$\frac{1}{2}$ pound firm white fish fillets, such as halibut, snapper, or striped or black bass, cut into $\frac{1}{2}$-inch pieces

$\frac{1}{2}$ pound medium shrimp (about 20), peeled and deveined

$\frac{1}{2}$ pound lump crabmeat, picked over for shells and cartilage

Salt

Reheat the sauce to a simmer in a medium saucepan if necessary. Stir in the cilantro, parsley, mint, olives, capers, and jalapeño liquid. Cook until almost all the liquid has evaporated from the sauce. (The seafood will give off liquid, so you need to start with a thick sauce to avoid a runny filling.)

Stir in the seafood. Bring to a simmer and cook, stirring often, just until the shrimp and fillets are opaque throughout, about 4 minutes. It is fine if some of the fish breaks up into smaller pieces. Season to taste with salt. Serve immediately.

TO ACCOMPANY SEAFOOD TACOS

Lime wedges

Chopped white onion

Chopped fresh cilantro

Grilled Spring Onions (page 95)

Mayonnaise or the seasoned mayonnaise from Grilled Corn Street Vendor–Style (page 227)

Pickled Red Onions (recipe follows)

pickled red onions · CEBOLLAS ROJAS ENCURTIDAS

These tart and flavorful onions are pretty too. They go with so many things—grilled fish, poultry, beef, or pork, any kind of taco—that we thought of bottling our own Rosa Mexicano pickled onions. Once you have them on hand, you will find your own uses, such as chopping them to season a finished soup, spooning them onto a burger, and a hundred more. ▪ makes about 2 cups

1½ pounds red onions, cut in half and then into very thin (about ⅛-inch-wide) strips (about 5 cups)

1½ teaspoons salt

½ teaspoon dried oregano, crumbled

½ cup white vinegar

1 cup freshly squeezed lime juice, or as needed

1 habanero chile

Toss the onions, salt, and oregano well in a mixing bowl. Pack them into a tall narrow glass or stainless steel container. Pour the vinegar over the onions, then add the lime juice. Press the onions down lightly; there should be enough juice to cover the onions. If not, add more lime juice. Cut a small slit in the tip of the habanero and tuck the habanero into the onions.

Weight the onions down lightly (a small heavy custard cup or ramekin works well). Refrigerate overnight. The onions can be stored in the refrigerator for up to 1 week. Bring to room temperature before serving.

slow-cooked achiote-marinated pork · COCHINITA PIBIL

The translation of the Maya word *pib* is "pit," as in a large pit dug in the ground in which a whole pig, rubbed with adobo and wrapped tightly in banana leaves, is cooked. Here is a citified version of this ancient dish: no pit, no whole pig, just tender, juicy meat and rich achiote flavor. The work can be divided among several days: rub one day, cook the next, rewarm the third.

Because it is difficult to properly cook a smaller amount of pork than what is given below, this recipe makes more than you will need to fill 15 tacos (as all the other filling recipes in this chapter do). But that is hardly a problem—rewarm leftovers and spoon them onto a roll for lunch: Mexico's version of a Carolina pulled pork sandwich. ▪ makes about 6 cups; enough to fill 15 tacos, with leftovers ▪ photograph on page 105

FOR THE ACHIOTE RUB

¼ cup orange juice

½ cup freshly squeezed bitter orange juice (see opposite) or cider vinegar or white vinegar

One 3½-ounce package achiote paste (see page 12)

Juice of 2 limes

5 teaspoons salt

3 garlic cloves

1 teaspoon dried oregano, crumbled

½ teaspoon cumin seeds

¼ teaspoon ground allspice

3½ pounds fatty pork butt or shoulder, cut into 1½- to 2-inch pieces

About half of a 10-ounce package banana leaves (see page 12)

Combine all the achiote rub ingredients in a blender jar. Blend at low speed until the achiote is broken into small pieces, then increase the speed to high and blend until smooth.

Put the pork in a large mixing bowl, pour the rub over it, and toss (wearing gloves, if you like) until the pork is evenly coated. The pork can be prepared in advance. Let stand at room temperature for up to 1 hour, or refrigerate for up to 1 day. Bring to room temperature before using.

Cut the thick edge from each banana leaf. Handling them gently to keep them in as large pieces as possible, wash the banana leaves under cold water, wiping away any white spots. Pat dry. Turn on a gas or electric burner to medium heat. Using tongs, pass each piece of leaf over the heat—quickly, so it doesn't scorch—until the top of the leaf turns shiny and the leaf is softened, about 5 seconds. Flip the leaf and repeat. With a damp kitchen towel, wipe both sides of the banana leaves to remove any remaining dirt or white spots.

Preheat the oven to 350°F.

Line an 11 by 9-inch baking dish (or any baking dish that holds the pork comfortably) with banana leaves, overlapping them as necessary in order to completely cover the bottom and sides; it is fine if some of the leaves overhang the sides. Transfer the pork and rub into the dish, scraping out all the rub from the bowl and making an even layer of pork. Fold any overhanging leaves over the pork and cover the top with the remaining pieces of banana leaf, tucking them between the baking dish and the leaves in the dish. Cover the dish tightly with a double thickness of aluminum foil.

Bake until the pork is tender enough to be pulled apart with a fork, about 2½ hours. (You can check after 2 hours, but not before. After checking, reseal the aluminum foil tightly, using new foil if necessary.) The pork can be prepared to this point up to 2 days in advance. Cool to room temperature, then refrigerate. Rewarm in a preheated 350°F oven for 20 to 30 minutes before continuing.

Remove the pork and let stand, covered, for 10 minutes. Remove the foil and top layer of leaves, and transfer the pork and its cooking juices to a serving bowl. Coarsely shred the pork with two forks. Serve hot.

TO ACCOMPANY ACHIOTE-MARINATED PORK TACOS

Pickled Red Onions (page 101)
Green Salsa (page 47)
Restaurant-Style Refried Beans (page 224)

NOTE: To serve the pork as a main course on its own, try this simple but stunning presentation: Use one of the plates you will be serving the pork on as a template and cut out 6 circles of banana leaf. Toast them lightly as described on page 102. After tossing the pork with the achiote rub, divide it among the circles, placing each portion in a mound in the center of the circle. Fold the top and bottom edges of the circle over the pork, then fold both sides over. Use kitchen twine to secure the bundles. Line a baking pan with banana leaves as described above and place the bundles side by side in the pan. Cover with banana leaves and foil and bake as described.

To serve, snip the strings and place the bundles folded side up on serving plates. Let each guest open the leaves to reveal the fragrant filling. The banana leaf circle will line the plate and look beautiful.

BITTER ORANGE (NARANJA AGRIA)

Bitter oranges (also called sour oranges) are ubiquitous in the cooking of Yucatán and Tabasco, as well as many other parts of southeast Mexico. A little larger than a lemon and pale green to yellow in color, they are not very sweet and have a very sour edge and a taste somewhat like lime. They were introduced to Mexico by the Spanish explorers. They add a nice puckery sensation to all kinds of sauces and salsas and in particular to cochinita pibil (see opposite). When not available, a mild vinegar does a similar job.

RIGHT: Slow-Cooked Achiote-
Marinated Pork (page 102)
BELOW: Banana leaf packet
(see Note, page 103)

lobster in "little adobo" • LANGOSTA EN ADOBILLO

Spanish is rich with diminutive nicknames, not just for people (think of Juanita or Paquito) but for food. One of the diminutives for adobo (see page 6) is *adobillo*. This amusing "little adobo"—made with an unconventional mixture of red guajillo and roasted habanero chiles—gives the lobster a hint of sweetness and a somewhat rusty color. The recipe makes more adobo than you will need for this dish, but it is very versatile. Freeze the leftover adobo in an ice cube tray, than transfer to a freezer bag. Use a cube or two to perk up the flavor of dishes like pork or beef stews. It will even add a new dimension of flavor to quick shrimp or fish stir-fries and sautés. ▪ makes enough to fill about 15 tacos

FOR THE "LITTLE ADOBO"

4 garlic cloves, peeled

1 habanero chile

2 guajillo chiles, wiped clean, stemmed, seeded, toasted, and soaked (see pages 2 and 3)

½ cup water

2 tablespoons white vinegar

½ cup olive oil

1½ teaspoons salt

Three 1½-pound live lobsters or 1¼ pounds cooked lobster meat

1½ teaspoons olive oil

MAKE THE LITTLE ADOBO: Place a rack about 6 inches from the broiler and preheat the broiler, to low if possible (you can do this while the chiles are soaking). Place the garlic and habanero chile on the broiler pan and broil, turning a few times, until the garlic is well browned, the chile is charred in spots, and both are softened, about 5 minutes.

Pull the stem from the habanero chile and put the chile and garlic in a blender jar. Drain the guajillo chiles and add them to the jar, along with the water and vinegar. Blend at low speed until smooth. With the motor running, pour in the olive oil in a thin stream. Blend until smooth; you will have about 1½ cups adobo. Add the salt, blend well, and scrape the mixture into a storage container. The adobo can be made up to 2 days in advance and refrigerated.

PREPARE THE LOBSTERS (IF USING LIVE LOBSTERS): Bring a large pot of salted water to a boil. Meanwhile, fill another large pot or a very large mixing bowl with ice and pour in enough cold water to cover the cubes. Plunge the lobsters into the boiling water and cook just until the shells are uniformly red, about 3 minutes. (The lobster meat will be undercooked—it will finish cooking in the sauce.) With tongs, transfer the lobsters to the ice water. Let stand for 5 minutes, then drain thoroughly in a colander.

REMOVE THE MEAT FROM THE LOBSTERS: Twist each tail to separate it from the body. Cut along the underside of the tail with a pair of shears and pull out the tail in one piece. Use a sturdy pair of nutcrackers or a wooden mallet to crack the claws and the two "knuckles" attached to them. Remove the meat from the claws and knuckles, using a seafood fork.

Cut the freshly cooked (or store-bought lobster) meat into ½-inch pieces. Drain the lobster on several sheets of paper towels, using another several sheets to blot the top dry. (Blotting the lobster as dry as possible before sautéing it will keep excess liquid out of the pan and cut the cooking time, which means tender, not overcooked, lobster.) The lobster meat may be prepared up to a few hours in advance. Cover and refrigerate.

Heat the oil in a large (at least 11-inch) heavy skillet over high heat just until the oil starts to smoke. Add the lobster and cook, stirring constantly, until any liquid in the pan has evaporated. Add 2 tablespoons of the adobo and cook, stirring until the lobster is coated, about 1 minute. Scrape into a serving bowl and serve immediately.

VARIATION · seafood for tacos

Cook one 1½-pound lobster as directed above and remove the meat (or substitute ½ pound cooked lobster meat); cut into ½-inch pieces. Cut ½ pound peeled and deveined small shrimp into ½-inch pieces. Cut ½ pound flaky fish fillets, such as bass or snapper, into ½-inch pieces. Toss the lobster, shrimp, and fish together in a bowl to mix them evenly. Cut a lime in half and squeeze the juice from both halves over the seafood, tossing again. Heat the oil as directed above, and cook the filling, stirring occasionally, until the seafood is just cooked through, 4 to 6 minutes.

TO ACCOMPANY LOBSTER (OR SEAFOOD) TACOS

Pickled Red Onions (page 101)
Grilled Corn Relish (page 228)

RIGHT: Jalapeños

4
ENCHILADAS

ENCHILADA IS REALLY A SHORT VERSION OF TORTILLA

enchilada, or, literally, "chileed tortilla"—in other words, a tortilla rubbed, mixed, cooked with, soaked in, or otherwise flavored with chiles of one type or another. That being said, there are infinite variations on the theme. For example, the masa for the tortillas (see page 90) can be made with chile paste or broth, as in the recipe for Red Masa on page 41 and then made into tortillas. *Enchiladas potosinas,* from San Luís Potosi, a state in the north of Mexico, are uncooked red masa tortillas that are filled with cheese, then fried and served with an assortment of salsas and toppings, which can even include scrambled eggs. *Enchiladas placeras,* from the central parts of Mexico (called *enchiladas mineras* in some states) are white corn tortillas rubbed with a dried chile paste and then gently fried, folded into quarters (without a filling), and topped with a scattering of poached carrots, potatoes, peas, chopped onion, cilantro, and cheese such as queso fresco or cotija.

Nowadays in Mexico, the modern concept of enchilada means corn masa tortillas topped or filled with seafood, poultry, or meat and served with any variety of chile-based sauces, salsas, or adobos (see page 6). They are usually garnished with greens or herbs, vegetables, grated cheese, and/or crema.

In the United States, we typically think of enchiladas as two or three corn tortillas gently fried in oil to soften them (or not), stuffed with some type of meat, poultry, cheese, and/or vegetable filling, and generously topped with a sauce (made, of course, with chiles). Toppings, as you see in the recipes in this chapter, can include chopped cilantro, onions, red or green cabbage, and sesame seeds (particularly good if the chile sauce is a mole).

In Mexico, one way to serve enchiladas that is seen in countryside restaurants and homes is to pass the softened tortillas (see page 115) through a hot sauce, then fold the unfilled tortillas into quarters, as described above, and overlap them on a plate. The sauced tortillas are topped with chicken or vegetables, buried under a small mountain of shredded lettuce, drizzled with crema, and finished with finely grated queso fresco and chopped fresh cilantro. Feel free to adapt any of the serving suggestions found at the end of each recipe to this family-style approach. Use the sauce to coat the softened tortillas before folding them, then scatter the filling (now a topping) over the tortillas, followed by the suggested toppings listed in the recipe.

At Rosa Mexicano, we take a slightly more formal approach to enchiladas. We fill the tortillas to order, douse them with sauce, and sprinkle them with cheese before putting them under a super-hot broiler to melt the cheese and warm the filling. We propose two ways for home cooks to serve enchiladas to guests. One is to fill the enchiladas up to a few hours in advance and refrigerate them right in their baking dish. Then, just before serving, sauce the casserole, top it with cheese, and bake until bubbly. This approach works well with looser sauces like Cooked Green Salsa (page 114) thinned with a little cream, paired here with the Crab Enchiladas (page 116), and the Swiss Enchiladas (page 113). There is no last-minute preparation for these two baked enchiladas except sprinkling on the toppings after they come out of the oven. The second approach, used with thicker sauces that won't stand up well to baking, is to prepare the sauce and filling in advance— up to 2 days ahead in most cases—and then to soften the tortillas (necessary only if using store-bought tortillas) up to an hour before serving. To serve, enlist a volunteer who can top the tortillas and take them to the table after you have filled and sauced them on the individual plates. With either method, most of the work is done in advance, and that makes enchiladas prime candidates for an entertaining menu.

swiss enchiladas · ENCHILADAS SUIZAS

Enchiladas suizas are an old staple of Sanborns, a very popular Mexican chain of cafeterias. It claims it named the dish and first served it more than fifty years ago. In the years that followed its debut, a number of Swiss restaurants with names like El Chalet Suizo opened in the capital. Enchiladas suizas are but one example of the cross-cultural nature and constant evolution of Mexico's cuisine.

To make this classic, chicken-filled corn tortillas are paired with Cooked Green Salsa that is enriched with cream and cheese. (Here we offer the green version; to prepare a red version, substitute Ranchera Sauce, page 122.) The casserole is topped with grated cheese and baked until bubbling and golden brown. The enchiladas can be filled hours in advance, and the tomatillo sauce made a day ahead. Before guests arrive, top the enchiladas with sauce and cheese and pop them in the oven. ▪ makes 6 servings

FOR THE SAUCE

4 cups Cooked Green Salsa (recipe follows)

2 poblano chiles, roasted (see page 21), peeled, seeded, and coarsely chopped

1 cup heavy cream

12 Fresh Corn Tortillas (page 92) or 6-inch store-bought corn tortillas

¼ cup vegetable oil or light olive oil if using store-bought tortillas

4 cups cooked shredded chicken (from Chicken Broth, page 66, leftovers or a store-bought rotisserie chicken)

FOR THE TOPPINGS

1½ cups shredded queso Chihuahua or Muenster cheese (about 6 ounces)

1 cup finely chopped white onion

⅓ cup chopped fresh cilantro

Preheat the oven to 375°F.

Make the sauce: Pour half the green sauce into a blender jar, add the poblanos, and blend at low speed until smooth. Pour into a medium saucepan, add the remaining green sauce and the cream, and bring to a simmer over low heat. Remove from the heat. If prepared in advance, reheat, adding water 1 tablespoon at a time if necessary to return the sauce to the right consistency, before ladling over the enchiladas.

If using store-bought tortillas, soften in the oil and drain them (see page 115). Fill and roll the tortillas, using ⅓ cup of the chicken for each one. Place the enchiladas seam side down in a 9 by 13-inch baking dish. The enchiladas can be prepared to this point up to 4 hours in advance. Cover them with a damp kitchen towel or paper towels, cover the dish with plastic wrap, and refrigerate. Remove from the refrigerator 30 minutes before baking.

Pour the hot sauce over the enchiladas. Jiggle the dish so the sauce settles in between the enchiladas. Sprinkle the cheese evenly over the top. Bake until the sauce around the edges is bubbling and the cheese is golden brown, about 20 minutes. Let stand for 5 minutes before serving.

Scatter the onion and cilantro over the enchiladas. Scoop 2 enchiladas and plenty of sauce onto each serving plate.

cooked green salsa · SALSA VERDE COCIDA

You will come across this tangy, cilantro-scented sauce not just in Enchiladas Suizas, but in countless Mexican recipes. At Rosa Mexicano we also turn it into a table salsa by boosting the heat and adding chopped onion and fresh cilantro (see the variation). You can also use the sauce as a base for stewing meat and poultry. · makes 4 cups

2 pounds tomatillos, husked and washed
2 jalapeños
3 small garlic cloves
1 teaspoon ground cumin

1 bunch cilantro, thick bottom stems removed, the remainder washed and shaken dry (see Note)
1 tablespoon vegetable oil
1 tablespoon salt, or to taste

Put the tomatillos and jalapeños in a medium saucepan, pour in enough cold water to barely cover (about 3½ cups), and bring to a boil. Cook until the jalapeños are soft and the tomatillos are tender, about 20 minutes. Remove from the heat and let stand for 15 minutes to finish cooking the inside of the tomatillos.

Drain the tomatillos and chiles (gently, to avoid breaking up the tomatillos) in a colander. Wipe out the saucepan and set aside. Put the tomatillos, jalapeños, garlic, and cumin in a blender jar and blend for a few seconds, just until the tomatillos are coarsely chopped. Add the cilantro and blend until the sauce is smooth and speckled with finely chopped cilantro. Do not overblend, or you will grind the tomatillo seeds and make a thick and pasty rather than smooth and shiny sauce.

Heat the oil in the cleaned pan over medium heat. Pour in the salsa, bring to a simmer, and simmer until lightly thickened, about 10 minutes. Season with the salt. The sauce can be stored in the refrigerator for up to 3 days. Reheat over low heat before using.

NOTE: When trimming, washing, and drying the cilantro, keep it more or less in bunch form, then add the bunch to the blender jar stems down; they will quickly be pulled into the liquid and chopped, avoiding overblending.

VARIATION · green salsa for the table

Coarsely grind 2 roasted and peeled jalapeños (see page 21) with a large pinch of salt in a molcajete or in a mortar with a pestle. Stir in 2 cups cooled Cooked Green Salsa, ½ cup finely chopped white onion, ½ cup chopped fresh cilantro, and salt to taste. (Alternatively, blend the chopped jalapeños and sauce in a blender jar using quick on/off pulses just until the jalapeños are coarsely chopped. Scrape into a bowl and stir in the onion, cilantro, and salt.) Let stand for 1 hour before serving.

SOFTENING AND FILLING TORTILLAS FOR ENCHILADAS

Regardless of the type of enchiladas you are making—rolled, folded, or dipped—store-bought tortillas need to be softened by briefly cooking them in hot oil. Once softened, tortillas destined for baked enchilada dishes (Swiss Enchiladas, page 113, or Crab Enchiladas, page 116) should be filled and then cooked or refrigerated as soon as possible. For enchiladas that are being filled and sauced just before serving (all the other recipes in this chapter), the softened tortillas can be stacked, wrapped in plastic, and held at room temperature for up to an hour. But here is another incentive to make your own fresh corn tortillas: they do not have to be softened before making enchiladas.

To soften tortillas: For 12 store-bought tortillas, you will need about ¼ cup vegetable or light olive oil. In a skillet large enough to hold a single tortilla, heat about half the oil over medium-low heat. To check whether the oil is at the right temperature, dip the edge of a tortilla in the oil—it should bubble briskly. Lay the tortilla in the pan and cook, turning once using tongs, until it starts to blister, about 15 seconds per side. Handle it carefully—once the tortilla softens, it can tear easily. Drain on paper towels. Repeat with the remaining tortillas, adding more oil as necessary.

To fill and roll tortillas: Imagine a line dividing each tortilla horizontally in half. Spread the filling evenly over the bottom half of the tortilla. Fold the bottom edge of the tortilla up over the filling, then roll up the tortilla. Place seam side down, to keep it from unrolling, in the baking dish or on a platter.

crab enchiladas · ENCHILADAS DE JAIBA

The sweetness of the crab and the onion acts as a terrific foil to the zip of the habanero chile. The crab stuffing is also delicious set over mixed greens as an appetizer.
These enchiladas are one of the most popular and spiciest dishes on Rosa Mexicano's
menu. ▪ *makes 6 servings*

FOR THE FILLING

1 pound lump crabmeat, picked over for shells
  and cartilage

1 cup Spicy Habanero Escabeche (recipe
  follows)

½ cup lightly packed chopped fresh cilantro

Salt

4 cups Cooked Green Salsa (page 114)

1 cup heavy cream

12 Fresh Corn Tortillas (page 92) or store-
  bought 6-inch corn tortillas

3 to 4 tablespoons vegetable oil if using store-
  bought tortillas

FOR THE TOPPINGS

1½ cups coarsely shredded Emmenthaler,
  Gruyère, queso Chihuahua, or Muenster
  cheese (about 6 ounces)

½ cup diced tomato

¼ cup toasted pumpkin seeds (see page 60)

¼ cup chopped fresh cilantro

Preheat the oven to 375°F.

Make the filling: Gently toss the crab, escabeche, cilantro, and salt to taste in a
medium bowl. Set aside.

Pour the green salsa into a medium saucepan, add the cream, and bring to a simmer over low heat. Remove the pan from the heat. (If filling the enchiladas in
advance, wait until just before you are ready to cook them to heat the sauce.)

If using store-bought tortillas, soften them in the oil and drain them. Fill and
roll the tortillas, using ⅓ cup of the crabmeat filling for each one (see page 115 for
tips on softening, filling, and rolling). Place the enchiladas seam side down in a 9
by 13-inch baking dish. (All 12 enchiladas will fit snugly if you arrange them in 2
crosswise rows of 6 in the dish.) The enchiladas can be filled up to 4 hours before
serving. Cover them with a damp kitchen towel or paper towels and plastic wrap
and refrigerate. Remove from the refrigerator 30 minutes before serving.

Pour the warm sauce over the enchiladas and jiggle the baking dish to settle the
sauce in between the enchiladas. Scatter the cheese in an even layer over the top.
Bake until the top is bubbling and golden brown and the filling is heated through,
about 20 minutes. Let the enchiladas stand for 5 minutes before serving.

To serve, scatter the tomato, pumpkin seeds, and cilantro over the enchiladas.
Scoop 2 enchiladas and plenty of sauce and toppings onto each serving plate.

spicy habanero escabeche · ESCABECHE PICOSO DE HABANERO

The habanero—generally considered the ultimate fire-breather of Mexican chiles—makes this a preparation that commands your attention. If you want to step back from the fire, use the milder jalapeño pepper. The chile's fire means that a little of this escabeche goes a long way. Try it as a condiment to store-bought rotisserie chicken or as a topping for a plain or filled omelet. Add a dab to the filling of any quesadilla or spread some on bread before assembling a sandwich. ▪ makes about 1¾ cups

½ cup mild olive oil

2 large (about 1 pound) white onions, skin and first outer layer removed, cut in half and then into thin slices

3 garlic cloves, cut in half

1 habanero chile, cut into quarters

5 small bay leaves

1½ teaspoons dried oregano, crumbled

¼ teaspoon dried thyme

3 tablespoons cider vinegar

1 teaspoon salt, or as needed

Heat the oil in a medium skillet over medium-low heat. Add the onions, garlic, chile, bay leaves, and dried herbs and cook, stirring, until the onions are translucent and wilted, without browning, about 10 minutes.

Add the vinegar and salt and bring to a boil. Remove the pan from the heat. Cool completely, then spoon into a small container and refrigerate for up to 2 weeks.

octopus enchiladas with roasted yellow tomato sauce
▪ ENCHILADAS DE PULPOS

This preparation is based on the Veracruz style of seafood cooking. To my taste, octopus and squid ink have a faint anise flavor, so I add anise seed to accentuate that.

Although this is a little more involved than most of the recipes in this chapter, you will be delighted with the results. And the recipe can easily be broken down into manageable steps. ▪ makes 6 servings

FOR THE FILLING

2½ pounds (completely drained weight) cleaned baby octopus, preferably fresh, or defrosted if frozen

1½ cups Salsa Mexicana (page 183)

½ cup small Manzanilla (Spanish) olives, halved and pitted

2 tablespoons small (nonpareil) capers

1 teaspoon squid ink (see Note)

¼ teaspoon ground anise seeds (see Note, page 61)

3 fresh mint sprigs, leaves only, finely chopped

½ cup lightly packed chopped fresh cilantro

¼ cup chopped fresh flat-leaf parsley

TO SERVE

12 Fresh Corn Tortillas (page 92) or store-bought 6-inch corn tortillas

3 to 4 tablespoons vegetable oil if using store-bought tortillas

Roasted Yellow Tomato Sauce (recipe follows)

Crema, crème fraîche, or thinned sour cream (see page 15)

About 2 cups finely shredded red cabbage

Make the filling: Cut the heads off the octopi and check to make sure the "beak"—the hard round sphere located between the head and tentacles—has been removed from each one; if not, cut it out. Cut the tentacles in half (into two sets of four each, not crosswise in half).

Remove the bay leaves from the tomato sauce and bring the sauce to a simmer in a large saucepan. Add the octopus, olives, capers, ink, and anise seeds. Bring to a boil, then adjust the heat so the liquid is simmering and cook, stirring occasionally, until the octopus is tender (even when tender, it will still be quite firm), the liquid given up by the octopus has cooked off, and the sauce is thick enough to coat the octopus, about 45 minutes. As more of the liquid evaporates, lower the heat slightly and stir more often. Depending on the octopus, it is possible the liquid will be thickened before the octopus is tender; if so, add water a few tablespoons at a time as necessary until the octopus is tender.

When the octopus is tender, stir in the mint, cilantro, and parsley and cook for 1 to 2 minutes. The sauce can be made up to 1 day in advance. Cool to room temperature, then refrigerate. Reheat over low heat, adding a small amount of water if necessary to return the sauce to the right consistency.

If using store-bought tortillas, up to an hour before serving, soften them in the oil and drain them (see page 115).

When ready to serve, reheat the yellow tomato sauce (and the octopus filling if necessary).

Place 2 tortillas on a warm plate. Fill and roll them, using ⅓ cup filling for each one (see page 115 for tips on filling and rolling). Center the enchiladas on the plate. Ladle about ⅔ cup of the roasted tomato sauce over them. Drizzle a little crema over the sauce in a zigzag pattern and scatter some of the cabbage over the center of the enchiladas. Repeat with the remaining tortillas, filling, sauce, and toppings.

NOTE: Squid ink is available online at www.markys.com.

roasted yellow tomato sauce ▪ SALSA DE TOMATES AMARILLOS

Yellow tomatoes make a beautiful sauce. They are not traditional in Mexican cooking, but the technique is. This sauce is good with other enchiladas, such as crab (page 116), or ladled over huevos rancheros or the beef-stuffed ancho chiles on page 207. If you increase the acidity of the salsa with a little lime juice, you can also serve it with grilled fish. ▪ makes 4 cups

6 medium yellow tomatoes (about 4 pounds), roasted (see page 23), cored, and peeled
1 habanero chile
3 garlic cloves

¼ cup vegetable oil
1 small white onion, finely chopped (about 1⅓ cups)
1 teaspoon salt
1 teaspoon sugar

Working in batches, combine the tomatoes, chile, and garlic in a blender and blend until smooth.

Heat the oil in a heavy medium saucepan over medium heat. Add the onion and cook, stirring, until the onion is translucent, about 4 minutes. Add the tomato mixture and bring to a boil. Adjust the heat so the sauce is simmering, and stir in the salt and sugar. Cook, stirring, until the sauce is a rich orange-yellow color and thickened enough to mound slightly on a spoon, about 40 minutes. Remove from the heat. The sauce can be made up to 2 days in advance. Let cool, then refrigerate. Reheat before using.

beef enchiladas with ranchera sauce
▪ ENCHILADAS DE PUNTAS DE RES Y SALSA RANCHERA

The word *puntas* translates as "tips," as in tenderloin tips. Usually much less expensive than the thick center-cut tenderloin steaks (filet mignon), they are perfect for this dish. You will find many versions of *puntas* across Mexico, including one dish known as *puntas al albañil* (bricklayers', or builders', style). Mexican builders are known for their healthy appetites and love of spicy food—they search out great eateries and also come up with dishes of their own. If you're into food, these are the guys you want to eat with. ▪ makes 6 servings

FOR THE FILLING

1½ pounds beef tenderloin tips

3 tablespoons light olive oil

1 large white onion (about 10 ounces), cut into ½-inch dice

2 garlic cloves, chopped

¾ cup slivered almonds

¾ cup chopped fresh cilantro

½ cup raisins

2 tablespoons juice from Rosa's Pickled Jalapeños (page 125) or bottled pickled jalapeños

1 teaspoon dried oregano, crumbled

Salt and freshly ground black pepper

Ranchera Sauce (recipe follows)

12 Fresh Corn Tortillas (page 92) or store-bought 6-inch corn tortillas

3 to 4 tablespoons vegetable oil if using store-bought tortillas

FOR THE TOPPINGS

2 cups very thinly sliced red cabbage

6 Rosa's Pickled Jalapeños (page 125) or bottled pickled jalapeños

⅓ cup chopped fresh cilantro

Raisins (optional)

Make the filling: Cut the beef into ¼ by ¼-inch strips. Heat the oil in a large (at least 11-inch) skillet over medium-high heat until it just starts to smoke. Immediately, but carefully, slide the beef, onion, and garlic into the pan. Cook, continuously stirring the ingredients up from the bottom of the pan, until the onion is wilted and the beef is cooked through, about 8 minutes. Add the almonds, cilantro, raisins, jalapeño juice, oregano and, salt and pepper to taste. Stir in ½ cup of the ranchera sauce and bring to a boil. Remove from the heat. The filling can be made up to 2 hours in advance. Let cool, then cover and refrigerate.

If using store-bought tortillas, up to an hour before serving, soften them in the oil and drain them (see page 115).

When ready to serve, reheat the ranchera sauce (and the beef filling if necessary).

Center 1 tortilla on each of six warm plates. Top each with an even layer of the beef filling, and then with a second tortilla. Spoon about ¾ cup of the ranchera sauce over each enchilada and let it run onto the plate. Scatter the red cabbage over the top, center a pickled jalapeño over the cabbage, and scatter the cilantro and raisins, if using, over the sauce.

ranchera sauce · SALSA RANCHERA

It's no wonder that we Mexicans make phenomenal tomato sauce. We gave the rest of the world tomatoes and taught them how to turn them into sauces, like this simple cinnamon-and-garlic-scented version that is another pillar of the Mexican kitchen. It has many, many uses, both on its own—spooned over eggs in the morning is one—and as the base for other dishes, such as the Beef Enchiladas. And why not make a potful of this instead of your usual tomato sauce next time spaghetti and meatballs are on the menu?

Terrible things are sometimes done in the name of salsa ranchera, like starting with raw tomatoes and blending them, skins and all, instead of beginning with peeled slowly roasted ripe tomatoes. The cinnamon stick is not traditional, but we always did it this way at home, and I still like it. It's not unusual to find cinnamon-seasoned sauces in some of the central Mexican states. ▪ makes 4 cups

3 pounds ripe tomatoes, roasted
  (see page 23), peeled, and cored

2 serrano chiles

2 large garlic cloves

A 2-inch piece of Mexican cinnamon stick
  (see page 16)

¼ cup vegetable oil

1 small white onion, finely chopped
  (about 1⅓ cups)

1½ teaspoons salt, or as needed

1 teaspoon sugar, or as needed

Working in batches if necessary, combine the tomatoes, chiles, and garlic in a blender and blend until smooth. Center the cinnamon stick on a 6-inch square of cheesecloth and tie the corners of the square together to make a neat bundle. (Mexican cinnamon will fall apart during cooking and the pieces can be difficult to remove from the finished dish. Wrapping the cinnamon in cheesecloth makes it easy to remove it all after cooking.)

Heat the vegetable oil in a medium saucepan over medium heat. Add the onion and cook, stirring, until the onion is translucent, about 4 minutes. Add the pureed tomato mixture and bring to a boil. Stir in the salt, sugar, and cinnamon bundle. Adjust the heat so the sauce is simmering. Cook until lightly thickened (just enough to coat a spoon), about 30 minutes. If the sauce thickens too much before that time, lower the heat slightly and add water, a tablespoon or two at a time.

Remove the sauce from the heat and check the seasonings, adding more salt and sugar if you like. The sauce can be made up to 3 days in advance. Let cool, then cover and refrigerate. Reheat over low heat, adding water 1 tablespoon at a time if necessary to return the sauce to the right consistency.

lamb enchiladas with tomatillo-pasilla sauce
• ENCHILADAS DE BORREGO EN SALSA DE PASILLA

The shredded lamb that serves as a stuffing for these unusual enchiladas is cooked "barbacoa style" (see page 127)—long, low-temperature baking that yields fork-tender, juicy, and intensely flavorful meat. The tangy-sweet tomatillo sauce is a marvelous accompaniment. Serve with steamed or roasted vegetables on the side. This recipe can be doubled, tripled, or more if need be. The lamb adobo is also great as a taco filling. • makes 6 servings

FOR THE ADOBO

4 guajillo chiles, wiped clean, stemmed, seeded, and toasted very lightly (see page 2)

4 chiles de árbol (with seeds), or less, depending on heat, wiped clean and well toasted (see page 2)

5 large garlic cloves

Scant 1 teaspoon cumin seeds

4 cloves

1 teaspoon dried oregano, crumbled

$1/2$ cup water

2 tablespoons cider vinegar

$2^1/_2$ pounds boneless leg of lamb (trimmed of most but not all fat) in one piece

1 tablespoon salt

3 large or 6 small avocado leaves

12 Fresh Corn Tortillas (page 92) or store-bought 6-inch corn tortillas

3 to 4 tablespoons vegetable oil if using store-bought tortillas

About 4 cups Tomatillo-Pasilla Sauce (recipe follows)

FOR THE TOPPINGS (ANY OR ALL)

About 2 cups finely shredded green cabbage

1 cup finely diced white onion

1 cup thinly sliced red radishes

$1/3$ cup chopped fresh cilantro

Preheat the oven to 300°F.

Make the adobo: Put both chiles, the garlic, cumin, cloves, oregano, water, and vinegar in a blender jar. Blend at low speed until smooth.

Put the lamb in a deep casserole or Dutch oven large enough to hold it snugly. Wearing gloves if you like, rub the salt, then the adobo into the lamb. Lay the avocado leaves over the lamb. Cover the casserole (with a double thickness of heavy-duty aluminum foil crimped tightly to the edges of the pot if there isn't a lid) and bake until the lamb is tender but not falling apart, about $2^1/_4$ hours. Remove and let cool to room temperature.

When the lamb is cool enough to handle, remove it and shred the meat fairly finely back into the sauce. The lamb can be prepared up to 1 day in advance. Cover and refrigerate.

If using store-bought tortillas, up to an hour before serving, soften them in the oil and drain them (see page 115).

When ready to serve, reheat the tomatillo-pasilla sauce (and the lamb filling if necessary).

[continued]

Place 2 tortillas on a warm plate. Spoon about ⅓ cup filling over one half of each, and fold the empty half over the filling. Center the tortillas on the plate, and ladle about ⅔ cup of the sauce over them. Repeat with the remaining tortillas, filling, and sauce. (There will be sauce left over.) Scatter the toppings of your choice over the enchiladas.

tomatillo-pasilla sauce · SALSA DE TOMATILLOS Y CHILES PASILLAS

Known primarily as a gutsy sauce for enchiladas, this can also be used as a braising liquid for meat or poultry. Or, if you have some leftover chicken, shred it into the sauce to make a quick filling for tacos. (One batch of this sauce makes enough to sauce the Lamb Enchiladas with enough left over to experiment with these or other techniques.)

You might want to substitute different chiles for the pasillas. For instance, guajillos produce a beautiful brick-red sauce with a distinctive flavor. The tomatillos can be boiled instead of roasted. Roasting them yields a sauce with a deeper flavor and color; boiling the tomatillos results in a more delicate sauce. ▪ makes 7 cups

2½ pounds tomatillos, husked, washed, and roasted (see page 23)

12 pasilla chiles, wiped clean, stemmed, seeded, toasted, and soaked (see pages 2 and 3)

9 garlic cloves

1 tablespoon sugar

1½ teaspoons salt

1½ teaspoons cumin seeds, very lightly toasted

1 teaspoon chile de árbol powder (see page 7) or other pure ground chile powder (optional)

½ teaspoon dried thyme, crumbled

½ teaspoon dried oregano, crumbled

¼ cup vegetable oil or mild olive oil

1 small white onion (about 6 ounces), coarsely chopped

Working in batches, combine the tomatillos, pasillas, garlic, sugar, salt, cumin, chile powder, if using, thyme, and oregano in a blender jar and blend just until smooth. Do not overblend, or the mixture will become pasty.

Heat the oil in a medium heavy saucepan over medium heat. Add the onion and cook, stirring, until the onion is translucent, about 1 minute. Scrape the tomatillo mixture into the oil and bring to a boil, stirring constantly. Adjust the heat so the sauce is simmering and cook, stirring often, until the sauce is thickened and shiny and little bubbles of oil appear on the surface, 20 to 25 minutes. If the sauce thickens enough that it starts to stick in places before it becomes shiny, add water, up to 1 cup, a little at a time. The sauce can be made up to 2 days in advance. Let cool, then cover and refrigerate. Heat to simmering, adding water a little at a time as necessary to restore the sauce to the right consistency, before using.

rosa's pickled jalapeños · JALAPEÑOS EN VINAGRE

These pickled peppers are a zesty addition to any meal, and the brine also serves as a terrific flavor booster for other dishes (such as the Beef Enchiladas with Ranchera Sauce on page 121). All sorts of vegetables, such as mushrooms, green beans, cauliflower, and *nopales* (cactus leaves), can be combined with the pickles.

Mustard may seem a little unusual in a Mexican recipe, but it is actually quite common in Mexico's urban areas. Use plain yellow (hot dog) mustard if that's what you have, or Dijon if you prefer. ▪ makes about 8 cups

20 medium jalapeños (about 1¼ pounds)
½ cup olive oil
2 medium white onions (about 14 ounces), cut into 2-inch chunks
2 large carrots (about 10 ounces), peeled and cut into ½-inch rounds
24 garlic cloves, peeled
3 cups cider vinegar
1 cup water
3 tablespoons salt

3 bay leaves
4 fresh thyme sprigs
4 fresh marjoram sprigs
½ lime, cut into ½-inch slices
1½ tablespoons sugar
2 teaspoons yellow or Dijon mustard
12 allspice berries, coarsely crushed
½ teaspoon black peppercorns, coarsely crushed

With a paring knife, cut two slits on opposite sides of each jalapeño, starting about ½ inch from the stem end and ending about 1 inch from the tapered end.

Heat the oil in a deep nonaluminum saucepan over medium-low heat. Add the jalapeños, onions, carrots, and garlic and cook, stirring often, until the vegetables are softened but not browned, about 10 minutes.

Add the vinegar, water, salt, bay leaves, thyme, marjoram, lime, sugar, mustard, allspice, and peppercorns. Bring to a boil, then adjust the heat so the liquid is simmering. Taste and add a little more water if the mixture seems too sharp to you. Remember, though, that it will mellow somewhat as it sits. Simmer for 15 minutes. Remove the pan from the heat and cool to room temperature.

Pack the vegetables and their liquid into clean glass jars and refrigerate. They will keep for up to 6 weeks, as long as they are kept refrigerated and all the vegetables are covered in liquid.

turkey-chorizo enchiladas with pecan-prune mole

▪ ENCHILADAS DE PAVO Y CHORIZO CON MOLE DE CIRUELAS

The rich, warm spiciness of the chorizo in the filling for these enchiladas balances the lean ground turkey and complements the sweet and fruity mole. (There's that Mexican love of sweet with spicy again.) The filling is based on a more traditional picadillo, made with ground beef or pork. *Picadillo* comes from the word *picado*, which means "chopped." Not only is the beef or pork chopped, but so are most of the other ingredients, which can include vegetables such as carrots, green beans, and chayote. Most picadillos are simmered in a tomato sauce like the Salsa Mexicana, as in this version, or Ranchera Sauce (page 122) and are seasoned with chiles (of course!) and herbs and spices. Picadillos are eaten by themselves or along with rice and/or beans or can serve as fillings for empanadas (turnovers). ▪ makes 6 servings

FOR THE FILLING

¾ pound chorizo (see page 205), removed from casings and crumbled

¾ pound ground turkey

⅓ cup very coarsely chopped pecans

⅓ cup raisins

2 tablespoons chopped fresh flat-leaf parsley

1½ cups Salsa Mexicana (page 183)

Salt

12 Fresh Corn Tortillas (page 92) or store-bought 6-inch corn tortillas

3 to 4 tablespoons vegetable oil if using store-bought tortillas

Pecan-Prune Mole (page 172)

FOR THE TOPPINGS

Crema, crème fraîche, or thinned sour cream (see page 15)

⅓ cup finely chopped white onion

⅓ cup chopped fresh cilantro

Sesame seeds

Make the filling: Put the chorizo in a large heavy skillet, set over low heat, and cook, stirring, until it begins to render its fat. Increase the heat to medium and cook until the chorizo is sizzling and starting to change color. Add the turkey and cook, stirring to break it up, until cooked through, about 5 minutes.

Add the pecans, raisins, and parsley and cook for 1 minute. Stir in the salsa, bring to a boil, and season with salt. Cook, stirring occasionally, until the sauce is lightly thickened. Remove from the heat. The filling can be made up to one day in advance. Let cool, then cover and refrigerate.

If using store-bought tortillas, up to an hour before serving, soften them in the oil and drain them (see page 115).

When ready to serve, reheat the mole, thinning it with a little water if necessary to restore it to the right consistency (and reheat the turkey-chorizo filling if necessary).

Place 2 tortillas on a warm plate. Spoon about ⅓ cup filling over one half of each. Fold the empty half over the filling and center the filled tortillas on the plate. Ladle about ⅔ cup of the sauce over the enchiladas. Drizzle some crema in a zigzag pattern over the enchiladas and scatter the onion, cilantro, and a small amount of sesame seeds over the sauce. Repeat with the remaining tortillas, filling, sauce, and toppings.

CHICKEN IN MOLE FOR TACOS

If you find yourself with a small amount of mole, such as the Pecan-Prune Mole, and half a chicken's worth of cooked and shredded meat, make this very simple taco filling. It will fill about 15 tacos and goes nicely with chopped white onion, chopped cilantro, lime wedges, and, if you like, Pasilla de Oaxaca Tomatillo Salsa (page 53).

Heat 2 tablespoons vegetable oil or light olive oil in a large skillet over medium heat. Add 1 medium white onion, chopped (about 1¼ cups), and cook, stirring, until translucent. Add the chicken, season with salt, and stir until heated through. Pour in 1 cup mole and bring to a simmer. Cook just until the sauce is lightly thickened.

BARBACOA

In Mexico, preparing barbacoa of lamb is an involved, ritualistic affair. After butchering the lamb, its innards are seasoned with chiles and cooked, then placed inside the lamb. Depending on the region or the cook, the lamb is then rubbed with chiles, and salt seasoned with other ingredients such as avocado leaves. The entire lamb, head and all, is wrapped in maguey leaves (see the headnote on page 166) and cooked overnight in a large pit holding glowing embers. It emerges just in time for lunch the next day.

If you ever attend an important Mexican family occasion—such as a wedding or anniversary—chances are barbacoa will be on the menu. All over the country, you'll find restaurants where this is a specialty.

Barbacoa can also be made with beef or goat.

5 QUESADILLAS AND TORTAS

QUESADILLAS

UNLIKE THE SMALLER HALF-MOON-SHAPED QUESADILLAS
made with corn tortillas in chapter 2, these large quesadillas are round and are made by layering
flour tortillas with various fillings. In Mexico, you would find these quesadillas made with flour
tortillas about the same size as corn tortillas—six inches or so in diameter—but at Rosa, we make
them with larger (ten-inch) flour tortillas. Quesadillas can be elegant, like the one made with serrano ham and Manchego cheese, or quite simple, using sliced deli ham and yellow cheese—every
Mexican schoolchild's favorite.

These larger quesadillas make a nice lunch or, cut into wedges, a good little nibble before dinner—especially for a dinner that comes off the grill.

cooking quesadillas

The perfect quesadilla is crisp and evenly browned outside with the cheese inside
melted and the filling warm. The key to success is steady, even heat—cooking
quesadillas over too high a heat crisps up the outside before the inside can become
gooey and warm.

TO COOK ON THE GRILL: The temperature is right if you can hold your hand
about an inch over the grill for 6 seconds or so before having to move it away. Any
less time, and the heat is too high—lower the temperature of a gas grill or wait
for the coals to die down a bit. Lay the quesadillas on the grill and cook until grill
marks start to form on the underside, about $1^1/_2$ minutes. Give the quesadillas a
quarter turn and cook until evenly golden brown and crosshatched, about another
$1^1/_2$ minutes. If the quesadillas start to brown before that, move them to a cooler
part of the grill. Flip and repeat.

TO COOK ON A GRIDDLE OR COMAL: Heat a heavy griddle or comal over
medium heat until a few drops of water flicked onto the surface dance around for
2 to 3 seconds before evaporating (if they evaporate any more quickly or slowly,
the griddle isn't the right temperature). Or preheat an electric griddle to 350°F.
Cook each quesadilla, turning once, until it is well browned in spots and the
cheese is melted, about 6 minutes.

EITHER WAY: Slide a large metal spatula under the quesadillas and transfer
them to a cutting board. Let the quesadillas cool for 1 minute before cutting into
8 wedges.

serrano ham and cheese quesadilla
▪ SINCRONIZADA DE JAMON SERRANO Y MANCHEGO

These simpler treats are also known as *sincronizadas,* a word that means just what it sounds like: synchronized. Where this odd name for a quesadilla came from is anyone's guess. My guess is that the name describes how, almost always, the layers—ham, cheese, and tortillas—are usually more or less the same thickness. ▪ makes 1 lunch or 4 appetizer servings

¾ cup coarsely shredded queso Chihuahua or
   Muenster cheese (about 3 ounces)
Two 10-inch flour tortillas

2½ ounces thinly sliced serrano ham or
   prosciutto
⅓ cup grated Manchego cheese (about 1 ounce)
Green Salsa (page 47; optional)

Make a thin layer of half the Chihuahua cheese on one of the tortillas. Cover with a layer of the ham, tearing or overlapping the slices as necessary to completely cover the tortilla. Top with an even layer of the remaining Chihuahua cheese and the Manchego. Cover with the second tortilla. Press down firmly to seal. The quesadilla can be assembled up to a few hours in advance. Wrap and refrigerate.

Cook the quesadilla as described on page 130. Pass the green salsa separately, if desired.

adobo-marinated chicken quesadilla ▪ QUESADILLA DE POLLO ADOBADO

In this simple quesadilla, getting the cooking right really matters. Slow, even heat will crisp the outside and give the cheese time to melt and absorb the flavor of the marinated chicken. ▪ makes 2 lunch or 8 appetizer servings ▪ photograph on page 132

1½ cups coarsely shredded queso Chihuahua
   (about 6 ounces)
Adobo-Marinated Chicken (recipe follows), cut
   into ¼-inch slices
Four 10-inch flour tortillas

Pico de Gallo (page 57; optional)
Guacamole (page 73; optional)
Pasilla de Oaxaca Tomatillo Salsa
   (page 53)

Make a thin layer of the Chihuahua cheese on 2 of the tortillas. Arrange half the chicken slices evenly on each tortilla. Top with an even layer of the remaining cheese. Cover with the remaining 2 tortillas and press them down firmly to seal. The quesadillas can be made up to a few hours in advance. Wrap and refrigerate.

Cook the quesadillas as described on page 130. Pass the pico de gallo and guacamole separately, if desired. Serve with the salsa.

adobo-marinated chicken · POLLO ADOBADO

This very simple adobo, which is a must-have in our quick dinner repertoire, is an example of the marinade type of adobo. In it, the nuttiness of toasted chiles is backed up by the fragrance of cumin and garlic and the bite of vinegar. Various recipes throughout the book call for this simple preparation, which gives you an idea of its versatility. Try the same adobo, or a slightly spicier version, for thin slices of pork loin or a whole pork tenderloin. The recipe can be easily doubled or tripled and the leftovers stored in the refrigerator for up to 2 days (or even frozen for up to 1 month).

▪ makes 2 to 3 main-course servings

FOR THE ADOBO

2 guajillo chiles, wiped clean, stemmed, seeded, and toasted very lightly (see page 2)

2 chiles de árbol (with seeds) or less, depending on heat, wiped clean and well toasted (see page 000)

3 large garlic cloves

½ teaspoon cumin seeds

⅛ teaspoon ground cloves

½ teaspoon dried oregano, crumbled

¼ cup water

1 tablespoon cider vinegar

1 pound boneless, skinless chicken breasts

Salt

Prepare the adobo: Put both chiles, the garlic, cumin, cloves, oregano, water, and vinegar in a blender jar and blend at low speed until smooth.

Pound the chicken with a meat mallet to an even thickness of about ¾ inch. Rub the chicken breasts generously with salt and put them in a shallow baking pan. Pour the adobo over the chicken and (wearing gloves, if you like) rub the marinade into the chicken. Cover and let stand at room temperature for up to 1 hour, or refrigerate for up to 1 day. Bring to room temperature if necessary before continuing.

Heat a gas grill to medium-high or prepare a hot charcoal fire.

Grill the chicken, turning once, until charred in places and cooked through, about 10 minutes. Remove to a carving board, cover with foil, and let stand for 5 minutes before slicing or serving.

Adobo-Marinated Chicken Quesadilla (page 131) accompanied by (from left) Green Salsa (page 47), Ranchera Sauce (page 117), Tomatillo and Chile de Arbol Salsa (page 149), and Guacamole (page 73)

TORTAS

TORTA IS A UNIQUELY MEXICAN WORD FOR A VARIETY of sandwiches, not found in other parts of Latin America or in Spain. Tortas can be made from various breads, depending on region and household, but the most commonly used roll is a *telera*, a flattish roll that is soft and porous inside, crusty on the outside. *Teleras* have two indentations that run along the top. You will generally find *teleras* still a little dusty with flour, which gives them a slightly nutty flavor. The same rolls are also typical of the Cordoba region in Spain, where legend has it that *teleras*, with the same two indentations as those in Mexico, are made that way so as to look like a *montera*, or bullfighter's hat. Whatever their origin, *teleras* are the bread of choice for making tortas, particularly in Mexico City and surrounding regions.

A torta can be stuffed with almost anything, but there are two main categories, hot, or *tortas calientes*, and cold, simply called *tortas*. Tortas calientes are more likely to be made with a fairly complex mix of ingredients, starting with a filling such as slices of slow-roasted leg of pork, ham with melted cheese, or seasoned shredded cooked chicken. In most cases, the bread is spread with refried black beans or pinto beans and crema (which can be replaced with crème fraîche or sour cream) and, in some cases, with mayonnaise as well! After the other ingredients have been heated and arranged on the rolls, then comes the final spreading of ripe avocado—adding the avocado before heating the torta would ruin the avocado—and a topping of a pile of sliced pickled jalapeños and sliced white onions. The resulting layers add up to a world of flavors and textures.

Everyone has a favorite *torteria*, and people may travel miles out of their way just to snack on their favorite torta. Generally, *torterias* are long-lasting businesses, passed from generation to generation. On a recent trip to Mexico, I took a friend to eat tortas at the same places I used to go in my childhood. Places like that, little corner-store *torterias*, inspired the sandwiches that are on our menu today.

No ordinary sandwiches, these tortas are meals in themselves. We have streamlined the recipes from their restaurant versions as much as possible without losing any of the flavor, but they do require some work. However, as throughout the book, most of the individual components can be prepared well in advance. You will not be disappointed.

"bald-headed ladies" · PELONAS

In the city of Puebla, the only place I know that they are found in Mexico, these sandwiches are prepared on rolls with round smooth tops that resemble bald heads. And since the word *torta* is feminine, it takes the feminine adjective for bald, *pelona*—hence, bald-headed ladies. Call them what you will, they are absolutely delicious. Make these on a day when you have a little leftover refried beans and/or a homemade salsa or two—better with both!—so half the work is already done. ▪ makes 4 sandwiches

4 ciabatta-style rolls, about 6 by 4½ inches, or 4 similar-sized sections from a long ciabatta loaf

Vegetable oil

4 firmly packed cups shredded cooked beef (see Note)

¾ cup Restaurant-Style Refried Beans (page 224), warm

4 firmly packed cups shredded romaine lettuce

⅔ cup finely chopped white onion

3 to 4 Rosa's Pickled Jalapeños (page 125) or bottled pickled jalapeños, seeded and cut into strips

Salt

1 tablespoon crema, crème fraîche, or thinned sour cream (see page 15)

¼ cup Green Salsa (page 47) or Pasilla de Oaxaca Tomatillo Salsa (page 53) or 2 tablespoons of each

Preheat the oven to 350°F.

Split the rolls or bread open, and reassemble the halves. Brush or rub the outsides (top and bottom) very lightly with oil. Place on a baking sheet and bake until crisp, 6 to 8 minutes.

Meanwhile, pour enough vegetable oil into a large skillet to film the bottom (you may be able to skip the oil if your beef has some fat) and heat over medium heat. Add the beef and toss and stir until sizzling, about 5 minutes. Remove the pan from the heat.

Spread the cut sides of the rolls with the refried beans. Pile the beef onto the bottoms of the sandwiches and top with the lettuce, then the onion, jalapeños, and a pinch of salt. Drizzle the crema and salsa(s) over the vegetables, put the tops on the sandwiches, and press down lightly but firmly. Cut the sandwiches in half from corner to corner.

NOTE: Prepare the beef as for the Shredded Flank Steak Salad on page 153, or substitute coarsely shredded leftover beef, such as from Slow-Braised Boneless Short Ribs (page 199) or pot roast.

Rosa's Mexican club sandwich

What everyone loves about a club sandwich—the different flavors and textures in every bite—makes our version one of our best sellers at lunch time. Avocado so ripe it is spreadable, sour cream, and mayonnaise add creaminess; chipotle and pickled jalapeño add heat; and bacon, chicken, and ham form the backbone. I hope by now I've convinced you to keep pickled jalapeños in your refrigerator, along with a can of chipotles. After that, if you set a small dollop of refried beans aside next time you make them, the rest of this sandwich is a breeze. ▪ makes 4 sandwiches

1½ tablespoons chipotle adobo puree
  (see page 7)
1½ tablespoons sour cream
1½ tablespoons mayonnaise
4 ciabatta-style rolls, about 6 by 4½ inches, or
  4 similar-sized sections from a long ciabatta
  loaf
½ cup Restaurant-Style Refried Beans
  (page 224), warm
Adobo-Marinated Chicken (page 133)

½ pound thick-sliced boiled ham
12 slices bacon, cooked until crisp
1⅓ cup shredded queso Chihuahua
  (see page 13; about 4 ounces)
¼ cup thinly sliced white onion
2 Rosa's Pickled Jalapeños (page 125) or bottled
  pickled jalapeños, cut lengthwise into strips
Olive oil
½ very ripe Hass avocado, peeled and
  cut into 4 slices

Whisk the chipotle puree, sour cream, and mayonnaise together in a small bowl. Split the rolls or bread open. Spread the chipotle mixture and refried beans evenly over the cut sides of the rolls. Cut the chicken into pieces as necessary to fit on the bottoms of the rolls and place on the rolls. Top with the ham and bacon. Sprinkle the cheese over the bacon, top with the sliced onion and pickled jalapeños, and close the sandwiches.

Pour a very thin coating of olive oil onto a heavy griddle or into a heavy skillet large enough to hold the sandwiches, and heat over medium-low heat. Add the sandwiches (bottom side down) and weight them: If cooking them on a griddle, cover them with a baking sheet topped with one or two cans of tomatoes or soup. If cooking the sandwiches in a skillet, weight them with a second heavy skillet or a plate topped with a can or two (depending on size). Cook until the underside is crisp and lightly browned, about 5 minutes. Flip, weight, and cook on the second side.

Lift off the bottoms of the sandwiches and spread 1 avocado slice evenly over each one. Replace the bottoms and set the sandwiches right side up on a cutting board. Press down gently but firmly and cut each sandwich in half.

Nearly all of the recipes in this book can by doubled, tripled, or more to suit your needs.

crispy chicken, avocado, and queso fresco sandwich
▪ CEMITA ESTILO ROSA MEXICANO

In some parts of Mexico, *cemita* means a type of bread, but in the city of Puebla, a *cemita* is a sandwich made with chicken, beef, or pork *milanesa* (cutlets coated with seasoned bread crumbs and fried) or simply ham and cheese. At Rosa we feature chicken *milanesa* in our *cemita,* but you can substitute plain cooked chicken. If you have pickled onions and pickled jalapeños on hand, this is a snap (and the recipe can easily be doubled). The breaded and panfried chicken is delicious on its own as a simple dinner or lunch.

Traditionally *cemitas* are made with *papalo quelite,* a pungent field green that grows wild. A mixture of cilantro and watercress is a tasty alternative.

Be sure to choose ripe, soft (but not brown) avocados. One of the keys to a successful *cemita* is an avocado that is ripe enough to spread over the bread.

▪ makes 2 sandwiches.

FOR THE CHICKEN

One 7- to 8-ounce boneless, skinless chicken breast

½ cup all-purpose flour

1 tablespoon salt, plus a pinch

1 tablespoon dried oregano, crumbled

½ teaspoon chile de árbol powder (see page 7) or other pure chile powder

1 egg

½ cup coarse dry bread crumbs

Vegetable oil

FOR THE SANDWICHES

2 ciabatta-style rolls, about 6 by 4½ inches, or 2 similar-sized sections from a long ciabatta loaf

4 teaspoons chipotle adobo puree (see page 7)

1 ripe Hass avocado, halved, pitted, peeled (see Note), and sliced

Two 5 by 4 by ½-inch-thick slices queso fresco (about 6 ounces)

1 firmly packed cup fresh cilantro sprigs (without thick stems)

1 firmly packed cup watercress sprigs (without thick stems)

2 tablespoons olive oil

¼ cup Pickled Red Onions (page 101)

2 Rosa's Pickled Jalapeños (page 125) or store-bought pickled jalapeños, cut into ½-inch-wide strips

BREAD THE CHICKEN: Set the chicken breast on a cutting board. Holding a knife parallel to the board, slice through the chicken starting at the thicker long side and stopping just before the chicken is sliced in half. Open the chicken like a book and cover with a sheet of plastic wrap. Pound with a meat mallet to a fairly even ¼-inch thickness. Cut the chicken in half.

Spread the flour on a plate and stir in 1 tablespoon of the salt, the oregano, and chile powder until evenly distributed. Beat the egg in a wide shallow bowl with the pinch of salt until very well blended. Spread the bread crumbs on a separate plate. Turn the chicken in the seasoned flour to coat all sides evenly, and tap off any excess flour. Turn the chicken in the egg to coat evenly, then hold it over the bowl to let any excess egg drip back into the bowl. Lay the chicken on the bread crumbs and turn once or twice, patting gently so the crumbs stick, until evenly coated.

Pour ½ inch of vegetable oil into a large skillet and heat over medium-high heat until rippling. Add the breaded chicken and cook until the underside is deep golden brown, about 4 minutes. Flip and repeat, adjusting the heat as necessary so the chicken gives off a lively sizzle without splattering while cooking. Remove to a small paper-towel-lined baking sheet to drain. The chicken can be cooked up to 1 hour before making the sandwiches. Keep at room temperature.

ASSEMBLE THE SANDWICHES: Preheat the oven to 350°F.

If necessary, remove the paper towel and rewarm the chicken on the baking sheet in the oven. Meanwhile, split the rolls or bread open, place on a baking sheet, and warm in the oven just until softened.

Spread the cut sides of each roll with the chipotle puree, then top both cut sides with the avocado slices and spread them evenly over the bread. Place the slices of queso fresco on the bottoms of the rolls and top with the warm chicken. Mound the cilantro and watercress over the chicken and drizzle the olive oil over the greens. Top with the pickled onions and jalapeños, dividing them evenly. Cover with the tops of the rolls, press down lightly but firmly, and cut the sandwiches in half.

NOTE: Here is a simpler way to deal with avocados—the result is more rustic, yielding coarse instead of neat slices, but that can be nice too. Cut the avocado in half and remove the pit. Using a large spoon, cut thick diagonal strips of the flesh down to the peel, then use the spoon to scoop them out.

6 ENSALADAS

THE KIND OF LARGE SALAD COMMON IN THE UNITED States full of protein and generous enough to serve as a main course, is not customary in Mexican cooking. Upon arriving at Rosa Mexicano, I was asked to come up with some interesting main course salads, Mexican style, because Americans loved them, especially at lunch. What could I do? I turned to colleagues and friends for advice, including Howard Greenstone, our company's CEO. I did not want to simply serve a Caesar-style salad with chopped jalapeños tossed in; it had to combine the best of American salads with authentic Mexican flavors. This, I concluded, called for a special dressing. As you can see in the recipes that follow, the dressings, like the Jalapeño Dressing (page 145) and the Pomegranate and Red Onion Dressing (page 61), are considerably more assertive than those common in the United States or Canada.

chicken hash salad · ENSALADA DE POLLO ROSA

Mexican cooks can't leave anything alone. If we're making a salad with leftover roast chicken—even if it's left over from a trip to the supermarket rotisserie—we doctor it up before we dress it. Warming the chicken with onion and oregano is a little step that adds a lot of flavor. The last time I made this salad, I realized that it started out like a chicken hash, so that's the name I picked. ▪ makes 4 servings

FOR THE CHICKEN

3 tablespoons olive oil

1 medium onion, finely chopped

2 jalapeños, finely chopped

Salt

6 garlic cloves, finely chopped

4 cups shredded cooked chicken (from Chicken broth, page 66, leftovers, or a store-bought rotisserie chicken)

½ teaspoon dried thyme

2 hearts of romaine

1 medium carrot, peeled and coarsely shredded

⅔ cup blanched almonds, toasted and coarsely chopped

¼ cup raisins

Jalapeño Dressing (recipe follows)

3 Golden Delicious or Fuji apples (see Note)

16 cherry tomatoes, halved

Season the chicken: Heat the olive oil in a large skillet over medium heat. Add the onion and jalapeños, season with salt, and cook, stirring, until the onion is translucent, about 5 minutes. Add the garlic and cook until softened, 1 to 2 minutes. Add the chicken and thyme and cook, stirring, until the chicken picks up some color and absorbs the seasoning, about 5 minutes. The chicken will stick to the pan in places—that's fine, just use the spoon to free any bits that stick. Take the pan off the heat and set aside.

Cut the dark leaf tips and thick white cores from the hearts of romaine. Cut each head lengthwise into quarters, then cut crosswide into 1-inch-wide strips. Put the romaine, carrot, almonds, and raisins in a mixing bowl or serving bowl. Toss with the dressing.

Stand an apple upright on a cutting board. Starting on one side, make very thin slices working toward the center. Stop when you see the first bits of core in the slices. Repeat three times, giving the apple a quarter turn each time. Then stack the slices several at a time and cut them lengthwise into thin strips. Add the strips to the bowl and toss them with the dressing to prevent browning as you work. Repeat with the remaining apples.

Scrape the seasoned chicken into the bowl and toss well to mix. Taste, and add salt if necessary. Serve the salad from the bowl or divide it among four serving plates. Scatter the cherry tomato halves over the bowl of salad or over individual salads.

NOTE: Do not peel the apples ahead of time. Doing so robs them of flavor and nutrients.

jalapeño dressing · ADAREZO DE JALAPEÑO

It is not unusual to see the French technique for making vinaigrette, with mustard as a flavoring and emulsifier, used throughout Mexico. But what is cooking, or life for that matter, without chiles? This dressing is also delicious on a simple salad of shredded chicken, celery, and onions. Or spruce up your favorite type of bagged mixed greens with the jalapeño dressing and a sliced avocado. ▪ makes about 1 cup

½ jalapeño
1 tablespoon Dijon mustard
Juice of 1 lime
2 tablespoons sherry vinegar or white wine vinegar
2 teaspoons salt

2 teaspoons sugar
1 garlic clove, minced
½ cup blended oil (olive and vegetable oils) or ¼ cup each olive oil and vegetable oil

Put the jalapeño, mustard, lime juice, vinegar, salt, sugar, and garlic in a blender jar and blend at low speed, using quick on/off pulses, until the jalapeño is finely chopped. With the motor running, pour in the oil in a thin stream.

Pour the dressing into a container with a tight-fitting lid. The dressing can be made up to a day in advance and refrigerated. Bring to room temperature and shake well before serving.

chicken salad fruit vendor–style · ENSALADA DE POLLO ESTILO VENDEDOR DE FRUTAS

No, fruit vendors don't usually sell chicken salad too. This salad was inspired by the street vendors in Mexico City and other parts of Mexico who sell all types of fruit. Big round slices of watermelon, papaya, pineapple, and even jicama sit atop blocks of ice, ready to be eaten as a cooling snack. Or, even better, these same fruits are cut into thick strips, sprinkled with lime juice, chile powder, and a little salt, and served in cone-shaped paper cups. One of my favorite treats is a whole green mango, cut to look like a flower and seasoned with lime juice, chile, and salt, served on a stick for easy eating. ▪ makes 6 servings

FOR THE CHICKEN

1½ pounds boneless, skinless chicken breasts

2 tablespoons chipotle adobo puree
(see page 7)

2 tablespoons honey

2 teaspoons salt

Juice of 1 lime

1 mango, peeled, pitted, and cut into ¾-inch cubes (about 1⅓ cups)

¼ ripe pineapple, rind and core removed, cut into ¾-inch pieces (about 2 cups; see Note)

1 small red bell pepper, cored, seeded, and cut into ¾-inch squares (about 1¼ cups)

½ seedless cucumber, peeled, cut lengthwise in half, and cut into ¼-inch slices (about 1 cup)

½ small jicama, peeled and cut into ¾-inch cubes (about 1½ cups)

Honey-Lime Dressing (recipe follows)

Salt

Red leaf lettuce or romaine lettuce leaves

Marinate the chicken: With a mallet, pound the chicken breasts to a fairly even ½ inch thickness, and lay them in a baking pan.

Whisk the chipotle puree, honey, salt, and lime juice together in a small bowl. Wearing gloves if you like, rub all sides of the chicken breasts with the marinade. Cover and refrigerate, turning once or twice, for at least 1 hour, or up to 1 day.

Heat a gas grill to medium-high or prepare a hot charcoal fire.

Remove the chicken from the marinade and arrange it on the grill. Grill, turning once, until charred in places and cooked through, about 10 minutes. Remove to a carving board, cover with foil, and let stand for 5 minutes.

In a large bowl, toss the mango, pineapple, red pepper, cucumber, and jicama with the dressing until coated. Cut the chicken into ¾-inch cubes, add them to the bowl, and toss again. Taste and add salt if necessary. Line the serving plates with lettuce leaves and top with the salad.

NOTE: Many supermarkets sell peeled and diced pineapple. If you like, substitute about 10 ounces store-bought pineapple cubes for the above.

honey-lime dressing · ADAREZO DE LIMÓN Y MIEL

Even with its sweetness, this very nice and simple dressing still carries a punch.

- makes about 1 cup

¼ cup freshly squeezed lime juice

2 tablespoons rice wine vinegar

2 tablespoons honey

1 serrano chile, coarsely chopped

2 teaspoons salt

1 garlic clove, coarsely chopped

1 teaspoon Dijon mustard

½ cup blended oil (vegetable and olive oils) or ¼ cup each olive oil and vegetable oil

Put the lime juice, vinegar, honey, chile, salt, garlic, and mustard in a blender jar and blend at low speed, using quick on/off pulses, until the chile and garlic are finely chopped. With the motor running, pour in the oil in a slow, steady stream.

Pour the dressing into a container with a tight-fitting lid. The dressing can be made up to a day in advance and refrigerated. Bring to room temperature and shake well before using.

Nearly all of the recipes in this book can by doubled, tripled, or more to suit your needs.

tomatillo and chile de árbol salsa - SALSA DE TOMATILLO Y CHILE DE ARBOL

Garlic can be roasted before adding it to a salsa made with cooked tomatillos or tomatoes, but when the chile that seasons the salsa is a chile de árbol, raw garlic tastes better to me.

When grinding toasted dried chiles, as for this salsa, make sure the molcajete is very dry so the chiles grind up nicely. ▪ makes about 1 cup ▪ photograph on page 93

5 chiles de árbol (with seeds), wiped clean, stemmed, and well toasted (see page 2)

1 large garlic clove

6 medium tomatillos (about 10 ounces), husked, washed, and roasted (see page 23)

Salt

Coarsely grind the chiles in a molcajete (or in a large mortar using a pestle). Add the garlic and grind to make a paste. Add the tomatillos and continue grinding until the tomatillos are liquefied and the chile-garlic paste is incorporated. (Alternatively, combine the chiles, garlic, and one-third of the tomatillos in a blender jar and blend at low speed until the chiles and garlic are finely chopped. Add the remaining tomatillos and blend, using quick on/off pulses, just until the tomatillos are liquefied. Blending too much will make a pasty, cloudy salsa.) Season to taste with salt.

The salsa can be made up to several hours in advance. Keep at room temperature until serving.

grilled shrimp salad with peanut-chipotle dressing
• ENSALADA DE CAMARONES CON ADEREZO DE CACAHUATE Y CHIPOTLE

This is a full-flavored, satisfying salad that fills the bill for a lighter meal. Crunchy sweet shrimp, tart oranges, and nuggets of golden corn tossed with greens in a nutty-spicy-smoky dressing cover all the flavor bases. ▪ makes 4 servings

FOR THE SHRIMP

1 pound peeled and deveined medium shrimp (about 36 per pound) or 1¼ pounds medium shrimp in the shell, peeled and deveined
1 tablespoon olive oil
Salt and freshly ground black pepper

2 oranges
2 hearts of romaine
5 lightly packed cups mesclun
2 lightly packed cups fresh cilantro leaves
½ small red bell pepper, cored, seeded, and cut into very thin strips (about ½ cup)
¾ cup Grilled Corn Relish (page 228)
Peanut-Chipotle Dressing (recipe follows)
About ⅓ cup Chile Peanuts (page 77; optional)

If using wooden skewers, soak them in cold water to cover for at least 1 hour before threading the shrimp onto them, to prevent the skewers from burning when grilled.

Marinate the shrimp: Toss the shrimp and oil together in a mixing bowl. Season generously with salt and pepper and toss again. Thread the shrimp onto four 8-inch metal or wooden skewers, leaving no space between them and making sure that the skewer passes through the tail and the thick end of the shrimp. Place in a baking dish or on a plate. The shrimp can be kept at room temperature for 30 minutes to 1 hour, or refrigerated for up to 4 hours.

Cut both ends off each orange and stand them on a cutting board. Using a paring knife, cut off the peel and white pith from the oranges, removing as little of the orange flesh as possible. Working over a bowl, cut the segments free of the membrane, letting the segments drop into the bowl. After you've cut all the segments, squeeze all the juice out of the membranes into the bowl.

Cut the dark green leaf tips and the cores with the thick white stems, from the romaine. Cut the head lengthwise into quarters, then cut crosswise into 1-inch-wide strips. Wash the romaine and mesclun and dry well, preferably in a salad spinner. Mix the greens with half the cilantro; reserve the rest. The greens can be prepared up to several hours in advance. Store them in a plastic bag in the refrigerator.

Heat a gas grill or light a charcoal fire, or set the rack about 6 inches from the broiler and preheat the broiler to high.

Place the shrimp on the grill or on the broiler pan and cook, turning once or twice, until cooked through, about 4 minutes. Remove to a plate.

Toss the greens, bell pepper, corn relish, and 1 cup of the dressing together in a large bowl until the greens are coated. Remove the shrimp from the skewers, add them to the bowl, and toss again. Divide among four plates, mounding the greens high in the centers and leaving some space around the edges. Top the salads with the reserved cilantro leaves and scatter the peanuts, if using, over them. If you like, spoon some of the remaining dressing around each salad.

peanut-chipotle dressing · ADOREZO DE CACAHUATE Y CHIPOTLE

Although I intended each of the dressings in this chapter to pair with a specific main-course salad, you will find many other uses for them. This recipe makes more than you will need to dress the shrimp salad. Toss the rest with a plain green salad, or spoon it over grilled or broiled fish, or even steamed asparagus or green beans.

Here I keep the heat level a bit on the high side, as the dressing will be tossed with a lot of greens and the heat will be diluted. ■ makes about 1½ cups

1 cup Chile Peanuts (page 77)
Juice of 3 limes
About 3 tablespoons white vinegar
½ cup orange juice

1½ tablespoons honey
2 to 2½ tablespoons chipotle adobo puree (see page 7)
⅓ cup olive oil

Chop the peanuts in a food processor, using quick on/off pulses, until finely ground. Set aside.

Pour the lime juice into a measuring cup. Add enough vinegar to total ⅓ cup, and pour the mixture into a small mixing bowl. Whisk in the orange juice, honey, and chipotle puree. Whisking constantly, drizzle in the olive oil. The honey and chipotle puree will help keep the dressing emulsified; if it starts to separate before you use it, just whisk it well. The dressing can be stored at room temperature for up to 4 hours or refrigerated for up to a day. Bring to room temperature before using.

NOTE: To keep the bowl steady when making this dressing (or any other one in this chapter), use this trick: Twist a well-dampened kitchen towel into a doughnut shape and place it on the counter. Center the bowl over the doughnut and press it firmly in place.

THE HIDDEN HEALTH BENEFITS OF MEXICAN COOKING

It may come as a surprise to many readers to learn that Mexican cooking is such a healthy, vegetarian-friendly cuisine. Here are a few examples.

▪ Most of our sauces are vegetable based, meaning that to achieve the wonderful velvety consistency in our sauces we do not use the thickening agents—such as butter mixed with flour, egg yolks, or reduced stocks—common in other cuisines. Many of our sauces are made of tomatoes, tomatillos, chiles, onions, garlic, and fresh herbs. Thick moles are made thick with healthful nuts and seeds, such as almonds, pumpkin seeds, peanuts, pecans, and sesame seeds—and more often than not all these moles and sauces are cooked with healthy vegetable oils.

▪ Because of their high vegetable content, all salsas, cooked or raw, pack a huge punch of vitamins and minerals. In its many forms, salsa has been cited as the healthiest snack in American supermarkets. (It is moreso if you are able to limit the chip consumption!) When salsa is eaten with a fresh corn tortilla (see page 92), you have a wholesome combination.

▪ Vegetarians can eat well from these recipes: all the bean and rice dishes (pages 216–224; omit the bacon from the Pinto Beans with Bacon and Onion on page 221), Swiss Chard with Beets, Queso Oaxaca, and Raisins (page 230), Rosa Mexicano's Corn Pudding (page 226; vegetarians omit ham and vegans omit the cheese); the spicy pickles (Mushrooms in Escabeche with Red Bell Peppers and Chiles; page 70, or Rosa's Pickled Jalapeños, page 125), Grilled Corn Relish (page 228) and any of the dressings for salads, which can be used on your creations or ours (see pages 145, 147, and 151). I hope that the basic preparation for cactus pads *(nopales)* and the simple salad that follows it will add a new staple to vegetarians' repertoires.

▪ Many of the savory preparations mentioned above and a few others can be substituted for the meat, poultry, and fish fillings in the enchilada and taco chapters. For example, the mushroom sauce for the Beef Tenderloin with Wild Mushrooms and Tequila (page 202) can be used in place of the chicken in the Swiss Enchiladas (page 113), as can the Swiss Chard with Beets, Queso Oaxaca, and Raisins, or, paired with the cheese of your choice, either of the refried bean recipes on page 224. Cactus-Leaf Salad (page 234) makes an unexpected but wonderful filling for tacos. With the omission of the tuna, the Ancho Chiles Stuffed with Tuna and Potato Salad on page 155 become vegetarian but stay delicious.

shredded flank steak salad · SALPICÓN DE RES

Salads with meat and vegetables are not typical in American homes, but in Mexico, many versions of such *salpicones* can be found. In Yucatán, for example, they are commonly made with venison. Pickled jalapeños are a must with this salad. ▪ makes 6 servings

FOR THE BEEF

2 pounds flank steak

1 medium white onion, cut in half

1 tablespoon salt

8 garlic cloves

2 teaspoons dried oregano, crumbled

10 fresh cilantro sprigs

1 large fresh mint sprig

FOR THE DRESSING

Juice of 3 limes

2 tablespoons chopped fresh cilantro

1½ teaspoons dried oregano, crumbled

6 tablespoons olive oil

Salt

1 heart of romaine

1 bunch radishes, trimmed, washed, and thinly sliced

1 pint cherry tomatoes, halved

6 ounces queso fresco, cut into ¼-inch cubes (about 1¼ cups)

½ medium red onion, thinly sliced (about ½ cup)

12 black olives, such as kalamata, pitted if necessary and coarsely chopped

Rosa's Pickled Jalapeños (page 125) or store-bought pickled jalapeños

PREPARE THE BEEF: Put the beef and all the seasonings in a large nonaluminum saucepan and pour in enough cold water to cover the beef by 4 inches. Bring to a boil over high heat, then adjust the heat so the liquid is simmering. Cover and cook until the beef is fork-tender, about 2 hours. Remove from the heat and cool the beef to room temperature in the liquid.

Remove the beef from the liquid and drain well. (Strain the cooking liquid and reserve for another use; it makes a delicious base for a soup, pot roast, or stew.) Cut the beef crosswise into strips about 2½ inches long, then finely shred the meat.

PREPARE THE DRESSING: Whisk the lime juice, cilantro, and oregano together in a small bowl (see Note, page 151). Whisking constantly, slowly drizzle in the olive oil. Season with salt.

Cut the dark green leaf tips and the core, with the thick white stems, from the romaine. Cut the head lengthwise in half and then crosswise into ½-inch-wide strips.

Set aside about one-quarter of the radishes and cherry tomatoes. Toss the beef together in a large bowl with the remaining radishes and tomatoes, the queso fresco, onion, and olives until well mixed. Pour the dressing over the salad and toss again. Season to taste with salt.

Divide the shredded romaine among four serving plates. Top each with a portion of the salad, and scatter the remaining tomatoes and radishes over all. Pass a bowl of pickled jalapeños at the table for people to help themselves.

ancho chiles stuffed with tuna and potato salad

• CHILES ANCHOS RELLENOS DE ATUN CON PAPA

A simple tuna and potato salad is transformed when stuffed into this lighter, more modern take on traditional chile rellenos. This recipe uses canned tuna, but since it's extraordinary with fresh tuna, I provide a variation.

The choice of potato is important here. For example, fingerlings may be too waxy to absorb the dressing. Yukon Gold potatoes are our number-one choice at Rosa, but the filling will also be delicious with red-skinned new potatoes. Very mealy potatoes, like russets, are too soft to hold their shape when mixed into the dressing.

■ makes 4 servings

FOR THE CHILES

4 large (about 5 inches long) ancho chiles

½ pound piloncillo (see page 16), broken into pieces, or ⅓ cup packed dark brown sugar plus 3 tablespoons molasses

1 cup cider vinegar

A 3-inch piece of Mexican cinnamon

½ teaspoon salt

FOR THE FILLING

1 pound small Yukon Gold potatoes or red-skinned new potatoes, scrubbed

3 tablespoons finely chopped red onion

2 scallions, trimmed and finely chopped

3 tablespoons chopped fresh flat-leaf parsley

1 jalapeño, roasted (see page 21), peeled, and finely chopped

2 to 4 tablespoons olive oil

2 tablespoons heavy cream

1 tablespoon mayonnaise

2 teaspoons freshly squeezed lime juice

1 teaspoon chopped garlic

Salt

Three 6½-ounce cans Italian or Spanish tuna packed in olive oil, drained

FOR THE SALAD

One 5-ounce bag mesclun lettuce or spring mix, washed and dried well

Pomegranate and Red Onion Dressing (page 61)

1 small (about 7 ounces) Hass avocado, halved, pitted, peeled (see Note, page 139), and cut into slices

PREPARE THE CHILES: Wipe clean with a damp towel. Carefully cut a lengthwise slit in each that runs from the shoulder to the tip.

Combine the piloncillo, vinegar, cinnamon, salt, and 2 cups water in a large saucepan and bring to a boil. Remove from the heat and add the chiles. Weight them down with a small plate and let soak until very pliable, about 1 hour.

MAKE THE FILLING: Put the potatoes in a large saucepan, pour in enough cold water to cover by 4 inches, and bring to a boil. Adjust the heat so the liquid is simmering and cook until the potatoes are tender when tested with a small knife, about 25 to 30 minutes.

While the potatoes are cooking, stir the red onion, scallions, parsley, jalapeño, 2 tablespoons olive oil, the heavy cream, mayonnaise, lime juice, and garlic together in a large bowl. Add salt to taste.

Drain the potatoes and let them stand until cool enough to handle. Cut them into 1-inch pieces and add to the dressing in the bowl. Toss gently to mix. Add the tuna and toss gently, to leave it in the largest pieces possible. If the filling appears a little dry, add up to 2 more tablespoons olive oil. Add salt to taste.

Drain the chiles, and gently remove as many of the seeds as possible without tearing the chiles. (Keeping the chiles whole will make a nicer presentation.) Gently open up one of the chiles and spoon just enough of the filling into it as you can without overfilling. Reshape the chile, closing up the opening. Repeat with the remaining chiles and filling.

ASSEMBLE THE SALAD: To serve, toss the greens together with the dressing until coated. Divide the greens among four plates, mounding them on one side of the plates. Set a stuffed chile opening side down next to the greens, and decorate the plates with the avocado slices.

VARIATION · ancho chiles stuffed with fresh tuna and potato salad

Rub 1 pound of thick tuna steaks with oil and season them generously with salt and pepper. Grill over high heat until seared outside but medium-rare in the center. Cool the tuna to room temperature and cut into bite-sized pieces. Substitute the fresh tuna for the canned.

Rosa's Cobb salad · ENSALADA MEXICANA COBB

There may be a couple of surprises in this recipe—besides the chorizo and pickled onion. First, the dressing (which would be welcome on just about any green salad, not to mention grilled fish or chicken) contains dill, which is not an herb that is usually associated with Mexican food. It is used, though very rarely, in the cities, where it is known as *eneldo*. The pairing of avocado and dill works beautifully. Watercress is another ingredient that may come as a surprise. But Mexicans love watercress in salads, probably because it is a little peppery. ▪ makes 4 servings

FOR THE GREENS

2 hearts of romaine

1 small head frisée, core and any brown leaf tips removed, cut into bite-sized pieces

1 bunch watercress, thick stems removed

Salt

Avocado-Dill Dressing (recipe follows)

FOR THE TOPPINGS

1 cup Pickled Red Onions (page 101)

2 links (about 6 ounces) chorizo (see page 205), cooked, removed from casings, and crumbled (see Note)

1½ cups cherry tomatoes, halved

1 cup crumbled Cabrales or other blue cheese (about 4 ounces)

Adobo-Marinated Chicken (page 133), cooled to room temperature and cut into ¾-inch cubes

1 ripe Hass avocado, halved, pitted, peeled (see Note, page 139), and cut into ½-inch cubes

4 cups Chile-Spiced Croutons (page 159)

PREPARE THE GREENS: Cut the dark green leaf tips and cores, with the thick white stems, from the hearts of romaine. Cut each head lengthwise into quarters, then cut crosswise into 1-inch-wide strips. Wash the romaine, frisée, and watercress in plenty of cool water and dry well, preferably in a salad spinner. The greens can be prepared up to several hours in advance. Store in a plastic bag in the refrigerator.

ASSEMBLE THE SALAD: Put the greens in a large mixing bowl, season lightly with salt, and toss with 1 cup of the dressing until coated. Divide the greens among four wide serving bowls. Arrange the toppings in bands across the greens, keeping the bands distinct. Serve immediately, passing the remaining dressing separately.

NOTE: To cook the chorizo, poke the sausages in a few places with a fork. Cook in a small skillet over medium-low heat, turning as necessary, until browned and cooked through, about 10 minutes.

avocado-dill dressing · ADAREZO DE AGUACATE Y ENELDO

Most salad dressings need an oil of some kind to make them creamy and rich-tasting; in this recipe, the rich, smooth avocado serves that function. ▪ makes about 1½ cups

1 large (about 10 ounces) ripe Hass avocado, halved, pitted, and peeled

½ cup packed fresh dill sprigs (thick stems removed)

3 tablespoons cider vinegar

2 tablespoons freshly squeezed lime juice

2 tablespoons finely chopped white onion

1 tablespoon Dijon mustard

1 serrano chile, coarsely chopped

2 teaspoons salt

1 garlic clove, chopped

Put the avocado in a blender jar. Top with the dill and then the remaining ingredients. Blend until smooth, adding water 1 tablespoon at a time, if necessary, to help the blending process. The dressing may be made up to 1 hour in advance. Pour into a bowl and cover with a piece of plastic wrap pressed directly against the surface to prevent the dressing from darkening.

chile-spiced croutons · CROUTONES DE BRIOCHE CON CHILE DE ARBOL

Part of Rosa's Cobb Salad, these spicy croutons would add kick and crunch to just about any green salad, as well as to thick and/or creamy soups.

Choose as square and even a loaf of brioche as possible—it will be easier to cut into neat cubes. If using challah, which is usually braided, start with a larger loaf.

▪ makes about 6 cups; enough for 6 generous servings

¼ cup olive oil

1 generous tablespoon chile de árbol powder (see page 7) or other pure chile powder

1 tablespoon dried oregano, crumbled

1 teaspoon salt

One 1-pound loaf brioche or one 1½-pound loaf dense challah, crusts removed and cut into 1-inch cubes (about 8 cups)

Preheat the oven to 325°F.

Stir the oil, chile powder, oregano, and salt together in a large mixing bowl. Tilt the bowl so the seasoned oil coats most of the sides, then add the bread cubes and toss gently until evenly coated.

Spread the croutons out on a baking sheet and bake until deep golden brown and crisp, about 15 minutes. Stir the croutons gently once during baking to turn them, bringing those around the edges into the center and vice versa. Let cool completely. The croutons can be kept in an airtight container at room temperature for up to 2 days.

RIGHT: Avocado Leaves

7 MAIN COURSES
PLATOS FUERTES

TO HELP OUR GUESTS BETTER UNDERSTAND THE PARTICULARS
of various regional Mexican cuisines, the dishes on the menus at Rosa Mexicano are grouped into several categories instead of only two, the more common appetizers and entrées sections, Rosa's menu has divisions for "appetizers," "tacos," "salads," and "enchiladas," as well as the one called "entrées." In this section you will find main courses or entrées that fit better within the realm of more conventional menus.

poblanos stuffed with spinach and goat cheese
· CHILES RELLENOS DE ESPINACAS

Quelites is a catch-all term that refers to many kinds of field greens and herbs—it comes from the ancient Nahuatl language and literally means "green things to eat." These greens grow wild all over Mexico and find their way into everything from quesadillas and stews to tortas. As *quelites* are not readily available in the United States, I have substituted baby spinach. The quantity of spinach in the recipe may seem enormous, but after cooking and squeezing, the volume shrinks dramatically.

The sauce can be made up to 1 day ahead and refrigerated; likewise, the chiles can be roasted a day in advance. · makes 6 servings

Seven 6-ounce bags (or six 7-ounce bags) baby spinach or 2½ pounds loose baby spinach

¼ cup mild olive oil

½ cup raisins

½ cup pine nuts

Salt

2 cups Ranchera Sauce (page 122)

6 large poblano chiles (about 1¼ pounds), roasted and prepared for stuffing (see page 21)

½ cup crema, crème fraîche, or thinned sour cream (see page 15)

Half an 11-ounce log plain goat cheese, cut into 6 slices

¼ cup coarsely chopped epazote (see page 15) or cilantro

Bring a large pot of salted water to a boil. Stir in the spinach a bagful at a time (or in 6 or 7 batches) and cook just until bright green, about 1 minute. Drain in a colander and rinse under cold water until cool enough to handle. Working in batches, squeeze as much water from the spinach as possible (be very serious about the squeezing!). Coarsely chop the spinach. There will be about 2 very tightly packed cups.

Heat the oil in a large skillet over medium heat. Add the spinach, raisins, and pine nuts and cook, stirring to break up the clumps of spinach, until the raisins are puffy, the pine nuts are starting to toast, and almost all the liquid has evaporated. Season the spinach with salt, then pour in ¾ cup water and cook until the water has evaporated. (It may seem odd to add water after taking the time to cook off the liquid, but there is a sound reason: the addition of water helps carry the salt evenly throughout the dense spinach mixture.) Remove from the heat and let cool.

Pour the sauce into an 11 by 9-inch baking dish or other baking dish that will hold the stuffed chiles snugly. Divide the filling among the chiles, filling them loosely. Put them opening side up in the baking dish. Cover tightly with aluminum foil and bake until heated through, about 25 minutes.

Drizzle the crema over the chiles while they are still in the baking dish, then transfer them to serving plates, spooning some of the cream-enriched sauce over and around them. (It is not necessary to blend the cream completely with the ranchera sauce; in fact, the plates will look nicer with a streaky sauce.) Top each chile with a round of goat cheese and some chopped epazote, and serve.

adobo-rubbed chicken steamed in parchment paper
▪ MIXIOTE DE POLLO

The term *mixiote* refers to the papery outer skin of the leaves of the maguey plant, which is also called the century plant. In cooking they serve as a waterproof container for various ingredients. Unfortunately, because of overharvesting, magueys are now in danger of extinction. Parchment paper is now used instead.

At Rosa Mexicano, we make mixiote with lamb shanks. Just about anything can be cooked *in mixiote,* including cactus leaves (see Cactus-Leaf Salad, page 232), rabbit, lamb, and poultry. The chiles used to make the adobo vary greatly from region to region, as do the herbs and spices.

Whenever you are steaming something for a long time—such as these chicken packets—toss a few coins (nickels and dimes work best) into the water in the pot. As long as you can hear the coins dancing on the bottom of the pot, there is still water left. Silence means the water has boiled away. ▪ makes 6 servings ▪ photographs on pages 168 and 169

6 large whole chicken legs, preferably with
   some of the backbone still attached (about
   4½ pounds), washed and patted dry
Salt
6 large avocado leaves (see page 12; optional)
Six 15 by 20-inch pieces of parchment paper

FOR THE ADOBO

A double recipe of adobo from the Lamb
   Enchiladas (page 123), made with the addition
   of 1 tablespoon salt, a 2-inch piece of
   Mexican cinnamon stick (see page 16), and,
   if not using avocado leaves in the parchment
   bundles, 1 teaspoon anise seeds
Six 10-inch pieces kitchen twine

Assemble the bundles: Season the chicken generously with salt. Center an avocado leaf, if using, over one piece of parchment paper. Center a chicken leg skin side down over the leaf. Spread about ⅓ cup of the adobo over the chicken, coating the top and sides well and letting it drip down onto the parchment. Bring the two long sides of the parchment up over the chicken so they meet, making a long rectangle with two open ends. Holding the two long sides together firmly with one hand, gather first one open end over the chicken, and then the other end, to create a neat little packet; both open ends should be completely closed in the process, to keep all the juices and flavor in the packet. Tie the packet securely with a length of twine. Repeat with the remaining chicken and adobo. The packages can be made up to a day in advance and refrigerated. Remove from the refrigerator 30 minutes before cooking.

To cook, fill a large pot that has a steamer insert with 2 inches of water (or to just below the bottom of the steamer insert). Bring to a boil over high heat. Arrange the packets in the steamer insert in as even a layer as possible. Ideally there will be some space between the packets, but it is okay if they are touching. Set the steamer over the boiling water, cover, and cook until the chicken is tender enough to fall from the bone, about 2 hours. (The only sure way to check if the chicken is done is to remove one of the bundles, untie it, and test the tenderness of the chicken with a fork. Be prepared with a fresh piece of string to retie the bundle if necessary.) Check the water occasionally and top it up with hot water if necessary.

Using tongs, transfer each packet to a shallow bowl. Let each person snip the string to untie the packet and let the fragrant steam escape, then simply and carefully slide the parchment out from under the chicken, leaving the chicken in the bowl with its delicious juices.

NOTE: To enjoy this in true Mexican style, serve the dish with warm tortillas and Green Salsa (page 47). Tear off a corner of a tortilla, top it with some of the fork-tender chicken and its juices and a drizzle of the green sauce, fold the whole thing up, and pop it in your mouth.

CUITLACOCHE-"STUFFED" CHICKEN BREAST

One of the more popular dishes at Rosa Mexicano over the years has been chicken breast stuffed with cuitlacoche. At the restaurant we first pound and butterfly bone-less chicken breasts, fill them generously with cuitlacoche (see page 15), wrap them tightly in plastic wrap, and poach them. When cooked we cool and then unwrap them. We then dip them in flour, eggs, and bread crumbs, fry them, and serve with a creamy poblano sauce.

Here is a less labor-intensive technique that yields the same combination of flavors and textures. For 4 servings:

1. Prepare ½ recipe of the Poblano Cream Sauce on page 170. This can be made up to 1 day in advance. Refrigerate the sauce until needed.
2. Prepare the Cuitlacoche-Mushroom Mixture on page 208. (This can be made up to 3 days in advance. Refrigerate until ready to use.)
3. Prepare a double batch of the chicken on page 138. (The chicken can be breaded up to a day ahead and refrigerated; bring to room temperature before cooking. Cook the chicken in two skillets.)
4. Just before serving, reheat the sauce and the cuitlacoche-mushroom mixture over low heat. Set each fried cutlet in the center of a serving plate and top with the cuitlacoche-mushroom mixture. Pour the poblano sauce over the top, letting it pool on the plates. Serve immediately.

ABOVE AND RIGHT: Adobo-Rubbed Chicken Steamed in Parchment Paper (page 166)

chicken and tortilla gratin · BUDIN

Budines can be composed of just about anything. They are usually homey dishes, which could be thought of as lasagnas, made with leftover tortillas or tamales layered with shredded chicken, beef, or pork and moistened with a variety of sauces. *Budines* (the name translates literally as pudding) seasoned with mole are called *budines aztecas*. Once you've made this version and have an idea of the typical proportions of filling, sauce, and tortillas, you can create your own *budin*. ▪ makes 8 generous servings

FOR THE GRATIN

12 day-old Fresh Corn Tortillas (page 92) or 12 store-bought 6-inch corn tortillas

¼ cup vegetable oil

2 cups shredded cooked chicken (from Chicken Broth, page 66, leftovers, or a store-bought rotisserie chicken)

2 poblano chiles, roasted (see page 21), peeled, seeded, and cut into ¼-inch-wide strips

Salt

3 Rosa's Pickled Jalapeños (page 125) or bottled pickled jalapeños, plus ¼ cup of the pickling liquid (optional)

1½ recipes Salsa Mexicana (page 183)

¼ cup heavy cream

2 cups coarsely shredded queso Chihuahua or Muenster cheese (about 8 ounces)

FOR THE POBLANO CREAM SAUCE

1½ cups heavy cream

2 large poblano chiles (about ½ pound), roasted, peeled, and seeded

½ lightly packed cup coarsely chopped fresh cilantro

⅓ cup fresh flat-leaf parsley leaves

10 fresh mint leaves

Salt

Soften the tortillas in the oil according to the directions on page 115, and drain them on paper towels. Season the chicken, if necessary, and the poblano strips with salt.

Preheat the oven to 375°F.

Line the bottom of a round 11 by 2½-inch-deep cazuela (see page 17) or a similar-sized baking dish with 4 of the tortillas—the tortillas will overlap in places and come partly up the sides of the cazuela; that is fine. Spread 1 cup of the chicken over the tortillas and top with half the poblanos and the jalapeños, if using. Spread one-third of the tomato sauce over them in an even layer and drizzle 2 tablespoons each of the cream and the pickling liquid, if using, over the sauce. Scatter ½ cup of the cheese over the top. Make another layer in the same way, using the remaining tortillas (the edges of the tortillas around the sides shouldn't extend above the rim of the dish), chicken, poblanos, and jalapeños, if using, half the remaining sauce, and all the remaining cream and pickling liquid, if using, and ½ cup cheese. Top with the remaining sauce. Push down any tortilla edges that have popped through the sauce, and scatter the remaining 1 cup cheese over the top. The casserole can be assembled up to 4 hours in advance. Cover with plastic and refrigerate; remove from the refrigerator 30 minutes before baking.

Bake the casserole until the top is golden brown and the sauce around the edges is bubbling, about 45 minutes. Remove from the oven and let stand for 5 minutes.

Meanwhile, make the cream sauce: Heat the cream in a small heavy saucepan over medium heat just until hot, not boiling. Pour into a blender jar and add the poblanos, cilantro, parsley, and mint. Blend until smooth. Add salt to taste. Return to the saucepan and set aside.

Just before serving, reheat the cream sauce. Serve the casserole hot with the cream sauce on the side.

Nearly all of the recipes in this book can by doubled, tripled, or more to suit your needs.

seared duck breasts with pecan-prune mole
▪ PECHUGA DE PATO CON MOLE DE CIRUELAS Y NUECES

Ducks were an important part of the diet in pre-Hispanic Mexico, particularly around the central regions. What is now Mexico City was a huge lake—in fact, the early city was constructed on landfill—and the region teemed with waterfowl.

This is a great-looking dish: slices of pink duck breast fanned over a rich mahogany sauce made with prunes, pecans, tomatillos, and chiles. The mole can be made ahead, but the duck must be cooked at the last minute. I recommend that you use an instant-read meat thermometer to check the duck. ▪ makes 4 servings

Two 1-pound moulard duck breasts (see Note)
Salt

FOR THE MOLE
¾ pound tomatillos, husked and washed
4 thick slices white onion
4 to 5 small garlic cloves, peeled
5 tablespoons vegetable oil
½ cup pecans
½ cup pitted prunes
5 cups Chicken Broth (page 66) or store-bought chicken broth, or as needed
½ cup freshly squeezed orange juice

3 mulato chiles, wiped clean, stemmed, seeded, and lightly toasted (see page 2)
4 pasilla chiles, wiped clean, stemmed, seeded, and lightly toasted (see page 2)
1 teaspoon chopped fresh thyme
½ teaspoon black peppercorns
1 tablespoon sugar
1 tablespoon salt, or to taste

FOR THE OPTIONAL TOPPINGS (ANY OR ALL)
Coarsely chopped pistachios (natural, not dyed)
Thinly sliced scallions
Sliced prunes

With a sharp paring knife, make diagonal cuts about ¾ inch apart through the skin and almost all of the fat of the duck breasts, without cutting into the meat. Make diagonal cuts in the opposite direction to score the skin and fat in a diamond pattern. (Cutting deep into the fat of the duck before cooking over low heat allows much of the fat to be rendered from the duck and also results in crisp skin.) Rub a generous amount of salt into both the meat and skin sides of the duck. Let stand at room temperature for up to 1 hour, or refrigerate for up to 1 day. Bring to room temperature before cooking.

Meanwhile, make the mole: Position a rack about 8 inches from the broiler and preheat the broiler, to low if possible. Put the tomatillos, onion, and garlic on the broiler pan, place under the broiler, and roast, turning each vegetable as necessary, until well browned, even charred in spots, on all sides: about 12 minutes for the garlic, about 15 minutes for the onions, and about 20 minutes for the tomatillos. Remove each ingredient as it is browned and set aside to cool.

While the vegetables are cooling, heat 2 tablespoons of the oil in a small skillet over medium heat. Add the pecans and cook, stirring, until lightly toasted, about 3

[continued]

minutes. Using a slotted spoon, transfer to a plate. Add the prunes to the skillet and cook, stirring, until softened and puffy, about 2 minutes. Scrape onto the plate with the pecans and let cool.

Working in batches, combine the pecans, prunes, tomatillos, onion, garlic, 3 cups of the chicken broth, the orange juice, mulato and pasilla chiles, thyme, and peppercorns in a blender jar and blend until smooth. Heat the remaining 3 tablespoons oil in a large heavy saucepan over medium heat. Add the prune mixture and cook, stirring, until it comes to a boil. Adjust the heat so the sauce is simmering, stir in the sugar and salt, and cook, stirring often, until lightly thickened and shiny, about 30 minutes. As the sauce simmers, add as much of the remaining 2 cups broth ¼ cup at a time as necessary to prevent it from becoming too thick. The sauce can be made up to 1 day in advance and refrigerated. Just before serving, reheat the sauce over low heat, adding small amounts of water as necessary to return it to the right consistency.

Put a heavy medium skillet over medium-low heat, add the duck breasts skin side down, and cook until much of the fat is rendered from the duck and the skin is a deep mahogany brown: the key to successful browning/rendering is to keep the heat even and fairly low. The whole process of rendering and browning can take up to 20 minutes; how much fat is rendered and how long it takes depends on the duck, but if the skin is taking on a fair amount of color before 10 minutes of cooking, lower the heat and continue cooking. Flip the duck breasts and cook until the second side is well browned and an instant-read thermometer inserted into the thickest part of the duck registers 140°F, about 8 minutes. This temperature will yield medium-rare to medium duck—i.e., a fairly pink center. Lower the heat slightly and increase the cooking time by 2 to 4 minutes for more well-done meat. Remove to a carving board and let stand for 5 to 10 minutes.

While the duck stands, reheat the sauce.

Holding the knife diagonally to the board, cut the duck into thin slices. Ladle about ⅓ cup sauce onto each of four plates. Top with overlapping slices of the duck. Scatter any or all of the toppings over the duck and serve.

NOTE: Moulard duck breasts are thick and meaty, with deep-red flesh and a rich flavor.

salmon with fruity mole · SALMON CON MANCHAMANTELES

Moles manchamanteles, literally "tablecloth stainers," are one of the numerous types of Mexican moles. This one is composed of tomatoes, fruit, and dried red chiles and is seasoned with cinnamon, cloves, and two kinds of sugar.

Like many Mexicans, I am not fond of salmon. Maybe it has something to do with salmon not being native to our waters, or with the fact that our seasonings and spices do not seem to complement its strong flavor and fatty flesh. This recipe is an exception—the sweetness and acidity of the fruit is a perfect match for the richness and full flavor of salmon. Choose thick fillets of this rich and elegant fish, which packs a truckload of omega-3 fatty acids. Because of its high fat content, it's well suited to broiling and grilling.

Simple sautéed spinach or the Swiss Chard with Beets, Queso Oaxaca, and Raisins (page 230) go nicely with this recipe. Grilled Corn Relish (page 228) makes a lively side dish.

The mole should be a pleasant balance of acidity, sweetness, and heat. Play with the amount of vinegar and piloncillo to adjust the sweet/sour balance to your liking and, if you like, add a little chile de árbol powder (see page 7) or other pure chile powder to pick up the heat a little. ▪ makes 4 servings

FOR THE MOLE

1 large tomato (about ½ pound)

1 thick slice white onion

4 garlic cloves, peeled

3 ancho chiles, wiped clean, stemmed, seeded, lightly toasted, and soaked (see pages 2 and 3)

2 guajillo chiles, wiped clean, stemmed, seeded, lightly toasted, and soaked (see pages 2 and 3)

A 2-inch piece of peeled ripe plantain

½ small Golden or Red Delicious apple, peeled, cored, and cut into 1-inch chunks (about 1 heaping cup)

1 cup 1-inch chunks pineapple (about ¼ pound)

6 allspice berries

3 cloves

A 1-inch piece of Mexican cinnamon bark (see page 16)

½ cup water

3 tablespoons vegetable oil

1½ tablespoons cider vinegar, or to taste

1 tablespoon shaved piloncillo (see page 16), or 1 tablespoon dark brown sugar and 1 teaspoon molasses, or to taste

1 teaspoon sugar

1½ teaspoons salt, or to taste

Four 8-ounce skinless salmon fillets, any pinbones removed

Salt and freshly ground black pepper

Juice of 1 lime

Position a rack about 8 inches from the broiler and preheat the broiler, to low if possible. Put the tomato, onion slice, and garlic on the broiler pan, place under the broiler, and broil, turning once, until well browned, even charred in spots, on both sides: about 12 minutes for the garlic, about 15 minutes for the onion, and about 20 minutes for the tomato. Remove the individual vegetables as they brown, and let cool.

[continued]

Put the tomato, onion, and garlic in a blender jar. Add the drained chiles, plantain, apple, pineapple, allspice, cloves, cinnamon, and water and blend at low speed until the fruit is finely chopped, then increase the speed to high and blend until smooth.

Heat the oil in a medium heavy saucepan over medium heat. Pour in the contents of the blender and bring to a boil, stirring constantly. Adjust the heat so the sauce is simmering and stir in the vinegar, piloncillo, sugar, and salt. Cook, stirring often, until the sauce is shiny and small beads of fat float on the surface, about 30 minutes. As the sauce cooks, add up to 1 cup water in small increments to prevent it from becoming too thick. Check for salt, adding more if necessary. You will have about 2¼ cups sauce. The sauce can be made up to 1 day in advance. Let cool, then cover and refrigerate. Reheat over low heat before serving, adding small amounts of water as necessary to restore the sauce to the right consistency.

Preheat the broiler. Line the broiling pan with aluminum foil. Season the salmon fillets with salt, pepper, and the lime juice, and place them skinned side down on the broiling pan. Place about 8 inches from the heat source and broil for about 7 minutes, or until nearly medium-rare. The salmon will continue to cook for a minute or so after it is removed from the oven.

Divide the sauce among four plates, letting it pool in the center of each. Top each pool of sauce with a salmon fillet.

VARIATIONS

To pan-sear the salmon, heat olive oil in a large nonstick sauté pan over high heat until almost smoking. Add the salmon fillets, seasoned as in the main recipe, skinned side up. Shake the pan slightly and cook for 3 minutes; turn and cook for 3 more minutes.

To bake salmon, preheat the oven to 375°F. Place the seasoned fillets on a baking sheet on the middle rack of the oven and cook for approximately 12 minutes.

MOLE

Derived from the ancient Nahuatl word *molli,* meaning "a concoction," a mole is basically a mixture that may include chiles, spices, seeds (sesame, pumpkin, and others), nuts (almonds or peanuts), herbs, and greens. Moles can be very thick or thin enough to eat as a soup.

Many moles are based on good homemade meat or poultry broth. Others are a paste that is added to simmering meat or poultry to stew.

Depending on the ingredients, moles can be green, red-brown, or even yellow. Contrary to popular belief, very few moles include chocolate. Here's a great way to understand the concept of mole: *aguacate* ("avocado") combines with the word *mole* to give us the well-known word *guacamole!*

trout with wild mushrooms cooked in foil · TRUCHA EMPAPELADA

This is one of my favorite ways to cook trout—wrapped in corn husks and then in foil—because it's rustic in presentation yet sophisticated in flavor. I learned it at the Díaz family compound in the mountains of the state of Mexico. Once the mushrooms and onion are cut, the packets can be put together in minutes and then refrigerated for up to 8 hours. The packets, which puff up dramatically in the oven, are best baked on the lowest oven rack, so if you would like to double the recipe to serve 4, be sure that you have two baking sheets that will fit side by side on the oven rack. It has become fairly easy to find farmed trout sold cleaned and boned with the heads on. These will contain an odd bone, however, so be aware while eating.

Extra-wide (18-inch) heavy-duty foil is essential for making the packets. Regular foil isn't wide enough to make the sturdy, completely sealed packets that result in the juices that make this dish so delicious. ▪ makes 2 servings ▪ photograph on page 178

6 large pieces (2 for insurance) dried corn husks (see page 13); (see Note)

Two 12- to 14-ounce cleaned and boned whole trout

About 2 teaspoons salt

6 large fresh epazote stalks or 12 large, leafy cilantro sprigs

½ large red or white onion, cut into very thin slices

½ pound mixed mushrooms, such as oyster, shiitake, and/or cremini (see Note)

4 serrano chiles, stemmed and cut lengthwise in half

4 scallions, trimmed

¼ cup olive oil

Put the corn husks in a bowl with enough cold water to cover them completely. Weight with a plate to submerge them and let soak until pliable, 30 minutes to an hour. Drain the husks, leaving them moist, and trim off any hard bits from the flat ends.

With a rack in the lowest position, preheat the oven to 400°F.

Rinse the trout under cold running water. Drain them well, but don't blot them dry, and lay them out skin side down. Season the inside of the fish with salt and divide half the epazote stalks between the cavities of the fish. Close up the fish and season the skin on both sides with salt.

Tear off two 30-inch-long pieces of 18-inch-wide heavy-duty foil and place them on your work surface with one of the long sides of each sheet closest to you. Arrange 2 of the corn husks in the center of each piece of foil so the pointed tips of the husks face outward and the two straight ends overlap a little in the center. Trim or, alternatively, overlap the husks, if necessary, so they are approximately the length of the trout. Position the husks so they are halfway between the center of each piece of foil and the long side closest to you.

[continued]

Scatter about two-thirds of the onion and two-thirds of the mushrooms over the husks. Season with salt and top with the trout. Scatter the remaining onions and mushrooms and the serranos over the trout. Season again with salt. Tuck 1 scallion along the fin side and 1 along the belly side of each trout. Drizzle the oil over the fish and vegetables. To seal the packages, one at a time, bring the long side of the foil farthest from you over the fish and line it up with the edge of the foil closest to you. Fold over ½ inch of the joined edges, then fold over again, making another ½-inch crease, to seal that side of the package. Make three or four ½-inch creases along the short sides to seal those sides. Transfer the packets—handling them carefully to prevent tearing the foil—to a baking sheet. The packages can be assembled up to 8 hours in advance and refrigerated. They can go directly from the refrigerator to the oven.

Bake until the packages puff up dramatically and the steam created inside makes the foil quiver, about 20 minutes (a few minutes more for packets that have been refrigerated). Gently transfer each packet to a large serving plate. Cut a slit along the long sealed edge and nudge the contents of the packet, along with all the juices, out onto the plate. Serve with the corn husks in place, or slide them out from under the trout.

NOTES: If you can't find corn husks, use two 30 x 15-inch sheets of parchment paper instead of foil. Assemble the ingredients in the order and position described in the recipe, only directly onto the parchment instead of over the husks. To make tight packets, fold the parchment exactly as you would the foil but be careful that the creases along the edges are good and tight.

Preparation of the mushrooms will vary depending on which type(s) you use: Stem shiitakes and cut the caps into ½-inch-wide strips; trim stem ends from cremini and cut the trimmed mushrooms into ¼-inch-wide slices; and remove the hard base from the clumps of oyster mushrooms and tear the individual mushrooms into 1-inch-wide strips.

red snapper veracruz-style · HUACHINANGO ESTILO VERACRUZANO

There are endless versions of this classic seafood dish from the Gulf of Mexico, and just as much debate about which are the "authentic" ingredients. Here is my interpretation, simplified for home cooks. It is usually served with rice and refried beans (see page 224), or with fried ripe plantains (see page 200). You could also serve it with grilled asparagus, steamed green beans, or sautéed spinach.

This casserole is ideal for company as it can be assembled in advance and refrigerated, then baked right before serving. ▪ makes 4 servings

Four 8-ounce skinless red (or other) snapper fillets
2 limes, cut in half
About 1 tablespoon salt
4 ripe large tomatoes (about 2 pounds)
1 large white onion, cut in half and then into very thin slices (about 3 cups)
6 bay leaves
½ cup chopped fresh cilantro

12 fresh sprigs thyme
3 Rosa's Pickled Jalapeños (page 125) or bottled pickled jalapeños, stemmed and coarsely chopped or sliced, plus 3 tablespoons of the pickling juices, plus (optional) chopped jalapeños for garnish
12 garlic cloves
½ cup pitted small Manzanilla (Spanish) olives
2 tablespoons tiny (nonpareil) capers
3 tablespoons olive oil

Put the fillets in a baking dish. Squeeze the juice from 1 of the limes over both sides of them, and season them generously with salt. Turn them once or twice in the seasonings. Marinate at room temperature for 30 minutes, or cover and refrigerate for up to 4 hours.

Bring a large saucepan of water to a boil. Set a bowl of ice water near the stove. Core the tomatoes and cut an X in the opposite end. Slip the tomatoes into the boiling water and leave them just until the skin starts to peel away from the X. The time depends on the tomatoes: very ripe tomatoes will need 10 seconds or so; less ripe tomatoes will take longer. With a slotted spoon, transfer the tomatoes to the bowl of ice water. Let them stand until cool enough to handle, then slip off the skins. Drain and cut into ¾-inch slices.

Preheat the oven to 425°F.

Scatter half the onions over the bottom of a 13 by 9-inch baking dish or another dish in which the fillets will fit snugly with a little overlap. Arrange a little less than half the tomato slices over the onions. (If you plan to present the finished dish at the table, use the smaller end slices of tomato here and save the prettier center slices for the top.) Top with the bay leaves, then scatter half the cilantro, thyme sprigs, and chopped jalapeño over that. Season with at least 1 teaspoon salt. Tuck the garlic cloves into the vegetables around the edges of the dish. Squeeze the juice from the remaining lime over the vegetables and top with the seasoned fillets, spacing them evenly but

[continued]

overlapping a little if necessary. Scatter the olives and capers over the fillets, then make another layer of the remaining onions and tomatoes to cover the fish. Scatter the remaining cilantro, thyme sprigs, and chopped jalapeño over that. Season again with salt, then drizzle the olive oil and pickled jalapeño juice over everything. Cover tightly with aluminum foil. The casserole can be prepared ahead and refrigerated for up to 6 hours. Remove from the refrigerator 30 minutes before baking.

Bake the casserole for 20 minutes. Uncover and bake until the juices given off by the vegetables are bubbling and the fillets are cooked through, 10 to 15 minutes.

To serve, scrape the vegetables covering the fish to the sides of the dish. Gently lift up the fillets and transfer them to serving plates. Most likely they will break apart a little; that is fine. Pick out the garlic cloves, bay leaves, and thyme sprigs and discard. Mash the remaining ingredients coarsely into the juices with a fork to make a chunky sauce. Check for seasoning, and add salt if necessary. Spoon the sauce over the fillets and scatter some chopped pickled jalapeños over each if you like.

SIX IF BY SEA

Here is a menu to share with six of your friends who love seafood and like to mingle in the kitchen before dinner. Most of the work is done well ahead but a few finishing touches are saved for the last minute.

- Guacamole with Seafood (page 74)
- Pumpkin-Seed-and-Crab-Crusted Halibut (page 184 prepare 1½ times the recipe); with Guajillo Chile and Pineapple Adobo (page 191)
- Simple White Rice (page 216) or Yellow Rice (page 218)
- Swiss Chard with Beets, Queso Oaxaca, and Raisins (page 230) or Steamed Vegetables
- Hibiscus, Mango, and Berry Trifle (page 245)

UP TO 2 DAYS BEFORE THE DINNER • Make the custard • Make the hibiscus syrup

UP TO 1 DAY BEFORE THE DINNER • Make the chile-pineapple adobo • Prepare the Swiss chard completely or prepare the green vegetable of your choice for steaming • Assemble and chill the individual trifles • Prepare the yellow rice seasoning mix (if using)

UP TO 4 HOURS BEFORE DINNER • Prepare the guacamole ingredients and refrigerate them • Marinate the seafood for the guacamole and refrigerate • Prepare the pumpkin seed topping, top the fish, and refrigerate

UP TO 2 HOURS BEFORE DINNER • Make the rice and remove from the heat

ABOUT 30 MINUTES BEFORE DINNER • Bring halibut, guacamole ingredients and marinated seafood to room temperature

ONCE GUESTS ARRIVE • Make the guacamole just before seating your guests • Reheat the rice, adobo, and chard over low heat (or steam a vegetable if that is your choice) • Begin cooking the halibut

salsa mexicana

You will find this sauce in almost every Mexican home. While the ingredients may be similar to many American and European tomato sauces, the technique—softening onions, then jalapeños, then garlic, then tomatoes and herbs—builds a different profile of flavors. The result is uniquely Mexican. ▪ makes 3 cups

¼ cup olive oil

1 large white onion, finely chopped

1 jalapeño, finely chopped

5 garlic cloves, finely chopped

2 pounds ripe, juicy tomatoes, cored and finely chopped

3 bay leaves

1 teaspoon dried oregano, crumbled

¼ teaspoon dried thyme, crumbled, or 2 fresh thyme sprigs, leaves only

2 teaspoons sugar

1 teaspoon salt, or to taste

Heat the olive oil in a medium nonaluminum saucepan over medium heat. Add the onion and cook until wilted, about 4 minutes. Stir in the jalapeño and cook until the onion is translucent, 3 to 4 minutes. Add the garlic and cook for 1 minute, then stir in the tomatoes, bay leaves, oregano, dried thyme, if using, sugar, and salt. Adjust the heat so the sauce is at a lively simmer and cook, stirring occasionally, until the liquid given off by the tomatoes has evaporated, about 20 minutes.

Stir in the fresh thyme, if using, and additional salt and sugar if needed. Cook 5 minutes. The sauce can be prepared 2 days ahead and refrigerated. Bring to a simmer, adding water a little at a time as necessary to return the sauce to its original consistency, before using.

USING SALSA MEXICANA

▪ To make *queso guisado,* a quick, delicious snack when spooned onto tortillas or pieces of crusty bread, gently stir chunks of queso fresco into a pan of the hot sauce and let sit until semi-melted.

▪ Stir some sauce into beaten eggs before scrambling them for a quick version of huevos a la mexicana.

▪ Shredded cooked chicken or sautéed tenderloin tips simmered with a little sauce make a quick dinner.

pumpkin-seed-and-crab-crusted halibut
▪ PESCADO EN COSTRA DE PEPITA Y CANGREJO

Crusting fish is a great technique, adding texture and flavor while protecting the fish from aggressive heat. The pumpkin-seed-and-crabmeat crust is both sweet and nutty, perfect with the firm texture and mild flavor of the halibut. The topping is simple to make and the fillets are easy to cook. You can also make the dish with cod, mahimahi, swordfish, salmon, or Chilean sea bass. ▪ makes 4 servings

FOR THE CRUST

½ cup pumpkin seeds, toasted (see page 60)

2 small jalapeños, roasted (see page 21) and peeled

4 garlic cloves, roasted along with the jalapeños

½ teaspoon salt

¼ teaspoon ground cumin

Scant ¼ teaspoon black peppercorns, coarsely cracked

¼ cup packed lump crabmeat, picked over for shells and cartilage

¼ cup packed chopped fresh cilantro

FOR THE FILLETS

¼ cup all-purpose flour

1 egg

Salt

Four 8-ounce halibut fillets (see Note)

3 tablespoons blended oil (olive and vegetable oils) or vegetable oil

1 cup Guajillo Chile and Pineapple Adobo (page 191), Cooked Green Salsa (page 114), or Poblano Cream Sauce (page 170)

Lime wedges

MAKE THE CRUST: Put about half the pumpkin seeds, the jalapeños, garlic, salt, cumin, and peppercorns in a food processor and process, using quick on/off pulses, until the seeds are finely chopped and the mixture is the texture of wet sand. Add the remaining pumpkin seeds and pulse until they are coarsely chopped. Spoon the mixture into a shallow bowl.

Add the crab and cilantro and rub everything together until the crab is coarsely shredded and evenly distributed throughout. The crust mixture can be made up to a few hours before using. Refrigerate until needed.

MAKE THE FISH: Put a rack in the center of the oven and preheat the oven to 425°F.

Spread the flour out on a small plate. Beat the egg with a pinch of salt in a shallow bowl until thoroughly blended. Determine which side is to be the "top" of the fillets (see Note); season the other sides with salt. Dip the top of one fillet into the flour, then into the egg. Lift out and let excess egg drip back into the bowl, then press the egged side of the fillet into the crust mixture, wiggling and pressing gently to get as much of the topping to stick as possible. Set the fillet coated side up on a plate and repeat with the remaining fillets. If there is any of the crust mixture left, divide it among the fillets, patting it to help it stick.

Pour the oil into a heavy ovenproof skillet (no plastic handles!) large enough to hold the fillets comfortably. Heat over medium-high heat until the oil thins and begins to ripple. Add the fillets topping side up and cook, spooning the hot oil over the topping occasionally, until the undersides are golden brown, about 4 minutes. Transfer the skillet to the oven and cook until the topping is lightly browned and the fillets feel firm to the touch, about 12 minutes for the size of fillets described in the Note.

Meanwhile, bring the sauce to a simmer in a medium saucepan, adding small amounts of water a little at a time if necessary to restore it to the right consistency. Keep warm.

Ladle ¼ cup sauce onto each serving plate and top with a fillet. Garnish with lime wedges and serve immediately.

NOTE: The shape of the fillets will determine how long they take to cook and how they will look on the plate. For fillets that will be done in the same time as the pumpkin-seed-crust takes to brown—and that will look impressive on the plate—choose evenly sized fillets that are about 3 inches thick and about 2 inches wide. Adjust the cooking time as necessary for thinner fillets. Use the flatter side of each fillet as the "bottom" and the more rounded side as the "top."

VARIATION · peanut-crusted halibut

Combine ½ cup Chile Peanuts (page 77), 14 garlic cloves, roasted (see page 22), 1 teaspoon dried oregano, crumbled, ½ teaspoon cracked black peppercorns, and ½ teaspoon chile de árbol powder (see page 7) or other pure chile powder (optional) in a food processor. Process, using quick on/off pulses, until the peanuts are finely chopped. Add another ½ cup Chile Peanuts, 4 scallions, trimmed and thinly sliced (about ½ cup), and ½ cup packed chopped fresh cilantro. Pulse a few times, just until the second batch of peanuts and the scallions are coarsely chopped. Substitute the peanut topping for the pumpkin-seed-crab topping; cooking time will remain the same.

OTHER USES FOR THE PUMPKIN-SEED-CRAB TOPPING

I love this topping so much that I started finding other uses for it. Here are a few:

- Sprinkle about 2 tablespoons of the topping over the filling of a ham and cheese quesadilla (page 131) before grilling.
- Fill a large, soft omelet with some of the warm crab topping.
- Cook ½ pound of angel hair pasta, drain it, and toss with 1 to 2 tablespoons of butter or olive oil and a full recipe of the crab topping. Season with salt and serve.

shrimp skewers · ALAMBRE DE CAMARONES

Alambres like this one are served at Rosa Mexicano over rice with pico de gallo. Luxurious shrimp skewers are not found so commonly in Mexico, but they make a great addition to a summer barbecue, especially for guests who don't eat meat or are simply into lighter fare. The simple marinade, made with ingredients you most likely have on hand, lets the flavors of the shrimp and vegetables shine through. If you prefer, the skewers can be broiled instead of grilled. ▪ makes 4 servings

FOR THE MARINADE

1 tablespoon olive oil
2 teaspoons freshly squeezed lime juice
1 teaspoon Worcestershire sauce
2 garlic cloves, minced
1 teaspoon dried oregano, crumbled
½ teaspoon salt
¼ teaspoon coarsely ground black pepper

12 jumbo shrimp (about 1 pound), peeled (tail segments and all) and deveined
1 small red onion, not peeled
1 ripe medium tomato
8 serrano chiles
Salt
Lime wedges
Pico de Gallo (page 57)

If using wooden skewers, soak them in cold water to cover for 1 to 2 hours.

Marinate the shrimp: Whisk the olive oil, lime juice, Worcestershire sauce, garlic, oregano, salt, and pepper together in a medium bowl until well blended. Add the shrimp and toss to coat. Let marinate at room temperature while you prepare the vegetables, or marinate in the refrigerator for up to 1 hour.

Cut the onion in half through the root and pull off all the papery outer layers. Pull off the two outer layers of each onion half, leaving the two layers joined. Reserve the inner layers for another use. Cut each of the two-layer pieces into 6 crescents. Cut the tomato in half through the core. Cut out the core and squeeze or scoop out most of the seeds, then cut each half into 6 wedges.

Heat a gas grill to medium-high or light a hot charcoal fire. Thread a serrano chile onto a skewer, pushing it almost all the way to the end. Follow with a piece of onion, then one of tomato. Follow the vegetables with a shrimp, making sure the skewer passes through the tail and the thick part of the shrimp. Repeat the vegetable-shrimp sequence twice, and finish off the skewer with a serrano. Repeat with the remaining vegetables and shrimp to make 3 more skewers. Brush the skewers with any remaining marinade. The skewers can be assembled up to 6 hours before cooking and refrigerated.

Grill the skewers, turning them once, until the shrimp are pink and cooked through and the vegetables are softened, about 6 minutes. Serve on the skewers or, using a fork, slide the shrimp and vegetables onto serving plates. (The shrimp and vegetables will most likely not slide off all at once; it is easiest to place a fork behind each piece of onion and slide one-third of the ingredients off the skewer at a time.) Serve with lime wedges and Pico de Gallo.

roasted seafood-stuffed pineapple · PINA RELLENA DE MARISCOS

Based on a recipe from a friend in the small Mexican state of Nayarit, on the Pacific coast, this is a terrific dish for a party because it looks impressive and all of the components can be made well ahead. The stuffed pineapple can be prepared early in the day and refrigerated until ready to bake. The result is dramatic and typically Mexican in its flavors—sweet pineapple, briny seafood, and spicy-sweet adobo. ▪ makes 4 servings

FOR THE PINEAPPLE

1 large ripe pineapple

3 tablespoons butter

1 small white onion, finely chopped (about 1 cup)

5 garlic cloves, minced

4 bay leaves

1 tablespoon sugar

½ teaspoon chile de árbol powder (see page 7) or other pure chile powder

¼ teaspoon *pimienta arabe* (see page 190)

Salt

FOR THE SEAFOOD

1¼ cups Guajillo Chile and Pineapple Adobo (page 191)

¾ pound skinless firm white fish fillets, such as halibut, or swordfish steak, cut into 1-inch cubes

8 large shrimp (about ½ pound), peeled and deveined

1 teaspoon salt

¼ teaspoon *pimienta arabe* (see page 190)

½ cup chopped fresh cilantro

8 littleneck clams or other small hard-shell clams, thoroughly scrubbed

¾ cup coarsely shredded Emmanthaler or Swiss cheese (about 3 ounces)

MAKE THE PINEAPPLE SHELLS: Lay the pineapple on its side on a cutting board. Starting at the bottom and using a heavy sharp knife, cut the pineapple and crown in half as evenly as you can—use slow, steady pressure on the knife and, if necessary, place a damp cloth on the board to keep the pineapple steady. Switch to a smaller knife and hollow out the pineapple halves: make a cut that runs around the cut edges of the pineapple, leaving about ½ inch of flesh attached to the shell; be careful not to cut through the shell, or the pineapple will leak during baking. Cut out the core from the center of each pineapple half and discard it. Continuing with the small knife, or switching to a large spoon if you find it easier, remove the pineapple flesh from the shell, again leaving at least ½ inch of pineapple attached to the shell. Set the shells aside and coarsely chop the pineapple.

Melt the butter in a medium skillet over medium heat. Add the onion and garlic and cook, stirring occasionally, until the onion is translucent, about 5 minutes. Add the chopped pineapple, bay leaves, sugar, chile powder, and *pimienta arabe*. Cook, stirring often, until the pineapple is very soft and the liquid it gives off has cooked down to a syrup, about 10 minutes. Season with salt and set aside to cool. The pineapple shells and pineapple mixture can be made up to a day in advance; refrigerate until needed. Discard the bay leaves before using.

With a rack in the center position, preheat the oven to 400°F. Line a baking sheet with aluminum foil.

[continued]

MAKE THE SEAFOOD MIXTURE: Heat the adobo sauce to a simmer, adding a small amount of water if necessary to restore the sauce to the right consistency. Remove from the heat.

Toss the fish fillet cubes and shrimp with the salt and *pimienta arabe* in a mixing bowl until the seafood is coated with the spices. Brush the insides of the pineapple shells with some of the adobo. Divide the seasoned seafood between the shells, keeping it in an even layer. Scatter the cilantro over the seafood, dividing it evenly. Spread ½ cup of the pineapple mixture over the seafood in each shell (reserve any extra pineapple to use as a condiment for grilled poultry or fish), then spread the remaining adobo over the pineapple in an even layer. The pineapple can be prepared to this point up to 6 hours in advance. Cover with plastic wrap and refrigerate.

Wrap the crowns of the pineapple in foil so they stay green and do not burn. Put the stuffed pineapples on the lined baking sheet and bake for 20 minutes.

Remove the baking sheet from the oven and tuck 4 clams into the stuffing of each pineapple half, spacing them evenly around the edges, then scatter the cheese over the adobo, dividing it evenly. Return the pineapples to the oven and bake until the clams are open, the filling is bubbling, and the cheese is lightly browned, about 20 minutes. Let stand for a few minutes before serving.

To serve, transfer the stuffed pineapples to a serving platter and bring them to the table. Scoop the filling onto serving plates, including some of each ingredient and some of the liquid from the pineapple in each serving.

PIMIENTA ARABE

Mexico has had a large Lebanese community for centuries, and so we have many Arab influences in our food. When I was growing up, my family had close ties to a Lebanese family and I learned a lot about their cooking methods, especially spicing.

Pimienta arabe, literally Arab pepper, is a blend of allspice, cloves, and black pepper. It is not common in Mexican cooking, but it was in our household. Proportions vary from kitchen to kitchen and chef to chef; mine is made with equal measures of allspice berries, whole cloves, and black peppercorns. For 2 tablespoons spice mixture, measure 1 tablespoon each allspice berries, black peppercorns, and cloves into a spice grinder and grind to a fairly fine powder. A little pinch of *pimienta arabe* adds an intriguing flavor to soups, stews, and sauces.

guajillo chile and pineapple adobo · ADOBO DE GUAJILLO Y PIÑA

The unusual combination of chiles and pineapple happens to be great with fish of any kind, but it's particularly good with the Pumpkin-Seed-and-Crab- or Peanut-Crusted Halibut on pages 184 and 185, as well as with the Roasted Seafood-Stuffed Pineapple (page 188). The recipe makes quite a bit of sauce, but the finished sauce keeps for 3 days refrigerated, or frozen up to a month. Or, if you prefer, set some of the uncooked sauce aside to use as a marinade (see below) and continue cooking the rest. ▪ makes 4½ cups

15 large guajillo chiles, wiped clean, stemmed, seeded, lightly toasted, and soaked (see pages 2 and 3)

4 cups diced (½-inch) peeled pineapple (about ½ pineapple) or store-bought diced fresh pineapple (1¼ pounds)

1 cup orange juice

6 chiles de árbol (with seeds), wiped clean and well toasted (see page 2)

10 to 12 garlic cloves

One 3-inch piece of Mexican cinnamon bark (see page 16), broken in half

1¼ teaspoons ground cumin

¼ teaspoon ground cloves

2 cups water

6 tablespoons olive oil

2 tablespoons sugar

1 tablespoon cider vinegar

Salt

Drain the guajillo chiles and rinse them well. Working in two batches, combine the guajillos, pineapple, orange juice, chiles de árbol, garlic, cinnamon, cumin, cloves, and water in a blender jar and blend until very smooth. (The uncooked adobo can be used as a marinade for meat, fish, or poultry.)

Heat the olive oil in a large heavy saucepan over medium heat. Pour in the adobo and bring to a boil. Adjust the heat so the sauce is simmering and cook, stirring occasionally, until the sauce is shiny and thickened, about 30 minutes. If the sauce thickens before taking on a nice sheen, add up to 1 cup more water, a few tablespoons at a time, and continue cooking.

Stir in the sugar, vinegar, and salt to taste. (Start with less of each if you've reserved some of the sauce for a marinade.) Strain the sauce through a very fine sieve, pushing in the solids left in the sieve to get as much liquid out of them as possible. The sauce can be made up to 4 days in advance and refrigerated. Bring to a simmer before using.

roasted poblanos with seafood stuffing and black bean sauce
▪ CHILES RELLENOS DE MARISCOS

Roasted poblano chiles can be the host of all sorts of fillings, from beefy to vegetarian. Here the combination of shrimp, calamari, crabmeat, and white fish fillets creates a wonderful mixture of flavor and texture. This seafood stuffing is similar to the taco filling on page 107, but it is richer in seafood and has a mysterious smoky flavor that comes from the pasilla de Oaxaca chiles in the tomato sauce base.

Be sure to choose straight-sided, not crinkly, poblanos. They will be easier to clean and fill and will sit up nicely without wobbling in the baking dish. ▪ makes 4 large or 8 smaller servings

Vegetable oil

FOR THE FILLING

Salsa Mexicana (page 183), made with 3 pasilla de Oaxaca chiles, wiped clean, stemmed, toasted, and seeded (see page 2), instead of jalapeños

1/2 cup chopped fresh flat-leaf parsley

1/2 cup chopped fresh cilantro

1/4 cup chopped fresh mint

1 tablespoon cider vinegar

1/2 pound skinless firm white fish fillets, such as halibut or mahimahi, or swordfish steak, cut into 1/2-inch cubes

1/2 pound peeled and deveined small shrimp (about 30)

1/2 pound cleaned calamari, bodies cut into 1/2-inch rings, tentacles left whole

1/2 pound lump crabmeat, picked over for shells and cartilage

8 large poblano chiles (about 1 1/2 pounds), roasted and prepared for stuffing (see page 195)

Black Bean Sauce (recipe follows)

About 1/2 cup crema, crème fraîche, or thinned sour cream (see page 15)

Chopped fresh cilantro

With a rack in the center position, preheat the oven to 350°F. Lightly oil a baking dish that will hold the stuffed chiles snugly.

Bring the salsa to a simmer in a medium saucepan over low heat. Stir in the parsley, cilantro, mint, and vinegar and cook for 1 minute. Stir in the fish and shrimp. Cook, stirring, for 1 minute. Stir in the calamari and cook, stirring, until the fish and shrimp are cooked through and the calamari is firm but tender, about 3 minutes. Stir in the crab and remove from the heat.

Using a large serving spoon, fill each pepper with the seafood mixture, filling them completely but not overstuffing. Mold the chiles back into their natural shape if necessary, leaving only a small amount of the stuffing exposed. Place the stuffed chiles in the baking dish cut side up. Cover tightly with aluminum foil and bake until heated through, about 20 minutes.

Meanwhile, reheat the bean sauce, adding water a tablespoon or two at a time in order to return the sauce to the right consistency.

To serve, ladle about ¾ cup of the sauce into a shallow serving bowl or a plate with a deep well and center 2 peppers over the sauce. Repeat with the remaining sauce and peppers. Or, for 8 servings, use a generous ⅓ cup sauce and 1 pepper per plate. Drizzle the crema over the peppers and sauce and sprinkle with cilantro.

LAND AND SEA FOR 6

This menu of contrasts is introduced by the herbal and citrus notes of the cool ceviche, which give way to the deep, meaty flavor of the pozole. The dessert, too, is a delicious contrast—a rich tasting but light chocolate sorbet balanced with a crisp cinnamon-scented cookie.

- Green Ceviche (page 30)
- Pozole (page 196)
- Chocolate Sorbet (page 257)
- Almond Cinnamon Cookies (page 254)

UP TO 2 DAYS BEFORE THE DINNER ▪ Make the sorbet and freeze ▪ Make the broth for the pozole (up to simmering the spare ribs) and refrigerate ▪ Make the cookie dough and refrigerate (or freeze a portion)

UP TO 1 DAY BEFORE THE DINNER ▪ Make the sauce for the pozole ▪ Prepare the chicken and roasted poblano for the pozole

EARLIER ON THE DAY OF DINNER ▪ Bake and cool the cookies ▪ Cut the seafood for ceviche and make the ceviche marinade ▪ Prepare the toppings for the pozole

ABOUT 1 HOUR BEFORE DINNER ▪ Marinate the ceviche ▪ Make the ceviche sauce ▪ Return the broth to a simmer

ABOUT 15 MINUTES BEFORE DINNER ▪ Drain the ceviche and add the sauce ▪ Add the chicken to the pozole ▪ Remove the pozole toppings from the refrigerator

black bean sauce · SALSA DE FRIJOLES NEGROS

Onions browned in oil add sweetness to this hearty sauce, as they do in the refried beans recipes on page 224. Black bean sauce is a natural with seafood, steaks, and chops. Another popular preparation using black bean sauce is called *enfrijoladas*, which is nothing more than tortillas dipped in black bean sauce and topped with all sorts of things, such as seafood, chicken, or even scrambled eggs for breakfast. Or top the sauced tortillas with salted air-dried beef, as they do in Oaxaca.

Thin this sauce with some chicken stock (or water, to keep it vegetarian) and add a little cream, and you have a delicious soup, especially when garnished with crumbled queso fresco, tortilla chips, and crema.

There are many variations of this basic sauce. I like to add hoja santa, a leaf from the sassafras family with a flavor reminiscent of mint and anise (its scientific name is *Pimpinella anisum*), and fresh epazote (see page 15). If you can't find these, use a little cumin and allspice. If you prepare the sauce ahead of time, you may want to make it extra spicy, because the sauce loses some of its punch in standing. ▪ makes 6 cups

½ cup vegetable oil
½ small white onion, thinly sliced
2 garlic cloves
1 small serrano chile, coarsely chopped
4 cups Soupy Black Beans (page 223)

3 avocado leaves, lightly toasted (see page 12; optional)
¼ teaspoon ground cumin
¼ teaspoon ground allspice
3 cups water
Salt

Heat the vegetable oil in a heavy medium saucepan over medium heat. Add the onion, garlic, and chile and cook, stirring, until the onion is light golden brown, about 8 minutes. Stir in the beans, then add the avocado leaves, cumin, allspice, and 1 cup of the water and season to taste with salt. Bring to a boil. Stir in the remaining 2 cups water, remove from the heat, and cool to room temperature.

Working in batches, pour the bean mixture into a blender jar and blend until very smooth. Strain the sauce into a clean saucepan, return to a simmer, and cook until lightly thickened, to the consistency of melted ice cream. Season to taste with salt. The sauce can be prepared up to 2 days in advance and refrigerated. Return to a simmer, adding small amounts of water as necessary to return the sauce to the right consistency, before serving.

roasted poblanos with cream · RAJAS CON CREMA

Rajas means "strips." In this case, the strips are roasted poblano chiles that are lightly cooked with onions. Their heat is tamed somewhat and their flavor enhanced by a splash of cream. Serve them hot or at room temperature with just about anything you like: scrambled eggs, warm corn tortillas, broiled fish, to name a few. They are absolutely delectable spooned over sliced grilled steak. There is some debate among Mexican cooks as to whether rajas should be made with oil or butter. Diplomatically, this version is made with both. ▪ makes 2 cups; about 4 servings ▪ photograph on page 198

2 tablespoons butter

1 tablespoon vegetable oil

1 medium white onion (about 6 ounces), cut in half and then into thin strips

4 poblano chiles, roasted (see page 21), peeled, seeded, and cut into ¼-inch-wide strips

½ teaspoon dried oregano, crumbled

Salt

½ cup heavy cream

Heat the butter and oil in a large skillet over medium heat. Add the onion and cook, stirring, until translucent and softened, about 5 minutes. Add the poblano strips and cook, stirring until softened (they should still have a little bite), about 3 minutes.

Add the oregano and season to taste with salt. Pour in the cream and bring to a boil. Cook until the cream is thickened and reduced enough so there is just enough to coat the vegetables generously. Serve hot or at room temperature.

pozole

This is a big, hearty soup/stew of pork and pozole (known in the United States as hominy). It is the hominy that makes it so special. To make it, corn kernels are soaked in hot water and powdered limestone, which has the effect of making the kernels taste meatier and become more firm. (Lime also adds nutritional value to the corn.) As the corn swells, it sheds its skin; the kernels are then dried. Using dried pozole requires soaking and long cooking; canned hominy is quick and it works well here.

This version of pozole, which contains chicken as well as pork, has been simplified somewhat from the traditional, but is still a big undertaking. It can be broken down into steps, however, with the various components prepared ahead and refrigerated. In that case, wait until reheating the pozole to add the chicken breasts. Pozole also freezes well.

To turn pozole into a real feast for a party, prepare Tostadas (page 96) and Traditional Refried Beans (page 224). Let guests spread their tostadas with the beans and munch on them in between spoonfuls of pozole. ▪ makes 7 cups; 6 generous servings

FOR THE SAUCE

2 large tomatoes (about 1 pound)

1 small white onion, cut into $\frac{1}{2}$-inch slices

5 to 6 large ancho chiles (about 3 ounces), wiped clean, stemmed, seeded, toasted, and soaked (see pages 2 and 3)

20 large garlic cloves (about $\frac{1}{2}$ cup)

$\frac{1}{2}$ teaspoon allspice berries

1 to 2 cups water, or as needed

2 tablespoons vegetable oil

FOR THE POZOLE

2 tablespoons vegetable oil

1 large white onion, finely chopped

10 garlic cloves, finely chopped

1 tablespoon dried oregano, crumbled

4 quarts water

1 rack (2 to $2\frac{1}{4}$ pounds) baby back ribs, cut between the bones into individual ribs

1 tablespoon salt

1 large bunch cilantro, folded in half and tied into a neat bundle with kitchen twine

One 4-pound chicken, cut into 10 pieces (see Note)

Four 15-ounce cans hominy, with its liquid

2 poblano chiles, roasted (see page 21), peeled, seeded, and coarsely chopped

FOR THE GARNISHES (ANY OR ALL)

1 head romaine lettuce, wilted leaves and core removed and cut into $\frac{1}{2}$-inch-wide strips

2 bunches radishes, trimmed and cut into $\frac{1}{4}$-inch slices

4 limes, cut in half

Chile de árbol powder (see page 7) or another pure chile powder of your choice

Crumbled dried oregano

MAKE THE SAUCE: Set the rack about 8 inches from the broiler and preheat the broiler, to low if possible. Arrange the tomatoes and onion slices on the broiler pan, in a single layer, and cook, turning once, until blackened in spots and softened, about 15 minutes for the onion and about 20 minutes for the tomatoes. Let cool slightly.

When the tomatoes are cool enough to handle, slip off the skins. Working in batches if necessary, combine the tomatoes, onion, anchos, garlic, and allspice berries in a blender jar and blend until very smooth. Add up to 1 cup water (total, not to each batch) if necessary to make a smooth puree.

Heat the oil in a heavy medium saucepan over medium heat. Pour in the puree and cook, stirring constantly, until slightly thickened; control the heat so the sauce doesn't spatter. Pour in 1 cup water and bring to a boil. Adjust the heat so the sauce is simmering and cook, stirring occasionally, for 1 hour. Add small amounts of water from time to time to keep the sauce more or less at the same consistency. The sauce can be made up to 2 days in advance; let cool, then cover and refrigerate until needed.

MAKE THE BROTH: Heat the 2 tablespoons oil in a large (about 8-quart) heavy pot or casserole over medium heat. Add the onion, garlic, and oregano and cook, stirring, until the onion is softened, about 4 minutes. Pour in the water, add the spareribs and salt, and bring to a boil. Adjust the heat so the liquid is simmering and cook for 45 minutes, skimming the foam from the surface occasionally. The broth can be made up to a day in advance, cooled, and refrigerated; bring to a simmer before continuing.

Stir the sauce into the broth and add the cilantro. Return to a simmer and cook for 15 minutes.

Add the chicken legs, thighs, and wings and cook for 15 minutes. The pozole can be made to this point up to 2 days in advance and refrigerated. Reheat to simmering before continuing.

Add the chicken breasts, the hominy, with its liquid, and the poblanos. Bring to a simmer and cook until the chicken is cooked through and the pork is tender, about 15 minutes. Remove and discard the cilantro.

While the pozole is finishing up, put whichever toppings you are using in serving bowls and set them on the table.

To serve, ladle the pozole into warm deep bowls, including some of each ingredient in every bowl. Pass the toppings around the table, letting people add them as they like.

NOTE: The easiest way to cut a chicken into 10 pieces is to buy a chicken already cut into 8 pieces (2 each: thighs, drumsticks, breasts, and wings). Then simply put the breast pieces bone side down on a cutting board and cut them crosswise in half with a heavy knife.

slow-braised boneless short ribs · TABLONES DE RES

These incredibly succulent short ribs are cooked on the bone for extra flavor and deboned before serving. They make an ideal party dish because they can be prepared up to 2 days ahead, before the final grilling or broiling. The roasted tomatillo sauce can be made ahead too. I recommend you buy chuck short ribs, because they are large and meaty. Although one pound of meat per person may sound like a lot, after trimming and cooking, you will have the right amount. ▪ makes 6 servings

Six 1-pound bone-in beef chuck short ribs

3 celery stalks, trimmed and cut into ½-inch slices

1 large carrot, peeled and cut into ¼-inch slices

1 large white onion, cut in half and then into thin slices

½ cup (peeled) garlic cloves

3 pasilla negro chiles, wiped clean, stemmed, seeded, and toasted (see page 2; optional)

10 bay leaves

2 tablespoons dried oregano

1 teaspoon black peppercorns

¼ cup chipotle adobo puree (see page 7)

3 tablespoons salt

2 cups water

Roasted Tomatillo-Chipotle Sauce (recipe follows)

Preheat the oven to 300°F.

Trim all the fat and silverskin (the thin whitish gray membrane) from the meaty sides of the ribs. Scatter about half the celery, carrot, onion, and garlic over the bottom of a deep 13 by 9-inch casserole or roasting pan with a tight-fitting lid or other casserole in which the ribs will fit snugly. Lay the ribs over the vegetables, meat side down, overlapping them a little if necessary. (The ribs will shrink as they cook and will end up not overlapping but lying meat side down to soak up all the juices.) Tuck the pasilla chiles, if using, and bay leaves between and around the ribs. Scatter the remaining celery, onion, carrot, and garlic, the oregano, and peppercorns over the ribs. Stir the chipotle puree, salt, and water together until the salt is dissolved. Pour over the ribs and wiggle the casserole to distribute the liquid evenly. Cover the casserole with its lid or a double thickness of heavy-duty foil, crimping it tightly to the sides to make a very tight seal.

Bake until the ribs are tender when poked with a fork; the meat should pull easily away from the bone, but it shouldn't be falling apart. This will take about 3 hours, but check at about 2½ hours. Remove the lid carefully or poke a hole in the foil to allow the steam to escape before removing the foil to check on the ribs. Replace it with new foil if further cooking is needed.

When the ribs are tender, let stand at room temperature until cool, then refrigerate for at least 6 hours, or up to 2 days.

[continued]

Slow-Braised Boneless Short Ribs with Roasted Tomatillo-Chipotle Sauce (page 201) and Roasted Poblanos with Cream (page 195)

When ready to finish the dish, wipe or scrape the solidified fat from the ribs and remove the meat from the bone. It may pull away easily or need to be cut away. Trim the cartilage that runs along the sides and back of each piece of beef. You will be left with neat little rectangles of beef. Broil or grill the ribs (see below). Whether broiling or grilling, you want to use low, steady heat to slowly heat the short ribs through while browning them. You'll know the ribs are heated through when fat begins to sizzle on the surface. If the beef starts to brown before the ribs soften and sizzle, remove them from the broiler and lower the heat (or move the rack farther away from the heat), or wait for the coals to die down a little, and try again.

TO BROIL THE SHORT RIBS: Position a rack about 8 inches from the broiler and preheat the broiler, to low if possible. Put the beef with what was the bone side up on the lightly oiled broiler pan. Broil until the top is browned and sizzling, about 6 minutes. Flip and repeat.

TO GRILL THE SHORT RIBS: Heat a gas grill to low or light a charcoal fire and wait for it to die down until you can hold your hand an inch from the grill for 5 seconds. Using tongs, oil the grill with a paper towel dipped in vegetable oil. Grill the short ribs, turning occasionally, until browned, softened, and sizzling, about 12 minutes.

Meanwhile, reheat the sauce over low heat, adding small amounts of water as necessary to restore the sauce to the right consistency. Keep warm.

To serve, ladle about 1/3 cup of sauce onto each plate and center a short rib on each.

FRIED PLANTAINS (PLATANOS FRITOS)

The sweet, earthy flavor of ripe—i.e., black—plantains contrasts nicely with savory preparations like these seafood-stuffed poblano peppers, as well as dishes such as the Red Snapper Veracruz-Style on page 180 or any grilled meats. In the coastal areas of Veracruz and Tabasco, fried plantains are part of daily life, just as rice and beans are elsewhere. They are very simple to prepare. Just before cooking, peel 2 ripe medium plantains and cut them on the bias into 1/2-inch slices. Pour a thin layer of vegetable oil into a large pan (a nonstick pan is helpful, especially if the plantains are very ripe) and heat it over medium heat until rippling. Add only as many plantain slices as will fit comfortably (cook the plantains in batches if necessary). Cook until the underside is browned, about 3 minutes. Flip and repeat. Drain on paper towels before serving hot or warm. (Makes about 6 servings.)

roasted tomatillo–chipotle sauce · SALSA DE TOMATILLO Y CHIPOTLE

The tart tomatillos, smoky chipotles, and sweet piloncillo (a type of raw sugar; see page 16) meld to create an exquisitely balanced sauce with delightful hints of cumin and oregano. It can be served as a sauce, as we do with the short ribs, or it can be diluted and used to braise meats, poultry, or game. ▪ makes 3 cups ▪ photograph on page 199

4 chipotle mora chiles (with seeds), wiped clean, stemmed, toasted, and soaked (see pages 2 and 3)

1 ancho chile, wiped clean, stemmed, seeded, toasted, and soaked (see pages 2 and 3)

6 garlic cloves

4 cloves

2 teaspoons dried oregano

2 teaspoons salt

¼ teaspoon ground cumin

¾ cup water

3 tablespoons vegetable oil

1½ pounds tomatillos, husked, washed, and roasted (see page 23)

2 tablespoons shaved piloncillo (see page 16) or 1½ tablespoons dark brown sugar plus 2 teaspoons molasses

Drain the chiles well and put them in a blender jar. Add the garlic, cloves, oregano, salt, cumin, and ½ cup of the water and blend until smooth.

Heat the oil in a medium heavy saucepan over medium heat. Pour in the chile mixture, then rinse out the blender with the remaining ¼ cup water and add that to the pan (set the blender jar aside). Bring the sauce to a boil, stirring to incorporate the oil. Adjust the heat so the sauce is simmering.

Blend the tomatillos, with their juices, until smooth (see Note). Pour into the sauce and stir in the piloncillo. Simmer, stirring occasionally, until the sauce is shiny and little dots of fat rise to the surface, about 30 minutes. Add water a small amount at a time if the sauce becomes too thick before turning shiny. The sauce can be prepared up to 2 days in advance and refrigerated. Bring to a simmer, adding water as necessary to restore it to the right consistency, before using.

NOTE: When blending tomatillos for any stewing sauce like this, "blend until smooth" means the tomatillos are pureed but you still should be able to see the little tomatillo seeds. If you blend more—so that the seeds are broken up—the sauce will become pasty or cloudy and will take on an unpleasant consistency.

beef tenderloin with wild mushrooms and tequila
• FILETE DE RES CON HONGOS AL TEQUILA

Mushrooms grow plentifully in the cool, high moist forests of Michoacán, in central Mexico. Michoacanos prepare their mushrooms in the manner I use here, but I perk them up with a little tequila. The combination of these wild mushrooms spiked with tequila and enriched with cream and seared beef is hard to beat. The recipe calls for beef tenderloin, but you can use any boneless steak you like here, adjusting the cooking time if necessary. I like to serve sautéed *nopales* (cactus leaves; see page 232) with this dish. Other possible accompaniments include pickled poblano strips (page 43), asparagus, peas, fava beans, and glazed carrots. • makes 4 servings

Four 8-ounce filets mignons (center-cut beef tenderloin steaks)

Salt and freshly ground black pepper

5 tablespoons light olive oil

¼ pound cremini mushrooms, stems trimmed and cut into ¼-inch slices

¼ pound shiitake mushrooms, stems removed, caps wiped clean and cut into ½-inch slices

¼ pound oyster mushrooms, hard stem ends removed, mushrooms torn into ½-inch-wide strips

½ large white onion, finely chopped

2 serrano chiles, finely chopped

3 garlic cloves, minced

¼ cup good-quality silver tequila

1 cup heavy cream

10 large fresh epazote leaves, finely chopped (about 2 tablespoons) (optional)

If the fillets are thicker than 1 inch, set them (cut surface down) on a cutting board and pound them with the heel of your hand or a mallet to an even 1-inch thickness. Season them generously with salt and pepper.

Heat 2 tablespoons of the oil in a large heavy skillet over medium-high heat. Add the fillets and cook until well browned on the first side, about 5 minutes. (Adjust the heat during cooking so the steaks brown evenly without burning the little bits that stick to the pan; those little bits will be incorporated into the sauce later, and if they are burnt, they will impart a scorched flavor.) Flip the steaks and repeat. Transfer the fillets to a plate and set aside. They will be rare at this point; they will be cooked further in the sauce. Return the pan to the heat.

Add the remaining 3 tablespoons oil to the pan and heat over medium-high heat until very hot but not smoking. Meanwhile, toss the mushrooms, onion, chiles, and garlic together in a bowl. When the oil is hot, add the mushroom mixture all at once and cook, stirring, until the mushrooms are browned. The timing will depend on the mushrooms, the pan, and the heat—most likely the mushrooms will give off a little liquid first, which must then be cooked off before the mushrooms begin to brown. Season with salt and pepper.

Remove the pan from the heat and pour in the tequila. Carefully return the pan to the heat and stand back—the tequila will probably ignite. When any flames die down, pour in the cream, add the epazote, if using, and bring to a boil. Cook, stirring occasionally, until the sauce is thickened and reduced by about half.

Add the steaks to the sauce. Cook, turning once or twice, until the steaks are warmed through and cooked to medium-rare, about 4 minutes. An instant-read thermometer inserted into the thickest part of a steak will register 130°F. (If desired, lower the heat and cook longer for more-well-done steaks. Add water, a tablespoon at a time to keep the sauce at the right consistency.)

Divide the steaks among serving plates and top with the sauce.

beef and chorizo skewers · ALAMBRE MEXICANO

The word *alambre* means "wire" or "cable"; it is easy to imagine the metal skewers as the cables that hold all the ingredients together. At Rosa Mexicano, *alambres* are removed from the skewers before they are brought to the table and served on rice that is flanked with Cooked Green Salsa (page 114) and a sauce similar to Roasted Tomatillo-Chipotle Sauce (page 201), but with tomato added. At home, you can let your guests undo their own skewers or you can do it for them.

A delicious side note: In most *taquerias* in Mexico, skewers similar to these are prepared by the *taqueros,* who then remove the meat and vegetables from the skewers, chop all the ingredients together, and mix them together with melted cheese to use as a filling for *tacos de alambre.* With fresh tortillas (page 92) and a little raw Green Salsa (page 47), they are absolutely heavenly. ▪ makes 4 servings

1 large white onion
1½ pounds beef tenderloin, trimmed of any fat and cut into 1½-inch cubes
Salt

Twelve 1-inch pieces chorizo (about ¾ pound; see opposite)
12 serrano chiles
Olive oil

If using wooden skewers, soak them in cold water to cover for 1 to 2 hours.

Cut the onion lengthwise in half and peel off the tough outer, layers. Cut the onion halves through the root into 1½-inch-wide wedges. Remove 12 to 16 two-layer pieces, leaving the layers attached to each other; reserve the inner layers of the onion for another use. Toss the beef cubes in a bowl with a generous amount of salt.

Position a rack about 6 inches from the broiler and preheat the broiler to high.

Make the skewers: Thread a serrano onto each of four 12-inch wooden or metal skewers and push it almost to the end. Thread half of the onion, beef, and chorizo onto the skewers, alternating the ingredients. Thread another serrano onto each skewer, then add the remaining onion, beef, and chorizo. Finish each skewer with a serrano. Brush or rub the skewers lightly with olive oil and place them on the broiler pan. The skewers can be assembled up to several hours ahead and refrigerated. Remove from the refrigerator 30 minutes before cooking.

Broil the skewers, turning once, until well browned on all sides and the beef is done to your liking, about 8 minutes for rare. If the skewers are browning too quickly (within the first 3 minutes or so), remove the pan and reduce the broiler heat before continuing, or move the pan farther from the heat, and continue cooking. Transfer to a platter and let stand for a minute or two.

To serve, slip a fork behind the first serrano on each skewer and slowly but steadily pull the skewer away to free the meat and vegetables. If you meet resistance, first put the fork behind each center serrano and remove half the meat and vegetables at a time. Serve hot.

CHORIZO

There are many styles and brands of chorizo on the market. Some are smoked, some are quite garlicky; some are cooked and some raw. Those from Spain may feature paprika as the predominant seasoning. Mexican chorizo, as a rule, is not smoked and is seasoned with chiles (of course), such as guajillos and chiles de árbol, as well as cumin, clove, and coriander seed. Most Mexican chorizos are sold raw, and that is the type I prefer for these recipes. Search out Mexican chorizo, which isn't hard to find, or, if you already have a brand you like, stick with it.

ancho chiles stuffed with beef tenderloin, shiitakes, and cremini

▪ CHILES ANCHOS RELLENOS DE PUNTITAS DE RES

I like to rehydrate dried ancho chiles in a mixture of water and cider vinegar flavored with piloncillo. Here, the sweetness from the piloncillo and the acidity from the vinegar make a well-balanced and delicious finished dish. Serve with one of the tangy sauces suggested below. ▪ makes 6 servings

FOR THE FILLING

- ⅓ cup (about 3 ounces) soft goat cheese
- ¾ cup chopped fresh cilantro
- 1½ pounds trimmed beef tenderloin (see Note) or skirt steak, cut into ¼-inch dice
- 6 ounces shiitake mushrooms, stems removed, caps coarsely chopped (about 2½ cups)
- 6 ounces cremini mushrooms, stems trimmed, coarsely chopped (about 3 cups)
- 1 large white onion, finely chopped (about 1½ cups)
- 2 medium jalapeños, finely chopped (about 3 tablespoons)
- 1½ tablespoons finely chopped garlic
- 2½ teaspoons dried oregano, crumbled
- 2 teaspoons salt, or to taste
- ¾ teaspoon ground cumin
- 3 tablespoons olive oil
- Freshly ground black pepper

- 6 large (about 6 inches long) ancho chiles, prepared for stuffing (see page 5)
- 3 cups Cooked Green Salsa (page 114), Roasted Yellow Tomato Sauce (page 119), or Roasted Tomatillo-Chipotle Sauce (page 201)

With a rack in the center position, preheat the oven to 350°F.

Prepare the filling: Put the goat cheese and cilantro in a large bowl and set aside. Toss the beef, mushrooms, onion, jalapeños, garlic, oregano, salt, and cumin together in a bowl. Heat half the oil in a large skillet over high heat until very hot but not smoking. Carefully add half the beef mixture and cook, stirring constantly, until the beef is cooked through and the mushrooms are lightly browned, about 8 minutes. (The timing may vary, and the beef and mushrooms may give off liquid that will have to be cooked off before the mushrooms will brown.) Scrape into the bowl with the goat cheese and cilantro and repeat with the remaining beef-mushroom mixture, using the remaining oil. When all the beef-mushroom mixture has been cooked, stir well to blend in the cheese and cilantro. Season with salt and pepper.

Drain the chiles and stuff them. There should be enough beef mixture to fill each chile, open side up, without overstuffing, so the cut in the chile can be closed over the filling. Place the chiles in a baking dish that holds them comfortably. Cover with aluminum foil and bake until warmed through, about 20 minutes.

Meanwhile, reheat the sauce to simmering.

Ladle about ¾ cup of the sauce onto each plate, top with a chile, and serve.

NOTE: If possible, use tenderloin "tails" (the thin tapered ends) or "heads" (the wider end opposite the tails) for this dish. Both have a less compact texture than cuts from the center that works well in this dish. These cuts may be less expensive than center-cut tenderloin.

pork chops with cuitlacoche and roquefort sauce
▪ CHULETAS CON CUITLACOCHE Y SALSA DE ROQUEFORT

Roquefort cheese may seem a little out of place in a Mexican cookbook, but the French are, after all, a part of Mexico's history. (Cinco de Mayo is a celebration that commemorates the victory of the Mexican militia over the occupying French army at the Battle of Puebla in 1862.) We have always had a very intense relationship with the French and share a lot of cultural similarities and food passions. Our bread making, to give one of many examples, is very similar to the French technique, as is the way we enjoy breads. A croissant in the morning or a trip to the bakery to buy a baguette or *pan frances*—which nowadays we call *bolillos*—have always been a part of everyday life in Mexico. And the cuitlacoche brings these pork chops right back into the Mexican arena. Although this dish isn't part of traditional cooking, it is one of those modern contributions to the new Mexican table. The chops would be delicious with Slow-Baked Haricots Verts (page 235) and some glazed carrots or mashed potatoes. ▪ makes 4 servings

FOR THE SAUCE

²/₃ cup Cooked Green Salsa (page 114)
²/₃ cup heavy cream
1¼ cups crumbled Roquefort cheese (about 5 ounces)

Four 10-ounce loin pork chops, 1 inch thick
Salt and freshly ground black pepper
2 tablespoons light olive oil

FOR THE CUITLACOCHE-MUSHROOM MIXTURE

½ pound cremini mushrooms, stems trimmed and cut into ¼-inch slices
¼ pound shiitake mushrooms, stems removed, caps wiped clean and cut into ½-inch slices
1 small white onion, finely chopped (about 1 cup)
2 serrano chiles, finely chopped
3 garlic cloves, minced
2 tablespoons light olive oil
Salt and freshly ground black pepper
One 7-ounce can cuitlacoche (see page 15), drained, liquid reserved

With a rack in the center position, preheat the oven to 400°F.

MAKE THE SAUCE: Bring the green sauce and cream to a simmer in a nonaluminum saucepan over medium heat. Remove from the heat and add the Roquefort. Whisk until the cheese is melted and blended into the sauce. Cover the pan and keep the sauce warm off the heat.

COOK THE PORK: Pat the pork chops dry. Season both sides generously with salt and pepper. Heat the oil over medium-high heat in a heavy skillet large enough to hold all the chops. (If you don't have a pan large enough to hold them all, cook them in batches.) Add the chops and cook until the underside is brown, about 5 minutes. Flip and repeat. The chops will not be fully cooked at this point.

Put the chops on a baking sheet (set the skillet aside) and bake until cooked to your liking—just a slight trace of pink closest to the bone is ideal. The best way to test for doneness is to insert an instant-read thermometer into the thickest part of a chop, next to the bone; the chops are done when the temperature reaches 150°F. Let the chops rest on the baking sheet for about 5 minutes before serving. (Meat continues cooking after it is removed from the heat; in the case of 1-inch-thick pork chops, the temperature will likely climb by 3 or 4 degrees.)

MAKE THE CUITLACOCHE-MUSHROOM MIXTURE: Toss the mushrooms, onion, chiles, and garlic together in a bowl. Heat the oil in the pan you used for the pork over medium-high heat until very hot but not smoking. Add the mushroom mixture all at once and cook, stirring, until the mushrooms are browned. The timing will depend on the mushrooms, the pan, and the heat—most likely the mushrooms will give off a little liquid first, which must then be cooked off before the mushrooms begin to brown. Season with salt and pepper.

Stir the drained cuitlacoche into the mushrooms. Add enough of the reserved liquid, about 2 tablespoons, to moisten the mixture if necessary. Remove from the heat.

Center a pork chop on each serving plate and top with the mushroom-cuitlacoche mixture, dividing it evenly. Pour the sauce over the chops and topping, allowing it to pool onto the plates. Serve immediately.

rack of lamb with pistachio
▪ COSTILLAS DE CORDERO CON PIPIAN DE PISTACHE

I am wild about this dish. It is based on a little trick from my good friend Maria Dolores Torres-Izabal. Good Mexican cooks always save the seeds that they tap out of dried chiles before toasting and soaking them. Maria Dolores toasts her seeds and uses them to coat steaks before searing them. Most of the seeds fall off during cooking, but they leave their mysterious, nutty, toasty flavor behind—along with a dash of heat. Here I use toasted chile seeds as the base for a dried rub that mostly stays in place during roasting and tastes terrific with the elegant pistachio sauce. The sauce (like almost every sauce in this book) can be done ahead, which also is true of the rub and seasoning the lamb.

Don't limit this rub to lamb: it is delicious on any steak, chop, or piece of chicken headed for the broiler or grill. Just be sure that whatever you're cooking is fairly quick. Some cooking intensifies the flavors of the rub, but too much will burn it.

▪ makes 4 servings

2 small 8-bone racks of lamb (see Note)
4 teaspoons salt

FOR THE CHILE-SEED RUB

¼ cup chile seeds (reserved from dried chiles;
   see page 2)
½ teaspoon allspice berries (about 15)
¾ teaspoon anise seeds
A 1-inch piece of Mexican cinnamon stick
   (see page 16)
3 cloves

FOR THE PISTACHIO SAUCE

3 cups Chicken Broth (page 66) or
   store-bought chicken broth
1 poblano chile, roasted (see page 21),
   peeled, seeded, and coarsely chopped
1 small serrano chile, coarsely chopped
½ cup shelled pistachios (natural, not dyed)
¼ cup unhulled sesame seeds
1 garlic clove
¼ teaspoon anise seeds
1 avocado leaf (see page 12; optional)

Quick Pickled Poblano Strips
   (page 43; optional)

Pat the lamb completely dry with paper towels. Rub the salt into all sides of the lamb, including the little spaces between the ribs. Let them stand while you make the rub.

MAKE THE RUB: Put the chile seeds in a medium skillet. Place over medium-low heat and cook, stirring and shaking the pan so the seeds toast evenly, until they turn slightly shiny and give off a sweet, nutty aroma, about 5 minutes. Pour the seeds onto a plate. Add the allspice, anise seeds, cinnamon, and cloves to the skillet and toast, stirring, until fragrant, about 2 minutes. Add them to the chile seeds.

When the seeds and spices are cool, grind them all together in a spice mill to a coarse powder. Rub the spice mixture into all sides of the lamb, coating it well and evenly, as if you were breading it. Let the lamb stand at room temperature for up to 45 minutes before cooking, or refrigerate for up to 8 hours. Remove from the refrigerator 45 minutes before cooking.

MAKE THE SAUCE: Combine 1½ cups of the broth, the poblano, serrano, pistachios, sesame seeds, garlic, and anise seeds in a blender jar and blend until smooth. Pour into a medium heavy saucepan and bring to a boil. Adjust the heat so the sauce is simmering and cook, stirring often, until the sauce is shiny and lightly thickened, about 30 minutes. If the sauce thickens too much—more than enough to coat a spoon lightly—before it turns shiny, add a little water 1 or 2 tablespoons at a time. Remove from the heat.

With a rack in the center position, preheat the oven to 450°F. Line a baking sheet with heavy-duty aluminum foil.

Place the racks bone side down on the baking sheet and roast until an instant-read thermometer inserted into the center of a rack registers 130°F (for medium-rare), about 20 minutes. Or adjust the cooking time according to the degree of doneness you prefer. Transfer the racks to a carving board and let stand for 5 to 8 minutes.

Meanwhile, reheat the sauce to a simmer.

Cut the racks between the bones into individual chops. Pour about ½ cup of sauce onto each of four serving plates. Stand 4 chops with the bones pointing up in the center of each plate. (It is fine if the chops lean against each other or slump a little.) Arrange a little cluster of the poblano strips, if using, over the center of each group of chops. Serve immediately.

NOTE: It is fairly easy to find "frenched" racks of lamb from Colorado or New Zealand that weigh about ¾ pound each at upscale supermarkets or butchers. (If not, they can be ordered.) Often they are frozen; allow a day or two for defrosting them in the refrigerator rather than using a quicker method. Frenching means that the meat (there is little of this) and fat (there is much of this) has been trimmed from between the ends of the bones. Frenching sometimes includes cutting out the chine bone that runs along the eye of the meat. Removing the chine bone makes it easy to cut the roasted rack into neat chops.

8 ON THE SIDE
FRIJOLES, ARROZ, Y VERDURAS

WALK THROUGH ANY OF OUR DINING ROOMS DURING a busy dinner and you will see people gathered around tables crowded with festive drinks, colorful entrées, and lots of side dishes. Those side dishes are not an afterthought, but an integral part of the dining experience at Rosa, just as they are in Mexico. Following are a collection of recipes that include two staples—rice and black beans—as well as others that help shape a complete meal, Rosa style, or add a Mexican note to your favorite home-cooked meal. All include serving suggestions and, as is true throughout the book, tips for preparing each as much in advance as possible. And do check out the group of intensely flavored mixtures that tint plain white rice a rainbow of colors and add authentic Mexican flavor with little effort.

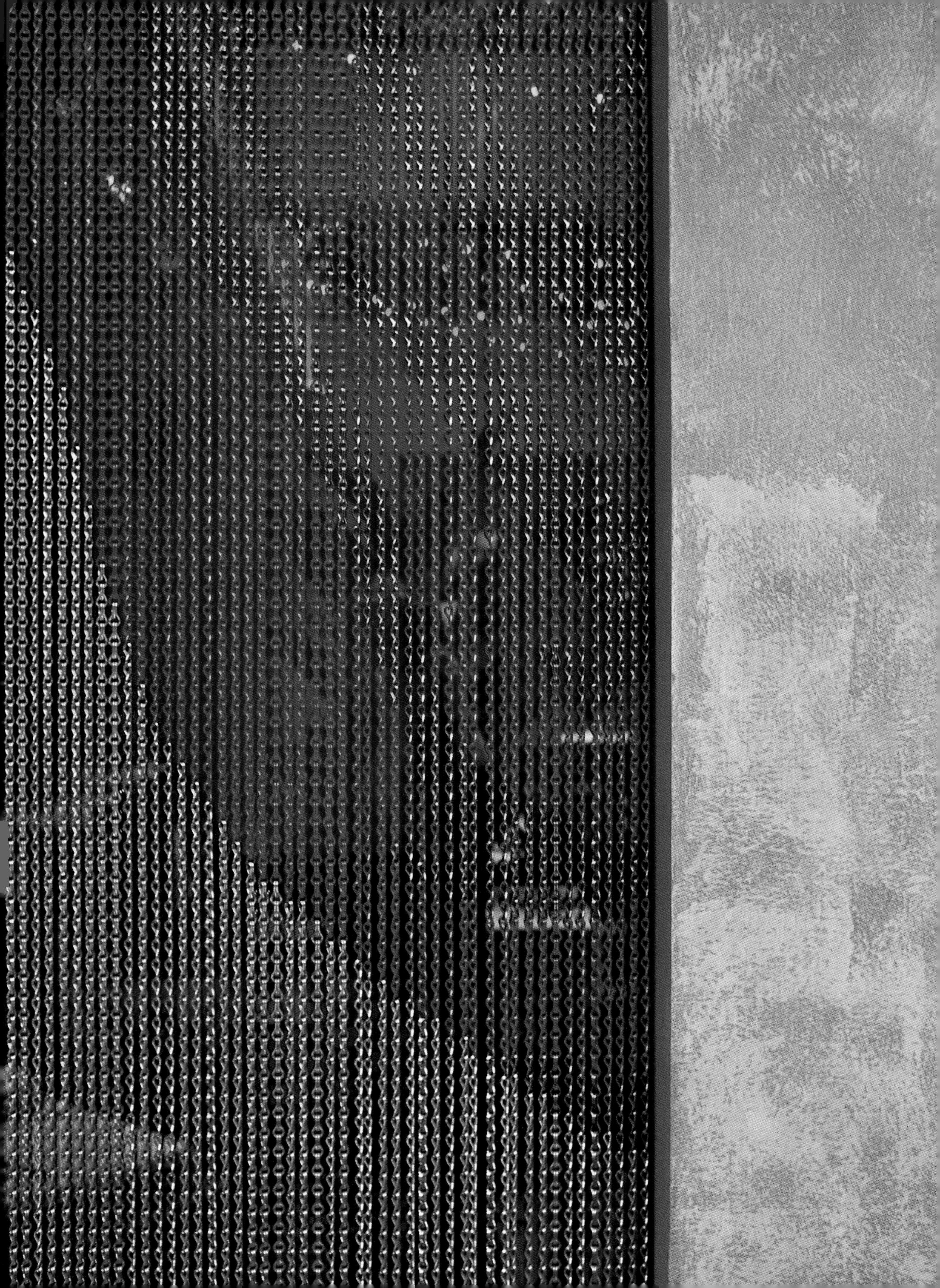

RICE

ALTHOUGH CORN AND BEANS ARE INDIGENOUS TO MEXICO, rice is not. It was introduced in the late 1500s by Spanish merchants who were already familiar with rice—the Moors had introduced it to Spain centuries earlier. But in the Philippines and China, these merchants came across other varieties of rice as well as a plethora of herbs, spices, and fruits unknown in Mexico and Spain at the time. A tropical grain, rice thrived in Mexico's steamy central and southern provinces. At Rosa Mexicano we use long-grain rice. You can use Carolina brand, basmati, or Texmati. Texmati and basmati will cook up firmer than Carolina.

simple white rice · ARROZ BLANCO SIMPLE

Mexicans almost never simply boil rice and serve it. We "fry" it first in a little oil until slightly crispy. This gives it a great texture and a toasty flavor. We then cook it in seasoned water (or chicken, vegetable, or fish broth). At Rosa Mexicano, we often add whole serrano peppers to the broth to flavor the rice, as in this basic recipe. Because they're added whole, the serranos don't impart heat at all, just flavor.

In Mexico, home cooks usually pick one of two methods; chopping the onion and garlic finely and sautéing them before adding the rice, or leaving the garlic cloves whole and the onion in large pieces so they can be easily removed before serving the rice. Blending in the onion and garlic—the method used here—will add flavor, make preparation easier, and save the trouble of picking the onion out of the finished dish.

- makes 4½ cups; 6 generous servings

1½ cups long-grain rice, such as basmati or Texmati
3 cups water
⅓ cup coarsely chopped white onion

1 small garlic clove
1¼ teaspoons salt
1½ tablespoons vegetable oil or mild olive oil
2 serrano chiles

Rinse the rice in a strainer under cold running water until the water runs clear, not milky, 3 to 4 minutes. Bounce the rice in the strainer to remove excess liquid, then place the strainer over a bowl and set aside until as much liquid as possible is drained from the rice, about 20 minutes. The grains of rice should feel dry or only very lightly damp to the touch.

Combine the water, onion, garlic, and salt in a blender jar and blend until smooth.

Heat the oil in a 2-quart saucepan over medium heat. Add the rice and cook, stirring constantly, until it turns translucent. There should be an occasional crackle and sizzle. If the rice starts to color or pop, lower the heat. Pour in the onion-garlic liquid and add the chiles. Bring to a boil and cook until the liquid is reduced to the level of the rice, about 10 minutes.

Turn the heat to low, cover the pan very tightly, and cook until the rice is tender and all the liquid is absorbed, about 10 minutes. The rice will look dense and very moist. Cover the pan and set aside, without lifting the cover again, for 15 minutes.

Remove the chiles (save them for another use; see Red Salsa Molcajete, page 99). Stir the rice with a fork to separate the grains, and serve immediately.

coloring and flavoring rice

Here is a neat little restaurant trick that home cooks can make their own. Each of these simple seasoning mixes will season and beautify the basic recipe (about 4½ cups) of rice. Make whichever of the seasoning mixes you choose, then stir it into the cooked rice after separating the grains.

green rice · ARROZ VERDE

With the addition of a little more cilantro and ¼ pound or so of lump crabmeat, this becomes a very nice dish by itself; we serve something like that at Rosa. You might find plain green rice as a *sopa seca,* or "dry soup" course, at one of Mexico's thousands of *comidas corridas,* small, informal restaurants that specialize in inexpensive multi-course meals. ▪ makes 4½ cups

3 packed cups (about 3 ounces) baby
  spinach, washed and drained
¼ cup water
⅓ cup packed chopped fresh cilantro

1 jalapeño, coarsely chopped
2 garlic cloves
1 teaspoon salt
Simple White Rice (opposite)

Put the spinach and water in a small saucepan. Put over medium heat, cover the pan, and cook just until the spinach is wilted and bright green, about 2 minutes. Scrape the spinach and water into a blender jar, and let cool.

Add the cilantro, jalapeño, garlic, and salt to the blender and blend until smooth. When the rice is ready, empty it into a serving bowl and toss with the seasoning mix until thoroughly blended and all the grains are coated.

yellow rice · ARROZ AMARILLO

Just because this is a Mexican cookbook does not mean that we can't occasionally reach into the global pantry for inspiration—after all, creativity is a hallmark of a good cook. This colorful recipe is a cinch to make and, for convenience sake, at Rosa we utilize two common types of mustard. If you choose a brand like French's or Gulden's—the common escorts to ballpark hot dogs—the rice will have a yellowish tint and a mild flavor; if you go for a spicier Dijon-style mustard, it will have more zip and a paler appearance.

My grandmother often served this dish accompanied by deviled eggs. ▪ makes 4½ cups

2 tablespoons vegetable oil or mild olive oil

2 tablespoons finely chopped white onion

1 large serrano chile, finely chopped

2 generous teaspoons finely chopped garlic

2 tablespoons prepared mustard (see headnote above)

3 medium scallions, trimmed and finely chopped

⅓ cup chopped fresh cilantro (including some stems)

2 tablespoons minced fresh mint

½ teaspoon salt

Simple White Rice (page 216)

Heat the oil in a medium skillet over medium heat. Add the onion, chile, and garlic and cook, stirring, until the onion is translucent, about 4 minutes. Stir in the mustard and cook for 1 minute, then stir in the scallions, cilantro, mint, and salt. Cook for 1 minute, and scrape into a small bowl.

When the rice is ready, empty it into a serving bowl and toss it together with the seasoning mix until thoroughly blended.

red rice · ARROZO ADOBADO

This simple adobo (see page 6) gives the rice a beautiful brick color and great chile taste. ■ makes 4½ cups

3 guajillo chiles, wiped clean, stemmed, seeded, and soaked (see page 3)

1 chile de árbol (with seeds), wiped clean, stemmed, and soaked (see page 3)

2½ tablespoons white vinegar

2 garlic cloves

A 1-inch piece of Mexican cinnamon bark (see page 16)

½ teaspoon cumin seeds

¼ teaspoon dried oregano, crumbled

2 cloves

⅓ cup water

1 tablespoon vegetable oil or light olive oil

½ teaspoon salt

Simple White Rice (page 216)

Drain the chiles and put them in a blender jar with the vinegar, garlic, cinnamon, cumin, oregano, cloves, and water. Blend until smooth.

Heat the oil in a small skillet over medium heat. Pour in the chile mixture, bring to a boil, and cook until reduced by about half. Stir in the salt, remove from the heat, and let cool.

When the rice is ready, empty it into a serving bowl, pour the seasoning mixture over it, and stir until thoroughly blended.

rice with achiote · ARROZ CON ACHIOTE

At Rosa Mexicano we like to be creative with rice, which is such a benchmark in our cuisine. Of course, rice and beans are staples in every Mexican restaurant in the United States, but I find that usually they taste as dull as they look, almost as if they had been treated as an afterthought. This is not to say that authentic rice should be spiced up. In fact, in Mexico it is rarely hot; it is, however, cooked with care and well seasoned.

This delicious, full-flavored recipe contains no firecrackers. It combines the flavors of earthy achiote with fragrant orange zest—a wonderful match. ▪ makes 4½ cups

1 tablespoon achiote paste
  (see page 12)
4 cloves
3 allspice berries
½ teaspoon salt
½ teaspoon dried oregano, crumbled
¼ teaspoon cumin seeds
2 garlic cloves

¼ teaspoon chile de árbol powder
  (see page 7) or other pure chile
  powder
½ cup water
2 tablespoons vegetable oil or
  light olive oil
Grated zest of ½ orange
  (about 2 teaspoons)
Simple White Rice (page 216)

Combine the achiote paste, cloves, allspice, salt, oregano, cumin seeds, garlic, chile powder, and water in a blender jar and blend until smooth. (The allspice may bounce around in the blender for a bit, but it will eventually succumb.)

Heat the oil in a small skillet over medium heat. Pour in the achiote mixture, bring to a boil, and cook until reduced by about half. Stir in the orange zest. Remove from the heat and let cool.

When the rice is ready, empty it into a serving bowl and toss with the seasoning mix until thoroughly blended.

pinto beans · *FRIJOLES BAYOS*

While black beans are associated with coastal Mexico, pinto beans are common throughout the central and northern regions. Pinto beans have softer skins and are less starchy than black beans. As mentioned on page 223, presoaking is not recommended. These beans are a delicious side dish on their own or use them as the starting point for the recipe that follows. ▪ makes 6 cups; 6 servings

1 pound pinto beans, rinsed and picked over

½ small white onion, coarsely chopped
(about ⅓ cup)

2 teaspoons salt

Put the beans, onion, and 10 cups water in a large saucepan and bring to a boil over high heat. Adjust the heat so the liquid is at a gentle boil and cook until the beans are somewhat tender, about 1 hour.

Stir in the salt. Continue cooking until the beans are tender but not mushy, 40 to 50 minutes. There should be enough liquid to cover the beans throughout cooking; if not, add warm water as necessary. Serve warm.

pinto beans with bacon and onion · *FRIJOLES CHARROS*

The consistency of the finished beans should be a little soupy, so it's best to serve them in small bowls as a side dish or starter or in a larger bowl for a whole meal. *Frijoles charros* are delicious topped with pico de gallo and chopped cilantro, but these are optional.

▪ makes 6 cups; 6 to 8 side-dish or appetizer servings ▪ photograph on page 93

6 thick strips bacon (about 6 ounces),
cut into ½-inch dice

1 medium white onion, finely chopped
(about 1⅓ cups)

1 jalapeño, finely chopped

3 large garlic cloves, finely chopped

½ teaspoon ground cumin

Pinto Beans (above; see Note, page 224)

Salt if necessary

Pico de Gallo (page 57; optional)

Chopped fresh cilantro (optional)

Cook the bacon in a medium saucepan over medium heat until browned and crisp, about 6 minutes. Add the onion and jalapeño and cook, stirring, until the milky-white liquid given off by the onion has cooked away and the onion is softened, about 4 minutes.

Stir in the garlic and cumin. Add the beans and bring to a boil, then adjust the heat so the liquid is simmering. Cook until the liquid is lightly thickened, shiny, and has intensified in color, about 10 minutes. Add salt to taste if necessary. Serve with pico de gallo and/or cilantro, if desired.

soupy black beans · FRIJOLES NEGROS

In Mexico, black beans are often cooked with epazote, a pungent herb with a heady aroma that is not unlike cilantro. Like mint, it grows almost everywhere—even where you don't want it to. We use it extensively: in soups, stews, bean dishes, and more. You can sometimes find fresh epazote in Latin American and Mexican markets. Never buy dried epazote—it is virtually tasteless. If you cannot find epazote, do as they do in Oaxaca, and add avocado leaves to the beans as they cook. ▪ makes about 6 cups; 6 servings

1 pound (about 2½ cups) black beans, rinsed and picked over
½ small white onion, roughly chopped (about ½ cup)

3 large garlic cloves
3 large fresh epazote stalks
1 large jalapeño
1½ teaspoons salt, or to taste

Put the beans, onion, garlic, and 8 cups water in a large saucepan and bring to a boil. Adjust the heat so the liquid is simmering and cook, uncovered, until the beans are softened but not tender, about 1 hour.

Cut a slit in the jalapeño and add it to the beans, along with the epazote and salt. Continue cooking until the beans are tender but not mushy, about 30 minutes. There should be enough liquid to cover the beans throughout cooking; if not, add warm water as necessary. Remove the jalapeño, check the seasoning, and serve.

BEANS

It would be no exaggeration to say that beans are the mortar that binds Mexican cuisine, along with rice and corn. At Rosa Mexicano we prepare all kinds of beans in various ways. After they are simply simmered, drained, and seasoned, we use them in salads, relishes, and soups. A black bean puree can be fried to a porridge consistency for *frijoles chinos* (see page 224), which we serve together with a bowl of rice with every main course. We also cook pinto, white, and red beans in similar preparations.

DON'T SOAK BLACK BEANS

Many recipes call for soaking black beans before cooking. While this reduces cooking time, I do not recommend it. Presoaking breaks down the skins, leaving them mushy, and can turn them an unappetizing gray. The beans may also develop a musty, funky flavor. If you are in a big rush, instead try good-quality canned black beans, well drained. They are not the same, but they'll do in a pinch with the right seasoning.

restaurant-style refried beans · FRIJOLES CHINOS

This is what most Americans think of when they think of refried beans. See the variation following for a thicker, more traditional version. ▪ makes 4 cups; 8 generous side-dish servings or 12 generous appetizer servings

6 tablespoons vegetable oil
⅔ cup finely chopped white onion
Soupy Black Beans (page 223; see Note)

1 packed tablespoon chopped fresh epazote (optional)
Salt

Heat the oil in a medium skillet over medium-low heat. Add the onion and cook, stirring often, until very brown, 8 to 10 minutes.

Scrape the onion into the beans. If you have an immersion blender, use it to blend the beans to a coarse puree. If using a standard blender, work in batches and stop the blender often to avoid making the puree too smooth. Transfer the beans to a medium saucepan (or return them to the pan they were cooked in) and stir in the epazote, if using. Bring to a simmer over medium-low heat. Cook until thickened to the consistency of oatmeal, about 15 minutes. Stir often as the beans cook, especially after they start thickening and become more likely to stick to the pan. Check the seasonings and add salt if necessary, then serve.

NOTE: The beans may be prepared in advance and kept at room temperature for up to 2 hours or refrigerated for up to 2 days. If refrigerated, reheat the beans to simmering over low heat, adding water a little at a time to restore them to the original consistency.

VARIATION · traditional refried beans Frijoles Refritos

These are the real thing—beans cooked down to a thick, rich consistency; so thick, in fact, that they are shaped into a loaf almost like a pâté and served with chips and other accompaniments. Two of my favorite things to serve with *frijoles refritos* are sliced radishes and finely shredded queso fresco.

Authentic Mexican *frijoles refritos* are made with lard, not oil. A few years ago at Rosa Mexicano, we decided to change our recipe and use lard. The beans sure tasted better, but when customers caught on to what we were doing, there was a major backlash from those who didn't want to eat animal fat. We now cook our refried beans in oil.

Prepare the refried bean as above, leaving the skillet used for the onion off to the side. When the beans are thickened, pull them from the heat. Heat 5 tablespoons vegetable oil in the skillet over medium heat. Add the beans and cook, stirring and scraping the bottom and sides of the pan almost constantly, until the beans begin to pull away from the sides of the pan as you stir, about 15 minutes.

Lower the heat to low and cook, stirring and scraping, until the beans form a glossy, very firm mass that gathers together when the pan is tilted, about 20 more minutes. Transfer to a rectangular serving plate by tilting the pan and rolling the beans onto the plate. If you like, pat the beans into a neat loaf shape. Serve warm with chips.

VERY VEGETARIAN

Vegetables play an important part in Mexican cooking. Here is a meal where they really shine.

- Drinks (pages 78–84), or pour your favorites, and Chile Peanuts (page 77) or store-bought salted roasted nuts
- Mushroom Quesadillas (page 46)
- Pico de Gallo (page 57)
- Poblanos Stuffed with Spinach and Goat Cheese (page 165)
- Soupy Black Beans (page 223)
- Rosa Mexicano's Corn Pudding (page 226; made without ham)
- Watermelon Ice (page 256) or store-bought sorbet or ice cream

UP TO 2 DAYS BEFORE THE DINNER ▪ Make the peanuts (if doing so) ▪ Make the ranchera sauce

UP TO 1 DAY BEFORE THE DINNER ▪ Roast the poblanos and prepare them for stuffing ▪ Make the spinach-goat cheese filling ▪ Make the black beans

EARLIER ON THE DAY OF THE DINNER ▪ Assemble the quesadillas ▪ Prepare the corn pudding ingredients and refrigerate ▪ Make the watermelon ice (if doing so)

ABOUT 2 HOURS BEFORE DINNER ▪ Stuff the poblanos and put them in a baking dish with the sauce; cover with foil and leave at room temperature ▪ Make the pico de gallo

ABOUT 1 HOUR BEFORE DINNER ▪ Make the corn pudding and bake it

ONCE GUESTS ARRIVE ▪ Grill the quesadillas ▪ Bake the poblanos ▪ Reheat the black beans gently

Rosa Mexicano's corn pudding · TORTA DE ELOTE

With a green salad or Swiss Chard with Beets, Queso Oaxaca and Raisins (page 230), this corn pudding would make a meal—a nice vegetarian meal if you leave out the ham. As a side dish, pair it with pot roasts and stews. Thanks to my friend Robin Greenly for inspiring me with this recipe. ▪ makes 8 side-dish or 4 main-course servings

8 tablespoons (1 stick) butter, melted, plus
  1 tablespoon melted butter for the baking
  dish

1 cup sour cream

2 large eggs

2 cups corn kernels (from about 4 ears corn)

1½ teaspoons salt

¼ teaspoon baking powder

½ cup masa for tortillas (see page 16)

1 cup diced (¼-inch) Manchego cheese
  (without rind; about 5 ounces before
  removing rind)

1 cup diced (¼-inch) boiled ham
  (about 4 ounces)

2 poblano chiles, roasted (see page 21), seeded,
  peeled, and cut into ⅛-inch-wide strips
  (optional)

With a rack in the center position, preheat the oven to 375°F. Using the 1 tablespoon melted butter, grease a 2-quart soufflé or other round baking dish. Set aside.

Put the sour cream, the remaining melted butter, and the eggs in a blender jar. Add the corn, salt, and baking powder and blend at low speed until smooth. Pour into a bowl and whisk in the masa. Stir in the cheese, ham, and chiles, if using.

Pour into the prepared baking dish, set on a baking sheet, and put in the oven. Immediately lower the heat to 350°F and bake until the pudding is puffed, the top and sides are deep golden brown, and the center feels firm, about 35 minutes. Let stand for 10 minutes before serving hot, or up to 30 minutes if serving warm.

grilled corn street vendor-style · ELOTES ASADOS CON CHILE

Try out this terrific summer recipe as an appetizer or as a side dish at your next barbecue and we guarantee rave reviews. It is simple to prepare, great looking, and absolutely addictive. The Mexican corn we use is quite different from American sweet corn. The Mexican variety has thicker cobs and larger kernels; it is also slightly chewier and not as sweet as its American counterpart. Both are equally good in this recipe.

This is typical Mexican street food, usually made with plain mayonnaise. At Rosa Mexicano I came up with a little addition that has turned out to be quite popular—mayonnaise seasoned with minced garlic and hot peppers. The mayonnaise can be prepared well in advance and refrigerated. ▪ makes 6 servings

FOR THE SEASONED MAYONNAISE

1/2 cup mayonnaise

1 jalapeño, roasted (see page 21), peeled, and minced

1 small garlic clove, minced

6 large ears corn with plenty of husks intact

1 1/2 cups finely grated queso fresco (about 4 ounces)

1 lime, cut into 6 wedges

Salt

Chile de árbol powder (see page 7) or other pure chile powder

MAKE THE SEASONED MAYONNAISE: Stir the mayonnaise, jalapeño, and garlic together in a small bowl. Cover and refrigerate for up to 1 day. Bring to room temperature before using.

ASSEMBLE THE DISH: Heat a gas or charcoal grill.

Leave any stalks attached to the corncobs in place. Peel back the outer firmer layers of husks from each ear one at a time, snapping them off at the base. If the husks snap off only partially, leaving the thick lower part still attached, remove that part as well, or you won't be able to bend the softer husks all the way back. When you reach the inner softer husks that peel back without breaking, peel them all the way back but leave them attached to the cob. Gather these softer husks together—they will be used as a handle to make eating the cooked corn easier—and tie with kitchen twine to keep them in place. Remove all the silk from the corn. If you like, wrap the husk-handles in aluminum foil to make sure they don't char during cooking.

Place the corn on the grill so the cobs are over the heat but the husks are extended over the edges. Cook, turning often, until the corn is evenly well browned with some charred spots, 12 to 15 minutes.

Put the cheese in a bowl. Spread each ear of corn with a thin, even layer of mayonnaise, then squeeze a lime wedge over each one and season lightly with salt. Hold each ear of corn over the bowl of cheese and rotate it as you sprinkle an even layer of the cheese over the corn, then season lightly with chile powder. Hand an ear to each guest, and let him or her season the corn with additional chile powder to taste.

grilled corn relish · ENSALADILLA DE ELOTE

One great thing about Mexican cooking is that so many preparations can be made in advance, so if you are entertaining you won't be ricocheting around the kitchen before mealtime. Here is a good example. This smoky and piquant corn relish, which has innumerable uses with fish, grilled meats, eggs, poultry and more, can be assembled earlier in the day, or the day before serving. ▪ makes about 5 cups

6 medium ears corn, husks and silks removed

1 small red onion (about 4 ounces), finely chopped

2 poblano chiles, roasted (see page 21), peeled, seeded, and cut into ½-inch squares

1 red bell pepper, roasted (see page 21), peeled, seeded, and cut into ½-inch squares

1 jalapeño, roasted (see page 21), peeled, and minced

3 tablespoons olive oil

3 tablespoons freshly squeezed lime juice, or to taste

Salt

½ to 1 teaspoon chile de árbol powder (see page 7) or other pure chile powder (optional)

½ cup tightly packed chopped fresh cilantro

Heat a gas or charcoal grill.

Place the corn on the grill and cook, turning often, until evenly well browned with some charred spots, 12 to 15 minutes. Cool to room temperature.

Trim the corn stalks (if any) even with the end of the cob so the ears will stand steady. Stand the ears of corn on a cutting board and, with a sharp knife, shave the kernels from the cob. There will be about 3 cups. Transfer the corn to a bowl and toss together with the onion, poblanos, bell pepper, jalapeño, olive oil, lime juice, and salt to taste. Add the chile powder if you like. Let stand at room temperature for 15 minutes or up to 2 hours. The relish may be prepared to this point up to 1 day in advance. Remove from the refrigerator 1 hour before serving.

Add the cilantro to the relish, toss again, and serve.

Nearly all of the recipes in this book can by doubled, tripled, or more to suit your needs.

lentil, apple, and banana salad
▪ ENSALADA DE LENTEJAS, MANZANAS, Y PLATANO

This may sound like high-fiber baby food, but don't knock it 'til you've tried it. The sweetness of the fruit, the earthiness of the lentils, and the sharp bite of the chiles conspire to create a surprisingly delightful and layered side dish. It's especially good with grilled fish and meat, and it can even be served alone as an appetizer. At Rosa Mexicano we sometimes substitute mature (black) plantains, cut into little cubes and fried, for the banana. ▪ makes 4½ cups; 6 servings

½ pound (about 1¼ cups) brown lentils, rinsed and picked over

½ small white onion, peeled

2 garlic cloves

Salt

1 Golden Delicious apple, quartered, peeled, cored, and cut into ¼-inch cubes (about 1½ cups)

1 firm banana, peeled and cut into ¼-inch cubes (about 1½ cups)

¼ cup finely chopped scallions

¼ cup chopped fresh cilantro

1 serrano chile, finely chopped

1 jalapeño, finely chopped

3 tablespoons olive oil

2 tablespoons mayonnaise

Juice of 1 lemon

Put the lentils, onion, and garlic in a large saucepan, pour in 8 cups water, and add a small handful of salt. Bring to a boil over high heat, then adjust the heat so the water is boiling gently, and cook until the lentils are tender but not mushy, about 20 minutes.

Drain the lentils thoroughly and transfer them to a serving bowl. Cool to room temperature, tossing occasionally.

Add the remaining ingredients to the bowl and stir gently until the lentils are coated and the fruits are distributed throughout. The salad can be covered and kept at room temperature for up to 2 hours (it is best if not refrigerated). Adjust the salt before serving.

Swiss chard with beets, queso Oaxaca, and raisins
▪ ACELGAS CON BETABELES, QUESO OAXACA, Y PASITAS

This recipe makes quite a large amount, but you won't mind. Leftovers reheat beautifully. Or, increase the amount of cheese a little and serve it as a hearty vegetarian main course. Queso Oaxaca, which is quite bland, goes nicely with the sweet and bitter flavors of the beets and chard, but so would a cheese with a little more character, such as queso añejo—an aged and slightly more robust version of queso blanco —or even a mild feta. ▪ makes 10 side-dish or 4 main-course servings

2 bunches medium (about 3½-inch diameter) red or gold beets, or 1 bunch of each

2 to 4 bunches Swiss chard, preferably white (see Note)

⅓ cup mild olive oil

1 large white onion, cut in half and then into thin slices

3 pencil-thin scallions, trimmed and thinly sliced

5 garlic cloves, finely chopped

2 serrano chiles, finely chopped

4 large ripe tomatoes, roasted (see page 23), peeled, and chopped

1 cup packed golden raisins

4 teaspoons salt

2 limes, halved

1 cup diced (½-inch) queso Oaxaca

Trim the greens from the beets and wash the beets well. If the greens are healthy looking, set them aside with the chard. Put the beets in a large saucepan and pour in enough cold water to cover them by 3 inches. Bring to a boil and cook until the beets are tender when poked with a small knife, 25 to 35 minutes, depending on the beets. Drain and let cool to room temperature.

While the beets are cooking and cooling, prepare the chard: Bring a large pot of salted water to a boil. While the chard is still in bunches (it's easier that way), trim off the bottom 1 inch or so of the stems; then separate the leaves. Cut out the thick stem from each leaf, or grasp the leaf on both sides of the stem with one hand and pull out the stem with the other; reserve the stems.

Wash the leaves and stems separately in plenty of cold water. Drain in a colander. Cut the stems crosswise into very thin slices and set them aside. Stir the leaves into the boiling water and cook for 1 minute after the water returns to the boil. Drain in the colander and rinse with cold water until cool enough to handle. Squeeze out the water from the chard and coarsely chop it.

Heat the oil in a wide deep skillet (or a cazuela, see page 17) over medium heat. Add the chard stems and cook, stirring often, until softened, 8 to 10 minutes. Add the onion, scallions, garlic, and chiles and cook, stirring, until the onion is softened, about 3 minutes. Add the tomatoes, all but 2 tablespoons of the raisins, and the salt. Cook until the stems are tender, the raisins are plump, and most of the tomato liquid has cooked off, about 15 minutes.

Meanwhile, slip the skins off the beets and cut beets into ½-inch dice. (Keep them separate if using red and gold beets.)

When the chard stems are tender, add the chard leaves and stir to separate them and coat them with sauce. Remove from the heat and squeeze in the juice from the limes. Transfer the chard to a platter and top with the diced beets, the remaining 2 tablespoons raisins, and the cheese. Serve hot, warm, or at room temperature.

NOTE: If the beets you are using have bushy, bright green tops, substitute those for part of the chard. Bunches of chard will vary in weight, so use the hanging scale in the produce department to come close to 4 pounds of chard, or less if using the beet tops. A little more or less won't dramatically affect the recipe.

QUESO OAXACA

Associated with Oaxaca, this ball-shaped, braided string cheese is somewhat salty and mildly tangy. It is a common ingredient in quesadillas because when it melts it retains its elastic texture.

The technique of making Oaxacan string cheese, which is Arabic in origin, arrived at our shores in the early sixteenth century with Cortez and the conquistadors. How it came to be specific to Oaxaca is anybody's guess. Interestingly enough, you won't find this string cheese in Spain today. Once the Moors were expelled from the Iberian peninsula in 1491, after eight centuries of domination, the Catholic monarchs expunged many vestiges of Arabic culture—even the cheese!

Similar braided cheeses are enjoyed in Armenia and in many Middle Eastern countries; Armenian string cheese is also widely found in the United States and makes a great substitute for its Oaxacan counterpart. You may find it plain or flavored with nigella seeds, which have a peppery, aniselike essence. For Mexican cooking, I prefer the plain variety.

prickly pear cactus leaves · NOPALES

The unique flavor and texture (similar to okra) of *nopales,* prickly pear cactus leaves, makes them universally popular in Mexico. The directions for trimming, cutting, and cooking the cactus leaves, also known as pads or paddles, stay the same no matter how you will prepare the finished leaves. And that's good to know, as *nopales* are infinitely adaptable, from simple preparations served as side dishes to pickles and salads, like the one that follows this recipe. Cactus leaves are available in Latin groceries and, increasingly, in larger or specialty supermarkets. If buying them whole, look for leaves with unblemished green skin and firm flesh. Some stores sell *nopales* already cleaned—a boon for home cooks. ▪ makes 2 to 2½ cups; 4 servings

6 large cactus leaves (about 1½ pounds)

2 cups water

½ small white onion (about 2 ounces), thinly sliced

1 tablespoon olive oil

1 teaspoon dried oregano, crumbled

1 chile de árbol (with seeds), wiped clean, well toasted (see page 2), and chopped

1½ teaspoons salt

If necessary, remove the spines from the cactus leaves: Put on a pair of heavy rubber or canvas gloves and hold a leaf firmly in place with one hand. With the other hand, run a knife along the leaf to scrape off the spines. Be sure to remove all the spines. Repeat with the remaining leaves.

Cactus leaves are thicker at one end than the other: cut the leaves crosswise into thin strips, making the strips a little thinner at the wide end.

Put the strips in a large saucepan, add the water, onion, olive oil, oregano, chile de árbol, and salt, and bring to a boil. Adjust the heat so the liquid is simmering and cook until the water is boiled off and the cactus is frying in the oil, about 10 minutes. The cactus should remain a little crunchy. Serve as is, hot or at room temperature, or use in other dishes.

cactus-leaf salad · ENSALADA DE NOPALES

Variations on this salad are found all over Mexico, served as a side dish, spooned into tacos, or even turned into a main course with the addition of diced queso fresco. Our version is lightened up with cherry tomatoes. ▪ makes 3½ cups; 4 servings ▪ photograph on page 28

Prickly Pear Cactus Leaves (page 232),
   at room temperature
2 cups yellow and/or red cherry tomatoes,
   cut in half
½ small red onion, very thinly sliced
¼ cup lightly packed chopped fresh cilantro

1 jalapeño, seeded and cut into very thin strips
1 tablespoon olive oil
Juice of 1 lime, or to taste
½ teaspoon dried oregano, crumbled
Salt to taste

Combine the cactus leaves and all the remaining ingredients in a bowl and toss well. Let stand for 20 minutes before serving.

Taste and add a little more salt and/or lime juice if you like.

slow-baked haricots verts · EJOTES AL ACHIOTE

One school of thought says that green beans should be cooked just until bright green and crisp. This recipe didn't go to that school. Long, slow cooking in a brightly flavored roasted tomato sauce brings out the deep flavor of the beans. We serve them with grilled salmon, halibut, and snapper, but they also go well with rice and beans for a vegetarian meal. ▪ makes 8 servings

½ cup mild olive oil

2 small red onions, thinly sliced

3 jalapeños, cut lengthwise into fine strips

5 garlic cloves, finely chopped

4 ripe large tomatoes (about 2 pounds), roasted (see page 23), peeled, and coarsely chopped

Juice of 2 oranges

4 teaspoons achiote paste (see page 12)

2 teaspoons sugar

2 teaspoons dried oregano, crumbled

3 bay leaves

2 tablespoons salt

2 pounds haricots verts (thin green beans), both ends trimmed

Preheat the oven to 325°F.

Heat the oil over medium-low heat in a 3-quart ovenproof casserole (such as an enameled cast-iron casserole with a tight-fitting lid or, even better, a cazuela—see page 17). Add the onions and jalapeños and cook, stirring, until the onions are tender but not browned, about 15 minutes. Add the garlic and cook for 3 to 4 minutes.

Add the tomatoes, orange juice, achiote paste, sugar, oregano, bay leaves, and salt and bring to a boil. Stir in the green beans and cook for 3 minutes.

Cover the casserole with its lid (or a double thickness of heavy-duty aluminum foil crimped tightly to the sides; wear oven mitts to do this). Bake until the beans are very tender and infused with the sauce, about 2 hours. Very fresh young beans may take a little less time; older, tougher beans a little more. Serve hot. The beans can be prepared up to 2 days in advance, cooled, and refrigerated. Reheat in the oven or on top of the stove.

RIGHT: Piloncillo

DESSERTS
POSTRES 9

IN THIS CHAPTER, I'VE GATHERED SOME OF MY FAVORITE desserts from a variety of sources—traditional Mexican home cooking, innovations on that theme, and a few very generous friends. There is something here for everyone, whether your thing is a light, chile-tinged watermelon ice or an over-the-top, creamy, and citrus-infused *tres leches* cake. Our guests, and yours, who, once the main course is cleared, swear that they "couldn't eat another bite" will find themselves reconsidering quickly when faced with any of the selections from this chapter. For simple and clever ways to combine these desserts or to integrate them into your regular repertoire, please see the box on page 255.

CAKES AND OTHER BAKED DESSERTS

OUR COLLECTION OF DESSERTS RUNS THE GAMUT FROM thin, elegant cookies to a homey cheesecake that is closer to a rice pudding with a graham cracker crust. And no Mexican cookbook would be complete without a flan. Ours is traditionally Mexican in its dense texture—thanks to a shot of cream cheese—and not so traditional in the addition of cajeta, a dense, rich-tasting cousin of dulce de leche. I hope you saved some room for dessert.

citrus "three milks" cake · TRES LECHES CITRICO

There are indeed "three milks" that go into this beloved dessert—not into the cake itself, but into the sweet syrup used for soaking the cake after it is baked and before it is frosted. My hunch is that the sudden appearance of this cake all over Latin America in the fairly recent past was a result of the recipe or some version of it being included on the label or in the recipe booklet that accompanied one or more of the canned milk products that go into the cake. (Much the same way as the onion dip craze that resulted when that recipe was printed on packages of instant onion soup mix.)

Although this recipe has several components, you can prepare each of them in advance. In fact, the cake must be baked a day ahead. And the whole cake can be completed hours or even a day before it is served. Of the many versions of *tres leches*, I like this one, topped with a citrus zest-seasoned whipped cream, best. ▪ makes 8 servings

FOR THE CAKE

Softened butter or vegetable oil cooking spray
⅔ cup all-purpose flour
½ teaspoon baking powder
4 large eggs
Pinch of salt
⅔ cup sugar
½ teaspoon pure vanilla extract
3 tablespoons water

FOR THE FROSTING

2 cups crème fraîche
2 tablespoons confectioners' sugar
1 teaspoon *each* grated lemon, orange, and lime zest

FOR THE "THREE MILKS"

One 14-ounce can sweetened condensed milk
One 12-ounce can evaporated milk
1 cup heavy cream
Grated zest of 1 orange (about 1 generous tablespoon)
Grated zest of 1 lemon (about 1 scant tablespoon)
Grated zest of 1 lime (about 2 teaspoons)
2 tablespoons Cointreau or other orange-flavored liqueur
1 tablespoon anisette or other anise-flavored liqueur

MAKE THE CAKE: With a rack in the center position, preheat the oven to 350°F. Cut a circle of parchment paper to line the bottom of an 8-inch springform pan, and place it in the pan. Using the softened butter or spray, grease the paper but *not the sides* of the pan.

Sift the flour and baking powder together into a small bowl. Set aside.

In the bowl of an electric mixer, or in a large mixing bowl, using a handheld electric mixer, beat the eggs and salt together at high speed until foamy. Gradually beat in the sugar, then continue beating until the eggs are pale yellow and about tripled in volume, about 5 minutes. Beat in the vanilla, then beat in the water 1 tablespoon at a time. Reduce the mixer speed to low and gradually beat in the flour mixture just until no trace of white remains.

With a rubber spatula, scrape the batter into the prepared pan. Bake until the cake is risen and deep golden brown, about 45 minutes. Cool in the pan on a rack for 5 minutes. Turn the pan upside down on the rack and let cool completely.

When the cake is completely cool, run a dull knife around the edge of the pan to release the cake, but leave the cake in the pan. Store, uncovered, at room temperature for 24 hours so it is nice and dry, ready for soaking.

MAKE THE FROSTING: Whisk the crème fraîche and confectioners' sugar together in a mixing bowl until stiff. Stir in the citrus zests. Cover and refrigerate. The frosting can be made up to a day in advance; use it right out of the refrigerator.

MAKE THE SOAKING LIQUID: Combine the condensed milk, evaporated milk, heavy cream, and orange, lemon, and lime zests in a large saucepan and bring to a boil over medium heat, stirring occasionally. Remove from the heat and strain into a pitcher or large measuring cup. Stir in the orange liqueur and anisette.

At least 2 hours or up to 1 day before serving, with the cake still in its pan, slowly pour about half the soaking liquid over the top, soaking the cake evenly. When the cake has absorbed all the liquid, add as much of the remaining liquid, a little at a time, as the cake will absorb. The best way to tell when the cake is fully soaked is to check the sides: After each addition of liquid, some will seep out of the cake into the space between the cake and the sides of the pan. When the cake no longer reabsorbs this liquid, it is fully soaked. If there is soaking liquid left, refrigerate it. Chill the soaked cake thoroughly, at least 4 hours or up to 1 day.

FROST THE CAKE: Up to 2 hours before serving, release the sides of the springform pan, place a serving platter upside down over the cake, and quickly invert the two. Gently remove the pan bottom. Coat the top and sides of the cake evenly with the frosting. (It is normal for some of the soaking liquid to seep out of the cake and onto the platter before it is served.) Let the cake stand at room temperature until ready to serve, then cut into wedges and pass any remaining soaking liquid separately.

rice pudding cheesecake · PASTEL DE ARROZ CON LECHE

Halfway between a creamy cheesecake and a dense rice pudding, this delicious dessert evolved, with many big twists, from a recipe originally devised by Fany Gerson, the former pastry chef at Rosa Mexicano. ▪ makes 12 generous servings

FOR THE CRUST

3 ounces Maria cookies or graham crackers, crushed (about 1 cup; see Note)

1 cup pecans, toasted and coarsely ground

1 tablespoon sugar

½ teaspoon ground Mexican cinnamon (see page 16)

¼ teaspoon salt

6 tablespoons unsalted butter, melted

FOR THE FILLING

Four 6-inch Mexican cinnamon sticks (see page 16)

2 vanilla beans

4 cups heavy cream

4 cups milk

1 cup basmati rice

Pinch of salt

¼ cup water

1 envelope plus 1⅛ teaspoons unflavored gelatin

Two 8-ounce packages cream cheese, cut into pieces, at room temperature

⅔ cup sugar

Mexican Caramel Sauce (page 266)

MAKE THE CRUST: With a rack in the center position, preheat the oven to 350°F.

Stir the crushed cookies, pecans, sugar, cinnamon, and salt together in a mixing bowl. Stir in the melted butter until the crumbs are evenly moistened. Press the crust mixture into an even layer over the bottom of a 9-inch springform pan. Bake until the crust is lightly browned and firm, about 15 minutes. Let cool completely.

MAKE THE FILLING: While the crust cooks, cut a 6-inch square from a double thickness of cheesecloth. Crumble the cinnamon sticks onto the square, add the vanilla beans, and tie the cheesecloth into a neat bundle. Put the cream, milk, and rice in a large saucepan. Drop in the spice bundle and heat, stirring, to a simmer. Add the salt and simmer, stirring occasionally, until the rice is tender, about 15 minutes.

While the rice is cooking, soften the gelatin: Pour the water into a small bowl. Sprinkle the gelatin over the surface, slowly and evenly to prevent lumps from forming. Whisk with a small fork until the gelatin is softened and the mixture is fluffy.

Stir the sugar into the cooked rice and remove from the heat. Stir in the cream cheese until the cheese is melted and the sugar is dissolved. Pour half the rice mixture into a sieve set over a bowl and, using a wooden spoon, mash the rice against the sieve to squeeze as much of the liquid from it as possible. Some rice will pass through the sieve too; that is fine. Scrape the mashed rice from the bottom of the sieve into the bowl with the liquid. Transfer the rice in the sieve to another bowl, and repeat with the remaining rice mixture. Measure out 2 cups of the reserved rice and stir into the liquid; discard the remaining rice. Whisk about 1 cup of the rice mixture into the softened gelatin until the gelatin is dissolved, then stir back into the rice mixture until thoroughly blended.

Pour the rice mixture over the cooled crust. Refrigerate the cake until completely chilled and set, at least 4 hours, or up to 1 day.

To serve, release the sides of the springform pan—run a knife dipped in warm water between the cake and the sides of the pan to free the cake completely. Cut the cake into wedges, making sure to cut all the way through the crust, and serve, passing the caramel sauce separately.

NOTE: Maria cookies are crisp round cookies with a pleasant, simple flavor, not unlike animal crackers—which make a good substitute. Maria cookies can be found in many Latin groceries and online at www.tienda.com.

hibiscus, mango, and berry trifle · ANTE DE FRUTAS A LA JAMAICA

Antes are a group of desserts that use leftover sponge cake as the starting point. Where the name comes from is a little mystery. In Spanish, *ante* means "suede," so maybe the name is a reference to the smooth, velvety texture of soaked sponge cake. Or it could be from the Latin *ante,* meaning "before," and stem from the old custom of serving such things before the main course.

There are a lot of versions of *antes.* Older ones involved soaking stale sponge cake in flavored syrups, then baking it; even after baking, the cakes remained moist. Nowadays, the term refers to any moist cake-based dessert layered with various nuts, fruit purees, and dry fruits—like a trifle.

It is difficult to give an exact amount for the cake (or ladyfingers) you will use—much depends on the size and shape of your glasses. Another nice thing about this dessert—apart from its good looks and wonderful flavor—is that it must be made ahead and chilled for the flavors and textures to really come together. That makes it a natural for entertaining. ▪ makes 6 servings

FOR THE HIBISCUS SYRUP

2 cups water

¾ cup sugar

A 1-inch piece of Mexican cinnamon stick (see page 16)

Two 2½ by 1-inch-wide strips orange zest (removed with a vegetable peeler)

Two 2½ by ½-inch-wide strips lime zest (removed with a vegetable peeler)

⅓ cup (about ½ ounce) dried hibiscus flowers or hibiscus tea (see Note)

1 tablespoon freshly squeezed lime juice

1 tablespoon anisette or other anise-flavored liqueur

TO ASSEMBLE

½ cup slivered almonds, lightly toasted

½ sponge cake from Citrus "Three Milks" Cake (page 240) or store-bought sponge cake or about 16 to 20 ladyfingers (day-old is best)

1 pint blueberries

½ pint raspberries

1 mango, pitted, peeled, and cut into ½-inch dice

Cinnamon Custard Sauce (page 264)

MAKE THE SYRUP: Combine the water, sugar, cinnamon stick, and citrus zests in a medium saucepan and bring to a boil over medium heat, stirring to dissolve the sugar. Remove from the heat and drop in the hibiscus flowers. (Hibiscus flowers or tea should steep in hot, not boiling, water—boiling will turn them sour.) Let steep until the syrup takes on a rich color and aroma, about 10 minutes.

Stir the lime juice and liqueur into the syrup, then strain the syrup. Set aside.

[continued]

ASSEMBLE THE DESSERT: Choose six large—about 12-ounce—wineglasses; glasses with long stems and wide bowls will make the nicest presentation. Cut the cake into ½-inch slices, then cut pieces large enough to line the bottom of the glasses. Or, if using ladyfingers, cut as necessary to fit into the bottom of the glasses. Brush both sides of the cake pieces or ladyfingers generously with warm syrup and line the bottoms of the glasses. Top each with 6 to 8 blueberries, 3 or 4 raspberries, and 1 tablespoon of the diced mango. Spoon 2 tablespoons of the cinnamon custard sauce over the fruit and top with 1½ teaspoons of the almonds. Make another layer of syrup-soaked cake, tearing or cutting the pieces of cake or ladyfingers as necessary. Reserve about half the pint of blueberries for serving, and make another layer of fruit and custard, using the remaining blueberries, raspberries, mango, and custard. Cover each glass with plastic wrap and chill for at least 2 hours, or up to 1 day.

Remove the *ante* from the refrigerator 30 minutes before serving. Scatter the reserved blueberries over the top and serve.

NOTE: In Mexico, dried hibiscus flowers, called *flores de Jamaica,* are steeped like tea and then made into a refreshing iced drink that is high in vitamin C. The flowers are available in Latin grocery stores and online from www.mexgrocer.com.

Peeling a mango with a uniquely Mexican mango fork, which helps you hold the fruit in place while you peel it.

brownie tamales · TAMALES DE CHOCOLATE

I have been fortunate to work with some truly gifted pastry chefs, one of whom is Nick Malgieri. Nick, a good friend as well as author of many well-respected dessert books, developed this twist on the *tamal* theme. The sweet tamales make a beautiful presentation, served in the rustic corn husks with a neat scoop of ice cream and an elegant drizzle of caramel sauce. Sweet Tomatillo Sauce (page 263) or even plain whipped cream would make a nice alternative to the caramel sauce. ■ makes 6 servings

FOR THE TAMALES

Three 6-inch store-bought corn tortillas

6 tablespoons unsalted butter, at room temperature

⅓ cup sugar

6½ ounces bittersweet chocolate, melted and cooled

4 large eggs, at room temperature

1⅓ cups ground pecans (4 ounces)

¼ teaspoon ground cinnamon

Grated zest of ½ orange

¼ cup bittersweet chocolate chips

6 large (at least 7 inches across the bottom and 7 inches long) dried corn husks, thoroughly soaked (see pages 13-15)

Vanilla ice cream, slightly softened

1½ cups Mexican Caramel Sauce (page 265)

Make the tamales: Tear the tortillas into 8 pieces each. Put them in a food processor and process until ground to the texture of coarse cornmeal (not powdery). Set aside.

In the bowl of an electric mixer fitted with the paddle attachment, or in a mixing bowl, using a handheld mixer, beat the butter and sugar together at medium speed until fluffy. Beat in the cooled melted chocolate. Beat in 2 of the eggs one at a time, then half the pecans and half the ground tortillas. Repeat with the remaining eggs, pecans, and tortillas, then beat in the cinnamon and orange zest. Fold in the chocolate chips.

Drain the corn husks, but do not blot them dry. Place a husk with the tapered end toward you. Center ½ cup of the filling on the husk. Fold the sides of the husk over the filling to enclose it completely, then fold the tapered end up to form a neat bundle with the top end open. Repeat with the remaining husks and filling. Stand the tamales open end up in a round 4-quart soufflé dish or other deep heatproof dish that will hold them snugly but comfortably; the idea is to keep them upright but not cramped.

Put the dish of tamales into a tamal steamer or a pot large enough to hold it comfortably. Pour in enough boiling water to come halfway up the sides of the dish, being careful not to get any water into the dish. Drop 2 or 3 coins into the water (see the headnote on page 166). Bring the water to a boil, then adjust the heat so the water is boiling gently. Cover the pot and steam until the tamales are semi-firm but still very moist in the center, about 25 minutes. (The only way to be certain the tamales are done is to unwrap one and cut into it. Handle it carefully because it will be quite hot.) Turn off the heat and let the tamales stand for 5 minutes.

To serve, using tongs, gently remove the tamales to serving plates. As soon as the husks are cool enough to handle, unwrap the tamales, leaving them on the corn husks in the center of the plates. Place a scoop of ice cream next to each tamale and drizzle the caramel sauce over and around the tamales and ice cream. Serve immediately.

TAMALES

We could devote an entire book to the incredibly versatile *tamal*. Tamales are vital components of the Mexican diet. We eat tamales as a main course as well as for breakfast; they are in attendance at every first communion and many other religious festivities.

Essentially, a *tamal* is made with some kind of corn masa paired with any number of additions. That filling is enclosed in a natural (but not edible) wrapper, most often corn husks or banana leaves. In certain parts of Mexico you might come across tamales wrapped in avocado leaves or *chaya* leaves, as well as all kinds of leaves from tropical and subtropical plants. Whatever the filling or wrapper, these little bundles are steamed and served still in their wrapper.

There is no end to the fillings that wind up inside: shredded chicken, turkey, pork, beef, beans, all kinds of stews and vegetables; and so on. Sometimes cheese, olives and assorted fruits join the party.

Americans may not be familiar with the spectacular sweet tamales. They come in many colors, including a lovely soft pink that is achieved by blending ground cochineal into the masa. Producing cochineal, a dye made from a microscopic insect that has been used for centuries to color everything from the human body to textiles and food, is still an important industry in Mexico and Peru. Today cochineal is used in such everyday things as ketchups, Campari, and many of red food items found in supermarkets.

Sweet tamales are made with all types of fruits—most commonly, pineapple, coconut, apples, and pears; some wear a garnish of raisins, prunes, nuts, or candied cactus. Chocolate is one of my favorite versions.

chile-spiked chocolate cakes · BOCAS NEGRAS

I thank my friend Fany Gerson, for creating this recipe for me. The cakes are spectacular served with Cinnamon Custard Sauce or Sweet Tomatillo Sauce, or both, but they are delicious on their own or with unsweetened whipped cream. ▪ makes 8 servings

¾ pound (3 sticks) unsalted butter, plus more for greasing the ramekins, at room temperature

1 cup sugar, plus more for coating the ramekins

6 medium chipotles mecos chiles, wiped clean, stemmed, seeded, lightly toasted, and soaked (see pages 2 and 3)

10 ounces bittersweet chocolate, finely chopped

⅓ cup freshly squeezed orange juice, strained

4 large eggs

4 teaspoons all-purpose flour

Pinch of salt

1½ cups Cinnamon Custard Sauce (page 265), 1½ cups Sweet Tomatillo Sauce (page 263), or ¾ cup of each

With a rack in the center position, preheat the oven to 325°F. Butter eight 4-ounce ramekins (see Note) and coat with an even layer of sugar. Tap out the excess sugar. Bring a kettle of water to a boil and remove it from the heat.

Drain the chiles and put them in a blender jar. Blend with just enough water (about 2 to 3 tablespoons) to make a thick, smooth puree. Pass the puree through a fine sieve and measure out 1½ tablespoons of the sieved puree. Reserve the rest for another use.

Put the chocolate in a large heatproof bowl. Bring the orange juice and the 1 cup sugar to a boil in a medium saucepan over medium heat, stirring until the sugar is dissolved.

Pour the sugar syrup over the chocolate and whisk gently just until the chocolate is melted. Add the butter and stir until blended. Beat in the eggs one at a time, beating well after each. Whisk in the chile paste, then stir in the flour and salt just until no streaks of white remain.

Divide the batter among the prepared ramekins and put them in a baking dish large enough to hold them comfortably (a 13 by 9-inch dish works well). Pull out the rack, put the baking dish on it, and pour enough hot water from the kettle into the dish to come halfway up the sides of the ramekins. Bake until the tops form an even, smooth, firm crust, 30 to 35 minutes.

Serve hot or at room temperature. In either case, unmold the cakes onto serving plates and garnish each with a ribbon of custard and/or tomatillo sauce, if desired.

NOTE: These cakes were baked in 4-ounce ramekins that measured 2¾ inches wide by 2 inches high. Other 4-ounce ramekins or custard cups can be used. Depending on their measurements, you may have to use more than one baking dish and/or adjust the cooking time.

cajeta and cream cheese flan · FLAN DE QUESO CON CAJETA

Mexican flans have a denser texture, sometimes created by blending almonds, pecans, or other nuts into the mix, than French crème caramel or even some of the lighter versions of flan better known to North Americans. In this case, the dense texture comes from the addition of cream cheese. This is a rich dessert, so a thin slice—no more than 1 inch thick—is plenty, especially if served with whipped cream and the almond cinnamon cookies on page 254 (both of which are strongly recommended). Cajeta is similar to dulce de leche, but it is made with goat's milk (dulce de leche is made from cow's milk) and has a little bit of a bite, which balances the sweetness nicely. Dulce de leche has become so popular in North America in recent years that everything from ice cream and chocolates to coffee shows off its rich, caramel flavor. Cajeta can't be far behind, but if necessary, store-bought dulce de leche can be substituted for the cajeta in this recipe; see the Note. ▪ makes 10 to 12 servings

FOR THE CARAMEL

½ cup sugar

2 tablespoons water

1 tablespoon light corn syrup

1 teaspoon freshly squeezed lime juice

FOR THE FLAN

One 12-ounce can evaporated milk

½ cup milk

4 ounces cream cheese, at room temperature

One 14-ounce can sweetened condensed milk

One 10.9-ounce jar cajeta (see Note)

1 tablespoon Kahlúa or other coffee-flavored liqueur

1 teaspoon instant espresso powder

8 large eggs

⅛ teaspoon salt

MAKE THE CARAMEL: Get out a 9 by 5-inch loaf pan (for the best presentation, choose a pan with sharp rather than rounded corners). Combine the sugar, water, corn syrup, and lime juice in a small saucepan and bring to a simmer over medium heat, stirring to dissolve the sugar. Stop stirring and bring to a boil, then cook the syrup until it turns a deep caramel color, about 4 to 4½ minutes. Once the caramel starts to color, lower the heat and watch it carefully—it can go from light to burnt quickly if left unchecked. If in doubt, use a spoon to drizzle a little of the caramel onto a white plate to check the color. When the caramel is ready, pour it into the loaf pan and set the pan on a rack to cool completely.

MAKE THE FLAN: With a rack in the center position, preheat the oven to 325°F. Choose a deep baking pan that will hold the loaf pan comfortably (an 11 by 9-inch pan works well), and set the pan on the oven rack. Bring a kettle of water to a boil, then take it off the heat.

Combine the evaporated milk, milk, and cream cheese in a blender jar and blend together until smooth. Scrape into a medium heavy saucepan. Add the condensed milk and cajeta and heat over medium heat, whisking constantly, until simmering.

Remove from the heat and add the liqueur and espresso powder.

Whisk the eggs and salt together in a medium mixing bowl. Whisking constantly, very slowly pour the cream cheese mixture into the eggs. Whisk gently until thoroughly blended. Strain through a fine strainer into the caramel-lined pan.

Pull out the oven rack and put the loaf pan in the baking pan. Pour enough hot water from the kettle into the baking pan to come one-third of the way up the sides of the loaf pan. Carefully slide the rack back in and bake until the center of the flan is set but still wiggles slightly, about 1½ hours. (Resist the temptation to check on the flan until it has been baked for at least 1 hour and 15 minutes: opening the oven door too many times will cool the oven down and throw off the cooking time.)

Slide out the rack and carefully transfer the pan of water and flan to a rack to cool to room temperature. Remove the pan from the water bath and refrigerate until completely chilled, at least 6 hours, or up to 1 day.

To serve, invert a rectangular or round serving platter over the flan, then quickly and bravely turn the flan upside down—it will slip out of the pan and onto the platter. Let it sit for a minute to make sure, then gently remove the loaf pan. Drizzle any caramel left in the pan over the flan. Cut the flan into 1-inch slices (or, if you like, cut into ½-inch slices and overlap 2 slices on each serving plate). Spoon some of the caramel from the platter over each serving.

NOTE: Cajeta is available in some Latin groceries or online from www.mexgrocer.com. If you can't get it, 1½ cups bottled dulce de leche can be substituted for the cajeta.

CAJETA

Cajeta is caramel made with goat's milk and sugar cooked together over very low heat for many hours (this is why most home cooks buy the perfectly acceptable commercial product found in supermarket). It's a sister product to dulce de leche, which is made with cow's milk and found all over the Spanish-speaking world. In Mexico it is made with goat's milk and called cajeta—from *cajita,* meaning "small box." (Other cultures make something similar and give it another name, such as *arequipe* in Colombia.) I still remember the little round boxes of cajeta, sealed with a colored paper band, that were sold by walking vendors on the highway to San Luis Potosí. With its dark tan color and wonderful smooth and sticky consistency, to my taste cajeta beats any dulce de leche on the market.

almond cinnamon cookies · GALLETAS DE ALMENDRA Y CANELA

This recipe makes a lot of cookies, but if you divide the dough into logs, it keeps frozen for a long time. I suggest you always keep a log in the freezer. Slice and bake as many as you need at a time. ■ makes about 160 thin cookies

3 cups all-purpose flour
1 teaspoon finely ground Mexican cinnamon (see page 16)
½ teaspoon baking soda
½ teaspoon baking powder
½ pound (2 sticks) butter, at room temperature
¾ cup sugar

¾ cup packed light brown sugar
1 large egg
1 large egg yolk
¼ teaspoon pure vanilla extract
Pinch of salt
1¾ cups raw (not toasted) slivered almonds
Confectioners' sugar for dusting (optional)

Sift the flour, cinnamon, baking soda, and baking powder together into a bowl and set aside.

In the bowl of an electric mixer fitted with the paddle attachment, or in a large mixing bowl, using a handheld mixer, beat the butter and two sugars together until fluffy. Add the egg and egg yolk and beat thoroughly. Beat in the vanilla extract and salt. Add the dry ingredients and almonds and mix at low speed just until thoroughly combined.

Divide the dough into 4 equal parts. Roll each one into a log about 10 inches long. Wrap each log individually with at least 2 layers of plastic wrap and freeze for at least 4 hours. The dough can be frozen for up to 2 months.

With the racks in the upper and lower thirds of the oven, preheat the oven to 350°F.

Bake as many or as few cookies at a time as you like: Cut the log(s) of dough into scant ¼-inch slices, and put the cookies on ungreased baking sheets with at least 1 inch between them. Bake until lightly golden brown around the edges, 10 to 12 minutes.

Cool the cookies on the pans for 5 minutes; then, using a spatula, transfer the cookies to a wire rack to cool completely. (If you wait longer than 5 minutes, the cookies will be too delicate to remove from the baking sheets without breaking them.) The cooled cookies can be stored in an airtight container for up to 3 days. If desired, dust with confectioners' sugar just before serving.

THE MATCH GAME

Throughout this chapter, I have offered suggestions for pairing various desserts with different sauces or toppings. Here are a few more ideas for quick and simple desserts.

- With a log of Almond Cinnamon Cookie dough (opposite) in the freezer, you can have an easy dessert in no time. Slice off as many cookies as you like, bake them, and serve them with store-bought ice cream. If you have time, whip up a batch of Sweet Tomatillo Sauce (page 263) or Sweet Raspberry-Guajillo-Chocolate-Chip "Salsa" (page 267), either of which marries beautifully with ice cream.

- Cinnamon Custard Sauce (page 264) can be used to create a simple dessert of store-bought pound cake sprinkled with liqueur, topped with toasted almonds and raisins, and finished with a drizzle of sauce.

- Dress up store-bought chocolate cake with a drizzle of Mexican Caramel Sauce (page 266)—which can be made days ahead and kept in the refrigerator—and some lightly whipped cream.

- For a killer parfait, layer Chocolate Sorbet (page 257) and/or Peanut-Cinnamon Ice Cream (page 262) with Mexican Caramel Sauce and toasted peanuts, salted or not, as you like.

- The plain sponge cake from the Citrus "Three Milks" Cake (page 240) is delicious when split into two layers and filled with whipped cream and strawberries or mixed berries. Toss the berries with a little sugar first, and they will give off delicious juices that will be soaked up by the cake. Top with more whipped cream and berries. Serve as is or, if you like, with the Sweet Tomatillo Sauce.

FROZEN DESSERTS

MEXICO'S MOUNTAINOUS GEOGRAPHY AND ITS LATITUDE result in the perfect conditions for astonishing and incredibly varied crops of fruit. Once a restaurateur (whose restaurant happened to have a pretty bad dessert menu) told me that the best desserts in Mexico are still on the trees! To some extent, he is right; to me, the quality and flavor of the fruits of Mexico have no parallel.

With all these wonderful fruits and other indigenous ingredients—did someone mention chocolate?—Mexicans are constantly creating the must tantalizing collections of frozen treats. Mexico has an old, deep-rooted tradition making frozen desserts. From big cities to small towns, and even at the sides of country roads, colorful ice creams, sorbets, and *raspados* (shaved ice flavored with syrups) are part of our everyday life.

Mexicans also indulge in ice creams made of the most unusual ingredients, such as pork cracklings, corn, or cucumber with chile, mole, and avocado, to name a few. Several large chains of ice cream shops around the country compete to impress their guests with newer, exciting, and sometimes downright eerie additions.

At Rosa, around midsummer, we hold the Festival de los Helados, an annual celebration of the vast assortment of these Mexican treats. On the following pages are a sampling of recipes from these festivals.

watermelon ice · RASPADO DE SANDIA

Raspados are similar to snow cones, but with a coarser and more uneven texture. Carts carrying huge blocks of ice, covered with thick fabric to slow melting, and a variety of sweetened syrups are a part of daily life in the parks, plazas, and downtown areas of Mexico. The ice is shaved by hand into a paper cone, then flavored with one of the syrups, which typically include tamarind, lime, *flores de Jamaica* (hibiscus), and red or white currant. Here is a home version, closer to granita, that makes a flavorful, chile-spiced ice with coarse crystals that melt slowly on the tongue. Line the serving bowls or glasses with thin slices of pineapple or mango, if you like, and scatter a few berries over each ice. ▪ makes about 1 pint

1 cup sugar
½ cup water
6 cups diced seeded watermelon (without rind)
3 tablespoons freshly squeezed lime juice

Pinch of chile de árbol powder (see page 7) or other pure chile powder
Lime wedges

Bring the sugar and water to a boil in a small saucepan over medium heat, stirring until the sugar is dissolved. Remove the syrup from the heat and cool to room temperature.

Combine the watermelon and ⅔ cup of the syrup in a blender jar and blend until smooth, stopping the blender occasionally to scrape down the sides. Pour the watermelon puree through a coarse sieve into a 9-inch square baking dish, preferably glass. Put the dish on a flat surface in the freezer.

When the edges of the ice start to freeze, about 30 minutes, stir the crystals from around the edges into the liquid in the center. Repeat each time the edges begin to freeze. It is important to stir the frozen parts into the still-liquid part of the mixture regularly (before they get too hard to break up), to develop the proper coarse crystals. Total freezing time will be about 3 to 3½ hours. The ice can be made up to a day in advance, but no longer.

To serve, spoon the ice into small bowls or cocktail glasses. Set a lime wedge atop each serving and serve immediately.

chocolate sorbet · NIEVE DE CHOCOLATE

One of the precious gifts to the world is chocolate. In its simplest and most ancient form, chocolate was a drink in which toasted, ground cacao beans were mixed with water, not milk, then foamed and served as an invigorating restorative reserved for nobles, clerics, and governors. (Mixing chocolate with milk is a fairly recent development.) While lean in calories but surprisingly creamy, this intensely chocolaty sorbet packs a double dose of flavor that comes from cocoa powder and chocolate. ▪ makes 1 quart ▪ photograph on page 258

2 cups sugar
1 cup unsweetened cocoa powder, sifted
⅛ teaspoon salt

4 cups water
12 ounces bittersweet chocolate chips or
    bittersweet chocolate, coarsely chopped

Put the sugar, cocoa, and salt in a heavy medium saucepan, and whisk in the water. Bring to a boil over medium heat, stirring to dissolve the sugar and cocoa. Remove from the heat and cool for 5 minutes. Add the chocolate and stir until melted.

Cool the sorbet base to room temperature, then cover and chill thoroughly.

At least 2 hours before serving, freeze the sorbet in an ice cream maker according to manufacturer's directions. Pack into a container with a tight-fitting lid and freeze until firm. The sorbet can be kept in the freezer for up to 4 days. If the sorbet is frozen solid, let stand at room temperature for 10 minutes before serving.

raspberry-rose ice cream · HELADO DE FRAMBUESA CON ESENCIA DE ROSA

The perfume of rose water blends beautifully with the flavor and color of raspberries. Rose water is a link to the Arab influences in Spain's (and therefore Mexico's) history. I love rose water, but some people don't. If you are one of them, simply omit it from the recipe, for a delicious raspberry ice cream. ▪ makes 5 cups ▪ photograph on page 259

Two ½-pint baskets (about 12 ounces)
   raspberries
1½ cups sugar
Juice of ½ lime
2 cups heavy cream

1 cup milk
6 large egg yolks
1 teaspoon rose water (see Note)
¾ cup white chocolate chips or chopped white
   chocolate (about 3 ounces)

In a small saucepan, stir together the raspberries, ¾ cup of the sugar, and the lime juice. Place over medium-high heat and bring to a boil, stirring to break up the raspberries. Adjust the heat so the liquid is simmering and cook for 6 minutes, stirring occasionally.

Strain the raspberry mixture through a fine sieve into a bowl, pressing on the berries to extract as much liquid and pulp as possible. Discard the seeds, and cool the raspberry mixture.

Combine the heavy cream and milk in a heavy nonaluminum saucepan and bring to a simmer over medium heat. Meanwhile, whisk the egg yolks and the remaining ¾ cup sugar together in a mixing bowl until pale yellow and fluffy. Whisking vigorously, pour about half of the hot cream onto the egg yolks in a slow, steady stream (see opposite for more on working with custards). Then pour in the remaining cream, whisking until thoroughly blended.

Return the custard to the saucepan and set over medium-low heat. Stir slowly with a wooden spoon or heatproof spatula, scraping the corners and bottom of the pan, until the foam disappears and the mixture thickens slightly, just enough to coat a wooden spoon and leave a clear mark when you pull your finger through it. Strain the custard into a bowl and stir in the rose water. Place a piece of plastic wrap directly on the surface to prevent a skin from forming and cool to room temperature.

Stir the cooled raspberry puree into the custard, cover, and chill thoroughly.

At least 3 hours before serving, freeze the custard base in an ice cream maker according to the manufacturer's directions. Pack into a container with a tight-fitting lid and freeze until firm. The ice cream is at its best when it has been frozen for 24 to 48 hours. If stored completely airtight, it will keep for more than a week.

NOTE: Rose water is available in specialty food stores and Mideastern grocery stores, and online from www.kalustyans.com.

CUSTARDS

Custards, whether baked or made on the stovetop, play an important role in Mexican desserts. The Cajeta and Cream Cheese Flan on page 252 is an example of a baked custard. Custard-based ice creams, like the raspberry-rose (opposite) and the peanut-cinnamon (page 262), and Cinnamon Custard Sauce (page 264) are the simplest examples of custards made on the stovetop. Whichever type of custard you are working with, here are a few pointers.

▪ Use gentle heat. On the stovetop, that means no higher than medium-low. Custards baked in the oven (such as the cream cheese flan) benefit from both a low temperature and a water bath, which regulates the heat and distributes it evenly all around the baking dish.

▪ Custards are thickened by the gentle heating of the egg yolks. It is important to heat the yolks gradually and not too much. Tempering egg yolks—that is, heating them slowly instead of adding the cold yolks directly to a hot liquid—ensures a smooth, rich custard. An overcooked custard has a telltale scrambled-egg look. Tempering yolks for a stovetop custard is a simple process: First, whisk the yolks well with the sugar in a mixing bowl. Then gradually add the hot cream (or milk, or a combination of the two) to the yolk mixture while whisking constantly. Start with small additions of the hot liquid and increase the amount a little with each addition. Once about half the hot cream has been added, pour in the remaining cream and whisk until the mixture is thoroughly blended and the sugar is dissolved. Now the custard is ready for its final cooking.

▪ Once the tempered egg yolk mixture is in the saucepan, stir the custard constantly with a wooden spoon or heatproof rubber spatula over medium-low heat. Be sure to get into the corners of the pan and all across the bottom—that is where the custard will stick and scorch first.

▪ Stovetop custards are done when they are thick enough to coat a wooden spoon lightly. (Pulling your finger through the custard on the back of the spoon or spatula will leave a clear trail.) Here is another good place for an instant-read thermometer: A stovetop custard is ready when the thermometer, inserted into the center of the custard, away from the bottom and sides of the pan, registers 175°F. At this point, immediately remove the pan from the heat and strain the custard into a bowl. Press a piece of plastic wrap against the surface of the custard to prevent a skin from forming, and cool to room temperature before refrigerating to chill.

▪ Baked custards are done when the edges are set but the center of the custard still jiggles lightly when the pan is moved gently back and forth.

peanut-cinnamon ice cream · HELADO DE CACAHUATE CON CANELA

Peanut butter is a familiar item in any supermarket in Mexico and a favorite among kids. Native to South America and introduced to Mexico in the pre-Colombian age, peanuts are used in a multitude of preparations from savory sauces to cookies and all kinds of desserts. This extra-chunky ice cream, rich with peanut flavor and scented with cinnamon, complements both the Brownie Tamales (page 248) and the Chile-Spiked Chocolate Cakes (page 250). Or serve it garnished with Almond Cinnamon Cookies (page 254) and drizzled with Mexican Caramel Sauce (page 266). ▪ makes 5 cups

2 cups milk

1 cup heavy cream

2 teaspoons pure vanilla extract

2 teaspoons ground Mexican cinnamon (see page 16)

6 large egg yolks

1 cup sugar

¼ teaspoon salt

1 cup super-chunky peanut butter

Combine the milk, cream, vanilla extract, and cinnamon in a heavy medium heavy saucepan and bring to a boil. Adjust the heat so the liquid is simmering and cook for 2 minutes. Meanwhile, whisk the egg yolks, sugar, and salt together in a mixing bowl until pale yellow and fluffy. Whisking vigorously, pour about half of the hot milk mixture onto the egg yolks in a slow, steady stream (see box on page 261 for more on working with custards). Then pour in the remaining cream, whisking until thoroughly blended.

Return the custard to the saucepan and set over medium-low heat. Stir slowly with a wooden spoon or heatproof spatula, scraping the corners and bottom of the pan, until the foam disappears and the mixture thickens slightly, just enough to coat a wooden spoon and leave a clear mark when you pull your finger through it.

Strain the custard through a fine strainer into a mixing bowl. Cool, whisking often, until lukewarm. Whisk in the peanut butter gently just until blended. Place a sheet of plastic wrap directly against the surface of the custard. Cool to room temperature, then chill thoroughly.

At least 4 hours before serving, freeze the custard base in an ice cream maker according to manufacturer's directions just until it is velvety and smooth and has reached a thick pouring consistency. Overmixing can give the ice cream a curdled look. Pack the ice cream into an airtight container and freeze until firm. Stored in an airtight container, the ice cream will keep for 3 to 4 days.

DESSERT SAUCES

the sauces? This section gives desserts their due with sauces that dress up, round out, and distinguish the sweet part of the meal. Some of the sauces are meant to be paired with specific desserts in this chapter, but that is where the fun begins. Consult individual recipe headnotes, the box on matching desserts on page 255, and your own inner pastry chef for more suggestions.

sweet tomatillo sauce · SALSA DULCE DE TOMATILLO

Yes, it is unusual to see tomatillos in a dessert sauce, but if you think of many desserts that balance the tartness of fruits such as green apples and sour cherries with sugar, the idea shouldn't really be shocking. ▪ makes about 1½ cups

½ pound small tomatillos, husked, washed, and coarsely chopped
⅓ cup shaved piloncillo (see page 16) or 3 tablespoons dark brown sugar and 1½ tablespoons molasses
2 tablespoons sugar

¼ cup water
½ vanilla bean, split lengthwise in half
One 3-inch piece of Mexican cinnamon bark (see page 16)

Put the tomatillos, piloncillo, sugar, and water into a small saucepan. Scrape the seeds from the vanilla bean with a paring knife (reserve the pod) and add the seeds to the saucepan.

Cut a 6-inch square from a double thickness of cheesecloth. Crumble the cinnamon stick onto the square, add the vanilla pod, and tie the cheesecloth into a neat bundle. Add the spice bundle to the pan and bring to a simmer over medium heat. Cook, stirring occasionally, until the tomatillos are very soft, about 15 minutes.

Pick out the spice bundle, and transfer the mixture to a blender jar. Blend the sauce on low speed, using quick on/off pulses, just until smooth; the tomatillo seeds should still be whole. Cool to room temperature, then chill for at least 2 hours before serving. The sauce will keep, covered and refrigerated, for up to 2 days.

UNO DE LOS INDISPENSABLES

cinnamon custard sauce · NATILLA DE CANELA

During Mexico's colonial past, egg whites were part of the mixture that plastered many church walls. The leftover egg yolks resulted in a rise in the popularity of this and other custard desserts, such as the flan on page 252. The name *natilla* comes from the word the Spanish use for cream—*nata*. Some people eat the custard sauce—spiked with a little anise liqueur, kirsch, brandy, or dark rum—all by itself for dessert.

▪ makes about 2 cups

2 cups heavy cream
One 5-inch Mexican cinnamon stick
  (see page 16)
Three 1-inch strips lime zest
  (removed with a vegetable peeler)

2 large eggs
½ cup sugar

Combine the heavy cream, cinnamon, and zest in a small heavy saucepan and bring just to a boil over medium heat. Remove from the heat.

Whisk the eggs and sugar together in a mixing bowl until thoroughly blended. Whisking constantly, slowly add the hot cream to the egg mixture. Return to the saucepan and cook over medium-low heat, stirring constantly with a wooden spoon or heatproof spatula, just until thickened, 5 to 10 minutes. (For more on cooking custards, see page 261.)

Strain the sauce through a fine sieve into a bowl. Cover the sauce with a piece of plastic wrap pressed directly against the surface and cool to room temperature. Then chill for at least 2 hours before serving. The sauce will keep, covered and refrigerated, for up to 2 days.

FROM TOP: Cinnamon Custard Sauce, Sweet Tomatillo Sauce (page 263), Sweet Raspberry-Guajillo-Chocolate-Chip "Salsa" (page 267)

UNO DE LOS INDISPENSABLES

Mexican caramel sauce · SALSA DE CAJETA

Caramel sauce of some kind or another is a staple of many dessert cultures. Made with cajeta (see page 253), this silky and light yet intense sauce is a perfect accompaniment for pound cakes and apple pies. It can turn a simple chocolate mousse into a world-champion dessert or drown an ordinary scoop of vanilla ice cream in happiness. It keeps well for up to 1 week in the refrigerator. ▪ makes a generous 2 cups

One 10.9-ounce jar cajeta (see Note, page 253)
1 cup heavy cream
¼ cup milk
½ teaspoon instant espresso powder

Pinch of salt
2 teaspoons Kahlúa or other coffee-flavored liqueur (optional but nice)

Remove the lid from the jar of cajeta and microwave the sauce right in the jar at medium power for 1 minute.

Scrape the cajeta into a small saucepan. Add the cream, milk, espresso powder, and salt and heat over medium-low heat, stirring constantly to prevent scorching, just until the mixture reaches a boil. Remove from the heat and stir in the liqueur, if using. Pour the sauce into a small bowl, cover with a piece of plastic wrap pressed directly against the surface of the sauce, and cool to room temperature. The sauce can be refrigerated, covered, for up to 1 week. Bring to room temperature before serving; if you would like to serve the sauce warm, heat it gently in a small saucepan over low heat until it reaches body temperature or slightly warmer.

sweet raspberry-guajillo-chocolate-chip "salsa"

▪ SALSA DULCE DE FRAMBUESAS CON CHILE GUAJILLO

I created this completely untraditional "salsa" for one of our special Valentine's Day dinner menus. Years after we served that dinner, one of our guests returned to ask for the recipe, saying that the dinner, and especially this salsa, had made a lasting impression. I was happy to come up with a small-batch recipe, and here it is.

▪ makes 2½ cups ▪ photograph on page 265

Two ½-pint baskets (about 12 ounces) raspberries

1 cup sugar

3 large guajillo chiles, wiped clean, stemmed, seeded, lightly toasted, and soaked (see page 2)

¼ cup water

Juice of ½ lime (about 1½ tablespoons)

1 teaspoon Tabasco sauce

1 teaspoon salt

4 ounces small bittersweet (62% cocoa solids is best) chocolate chips or 4 ounces bittersweet chocolate, finely chopped

⅓ cup pecans, toasted and coarsely chopped

⅓ cup dried cranberries

2 ounces dried apricots or peaches, cut into ¼-inch dice (about ⅔ cup)

2 ounces candied pineapple, cut into ¼-inch dice (about ⅔ cup)

Stir the raspberries, sugar, drained guajillos, water, lime juice, Tabasco, and salt together in a medium heavy saucepan. Place over medium-high heat and bring to a boil, stirring constantly to break down the raspberries. Adjust the heat so the mixture is simmering, and simmer for 5 minutes. Pour into a blender jar and blend just until smooth.

Srain the mixture through a fine sieve into a mixing bowl, pressing down hard to extract as much pulp and liquid as possible; discard the solids. Cool to room temperature.

When cooled, stir the chocolate, pecans, and dried fruit into the raspberry-chile puree. The salsa will be thick but pourable. Transfer to an airtight container and refrigerate until ready to serve. The salsa will keep in the refrigerator for up to 3 days. It will thicken as it sits (because of the pectin in the raspberries). Bring to room temperature before serving and, if necessary, thin the salsa by adding water 1 tablespoon at a time.

SOURCES

Cheese Supply
P.O. Box 515
Vashon, WA 98070
www.cheesesupply.com
Features over 700 cheeses—including
Spanish Manchego, which we use in
our Serrano Ham and Cheese
Quesadilla, and queso fresco from
Mexico.

D'Artagnan
280 Wilson Avenue
Newark, NJ 07105
800-327-8246 ext. 0
www.dartagnan.com
An extensive selection of foie gras,
pâtés, sausages, smoked delicacies,
and organic game and poultry—
including Moulard duck breasts, which
we use in our Seared Duck Breasts with
Pecan-Prune Mole.

DVO Enterprises
620 E. Windsor Court
Alpine, UT 84004
801-492-1290
www.dvo.com
Offers dehydrated masa, which is
used to make tortillas, and Mexican
cinnamon—an essential ingredient in
several of our sauces. Also sells
cooking equipment and kitchen
gadgets.

Gourmetsleuth
P.O. Box 508
Los Gatos, CA 95031
408-354-8281
www.gourmetsleuth.com
Sells avocado leaves, banana leaves (to
wrap tamales or for the Slow-Cooked
Achiote-Marinated Pork), dried corn
husks (for our Trout with Wild
Mushrooms), and piloncillo sugar. Also
sells molcajetes, which are essential
for preparing guacamole and salsa.

iGourmet
508 Delaware Avenue
Pittston, PA 18643
877-446-8763
www.igourmet.com
iGourmet sells specialty foods and
many interesting cheeses, including
Manchego and queso Oaxaca, which is
great in our Swiss Chard with Beets,
Queso Oaxaca, and Raisins.

Kalustyan's
123 Lexington Avenue
New York, NY 10016
800-352-3451
www.kalustyans.com
A great resource for spices, herbs, and
Indian and Middle Eastern products.
Sells more than thirty varieties of
chiles, as well as rose water, which we
use in our Raspberry-Rose Ice Cream.

La Tienda
3601 La Grange Parkway
Toano, VA 23168
800-710-4304
www.tienda.com
A wide selection of fresh and preserved
food products and kitchenware not
generally available outside of Spain—
including Maria cookies (used in our
Rice Pudding Cheesecake) and
cazuelas, which are the perfect baking
dish for our Slow-Baked Haricots Verts.

L'Epicerie
866-350-7575
www.lepicerie.com
A gourmet food purveyor with a section
for hard-to-find ingredients. A good
source for mango and passion fruit
purees.

Marky's
687 NE 79th Street
Miami, FL 33138
800-522-8427
www.markys.com
A gourmet food store specializing in
caviar, smoked salmon, foie gras, and
truffles. A good source for squid ink,
which we use in our octopus dish.

Melissa Guerra
4100 North 2nd, Suite 200
McAllen, TX 78504
877-875-2665
www.melissaguerra.com
Located on the border of Mexico, this
retailer provides high-quality Mexican
food products and kitchen equipment,
including canned cuitlacoche, a
delicious filling for quesadillas and a
key ingredient in our Pork Chops with
Cuitlacoche and Roquefort Sauce.

Mexgrocer
7445 Girard Avenue
La Jolla, CA 92037
858-459-0577
www.mexgrocer.com
Offers kitchenware, recipes, cooking
tips, and authentic Mexican food,
including spices and chiles, plus crema
to drizzle over our enchiladas, and
dried hibiscus flowers to make a
refreshing iced drink.

ACKNOWLEDGMENTS

In putting together this book, I discovered that writing, much like cooking in the kitchen of Rosa Mexicano, is very much a collaborative effort.

First of all, I would like to thank Doug Griebel and Dan Hickey, who for the past twenty-five years have kept Rosa Mexicano at the lead of the restaurant community in New York City. They have not only carefully guarded the "Mexicanism" that Rosa is known for but with their hard work and determination made Rosa one of the great restaurants in the nation.

My gratitude goes to Lila Lomeli, who has always provided great advice and friendship. Very special thanks as well to all the team (the family) at Rosa Mexicano Restaurants and corporate offices, for being such good buddies and so supportive.

I owe more than I can express to Chris Styler for writing so wonderfully and dealing with our crazy schedule! My agent, Lisa Queen, and my publisher, Ann Bramson, believed in me. Ann's team at Artisan were dedicated to making this a wonderful book: thanks to Anna Berns, Nicki Clendening, Danielle Costa, Jan Derevjanik, Trent Duffy, and Nancy Murray, as well as Judith Sutton. I couldn't have asked for more beautiful photographs than those shot by Christopher Hirsheimer; her stylist, Melissa Hamilton, helped make my food look extraordinary. Thanks are also due to Sandra Ciklik for her invaluable assistance, and to Bryan Miller for stepping up to the plate at a crucial moment.

Last but not least, thanks and all respect go to Howard Greenstone, Rosa's chief operating officer and partner, an incredible businessman, a comrade, and the most tenacious restaurateur I have ever met.

My days wouldn't be the same without the unconditional help of my partner, Marco.

INDEX

*acelgas con betabeles, queso Oaxaca,
      y pasitas,* 230–31
achiote paste, 12
    -marinated pork,
        slow-cooked, 102–3
    in slow-baked haricots verts, 235
aderezos:
    de aguacate y eneldo, 158
    de cacahuate y chipotle, 151
    de granada y cebolla morada, 61
    de jalapeno, 145
    de limón y miel, 147
adobo(s), 6
    for grilled chile-marinated
        skirt steak, 94–95
    guajillo chile and pineapple, 191
    lobster in "little adobo,"
        for tacos, 106–7
    -marinated chicken quesadilla,
        131–33
    -marinated chicken tacos,
        grilled, 96
    -rubbed chicken steamed
        in parchment paper, 166–67
adobo de guajillo y piña, 191
alambre de camarones, 187
alambre mexicano, 204
almond(s):
    in beef enchiladas with
        ranchera sauce, 121–22
    in chicken hash salad, 144
    cinnamon cookies, 254
ancho chile(s), 3–5
    paste, 5
    reconstituting, for stuffing, 5
    stuffed with beef tenderloin,
        shiitakes, and cremini, 207
    stuffed with tuna and potato
        salad, 154–55
ante de frutas a la Jamaica, 245–46
appetizers, 26–63
    basic ceviche, 29
    basic quesadillas, 44–45
    ceviche verde, 30
    chile peanuts, 77
    coconut ceviche, 35

crab turnovers, 40–41
crisp chicken flautas, 50–52
garlicky shrimp and
    mushrooms, 37
green salsa, 47
green salsa with avocado, 47
guacamole, 73–74
guacamole with fruit, 74
guacamole with seafood, 74
mushroom quesadillas, 46
mushrooms "en escabeche"
    with red bell peppers
    and chiles, 70
pasilla de Oaxaca tomatillo
    salsa, 53
peach pico de gallo, 42
pico de gallo, 57
quesadillas with poblanos, 45
queso fundido, 56
quick pickled poblano
    strips, 43
red masa dough, 41
red snapper ceviche
    with mango, 32
Rosa Mexicano house salad,
    60–61
shrimp with cilantro cream, 36
tomato, avocado, and red onion
    salad, 62
tortilla chips, 77
Yucatán-style baby back ribs,
    54–55
see also soups
apple, lentil, and banana salad, 229
arroz:
    adobado, 219
    amarillo, 218
    blanco simple, 216–17
    con achiote, 220
    verde, 217
avocado(s):
    crispy chicken, and queso fresco
        sandwiches, 138–39
    -dill dressing, 158
    green salsa with, 47
    for guacamole, 73–74

hot soup, 67
tomato, and red onion salad, 62
avocado leaves, 12

bacon:
    pinto beans with onion and, 221
    in Rosa's Mexican club
        sandwich, 137
banana, lentil, and apple salad, 229
banana leaves, 12
    for slow-cooked achiote-
        marinated pork, 102–3
barbacoa, 127
bean(s), 214, 223
    black, sauce, roasted poblanos
        with seafood stuffing and,
        192–93
    pinto, 221
    pinto, with bacon and onion, 221
    presoaking black, 223
    restaurant-style refried, 224
    soupy black, 223
    traditional refried, 224–25
beef:
    in "bald-headed ladies," 135
    and chorizo skewers, 204
    enchiladas with ranchera sauce,
        121–22
    grilled chile-marinated skirt steak,
        for tacos, 94–95
    shredded flank steak
        salad, 153
    slow-braised boneless short ribs,
        199–200
    tenderloin, ancho chiles
        stuffed with shiitakes,
        cremini and, 207
    tenderloin with wild mushrooms
        and tequila, 202–3
beets, Swiss chard with queso
    Oaxaca, raisins and, 230–31
berry, hibiscus, and mango trifle,
    245–46
bitter orange (naranja agria), 103
bocas negras, 250

botanas. *See* appetizers
broths:
    chicken, 66
    epazote, fresh corn in, 68
    for pozole, 196–97
brownie tamales, 248–49
budin, 170–71

cacahuates enchilados, 77
cajeta and cream cheese
    flan, 252–53
cakes:
    chile-spiked chocolate, 250
    citrus "three milks," 240–41
calamari, in roasted poblanos
    with seafood stuffing and
    black bean sauce, 192–93
caldo de pollo, 66
camarones:
    con hongos al ajillo, 37
    con rabos de cilantro, 36
caramel sauce, Mexican, 266
carne enchilada, 94–95
cascabel chiles, 6
cazuelas (earthenware
    casseroles), 17
cebollas rojas encurtidas, 101
cemita estilo Rosa Mexicano,
    138–39
ceviche, 29
    basic, 29
    coconut, 35
    pointers, 31
    red snapper, with mango, 32
    seafood to consider for, 31
    verde, 30
ceviche:
    al coco, 35
    de huachinango con mango, 32
cheese, 13
    and serrano ham quesadilla,
    131
    see also specific cheeses
cheesecake, rice pudding,
    243–44

chicken:
    adobo-marinated, quesadilla,
    131–33
    adobo-rubbed, steamed in
    parchment paper, 166–67
    breast, cuitlacoche-"stuffed," 167
    broth, 66
    crisp flautas, 50–52
    crispy, avocado, and queso fresco
    sandwich, 138–39
    grilled adobo-marinated, tacos,
    96
    hash salad, 144
    in mole for tacos, 127
    in pozole, 196–97
    salad fruit vendor-style, 146
    and tortilla gratin, 170–71
    in tortilla soup, 64
chile(s), 2–11
    ancho chile paste, 5
    disposable gloves for, 9
    heat levels of, 11, 49
    -marinated skirt steak, grilled, for
    tacos, 94–95
    mushrooms "en escabeche" with
    red bell peppers and, 70
    paste, for guacamole, 73–74
    powders, pure homemade, 7
    preparing roasted poblanos for
    stuffing, 11
    reconstituting ancho,
    for stuffing, 5
    roasting fresh, 21–22
    saving and toasting seeds of, 8
    -spiced croutons, 159
    -spiked chocolate cakes, 250
    toasting and soaking dried, 2–3
chile peanuts, 77
chiles anchos rellenos de atun
    con papa, 154–55
chiles anchos rellenos de puntitas
    de res, 207
chiles de árbol, 6
    and tomatillo salsa, 149
chiles rellenos de espinacas, 165
chiles rellenos de mariscos, 192–93

chipotle(s), 7
    -peanut dressing, grilled shrimp
    salad with, 150–51
    -roasted tomatillo sauce, 201
chocolate:
    in brownie tamales, 248–49
    chili-spiked, cakes, 250
    -chip-raspberry-guajillo
    "salsa," sweet, 267
    sorbet, 257
chorizo, 205
    and beef skewers, 204
    in Rosa's Cobb salad, 157
    -turkey enchiladas with
    pecan-prune mole, 126–27
chuletas con cuitlacoche y salsa
    de Roquefort, 208–9
cilantro:
    in ancho chiles stuffed with
    beef tenderloin, shiitakes,
    and cremini, 207
    in cooked green salsa, 114
    cream, shrimp with, 36
    in crispy chicken, avocado,
    and queso fresco sandwich,
    138–39
    in green salsa, 47
    in grilled shrimp salad with
    peanut-chipotle dressing,
    150–51
    in pico de gallo, 57
    in pozole, 196–97
    in red snapper ceviche
    with mango, 32
cinnamon, Mexican, 16
    almond cookies, 254
    custard sauce, 264
    in guajillo chile and
    pineapple adobo, 191
    -peanut ice cream, 262
    in rice pudding cheesecake,
    243–44
    in *salsa dulce de tomatillo,*
    263
citrus "three milks" cake,
    240–41

clams, in roasted seafood-stuffed
 pineapple, 188–90
cochinita pibil, 102–3
coconut ceviche, 35
comales (griddles), 17, 130
condiments:
 grilled corn relish, 228
 pico de gallo, 57
 rajas con crema, 195
 sangrita de Jalisco, 85
 spicy habanero escabeche, 117
cookies, almond cinnamon, 254
cooking techniques, 21–23
 rinsing food, 23
 roasting vegetables, 21–23
corn:
 fresh, in epazote broth, 68
 fresh, tortillas, 92
 grilled, relish, 228
 grilled, street vendor–style, 227
 pudding, Rosa Mexicano's, 226
corn husks:
 dried, 13–15
 for trout with wild mushrooms
  cooked in foil, 177–79
*costillas de cordero con pipian
 de pistache,* 210–11
costillitas con achiote, 54–55
crab:
 enchiladas, 116
 -and-pumpkin-seed-crusted
  halibut, 184–85
 in roasted poblanos with
  seafood stuffing and
  black bean sauce, 192–93
 in seafood stewed in tomato
  sauce, 100
 turnovers, 40–41
cream, heavy:
 in beef tenderloin with
  wild mushrooms
  and tequila, 202–3
 in chicken and tortilla gratin,
  170–71
 cilantro, shrimp with, 36
 in cinnamon-custard sauce, 264

in Mexican caramel sauce, 266
in peanut-cinnamon
 ice cream, 262
in rajas con crema, 195
in raspberry-rose ice cream, 260
in rice pudding cheesecake,
 243–44
cream cheese:
 and cajeta flan, 252–53
 in rice pudding cheesecake,
  243–44
crema, 15
 in "bald-headed ladies," 135
 in crab turnovers, 40–41
 for crisp chicken flautas, 50–52
 in poblanos stuffed with spinach
  and goat cheese, 165
 in queso fundido, 56
croutons, chile-spiced, 159
crust, for rice pudding cheesecake,
 243–44
cuitlacoche, 15
 pork chops with Roquefort sauce
  and, 208–9
 -"stuffed" chicken breast, 167
custard(s), 261
 cinnamon, sauce, 264

desserts, 238–67
 almond cinnamon cookies, 254
 brownie tamales, 248–49
 cajeta and cream cheese flan,
  252–53
 chile-spiked chocolate
  cakes, 250
 chocolate sorbet, 257
 cinnamon-crusted sauce, 264
 citrus "three milks" cake,
  240–41
 custards, 261
 hibiscus, mango, and berry trifle,
  245–46
 Mexican caramel sauce, 266
 peanut-cinnamon
  ice cream, 262

quick and simple dessert
 pairings, 255
raspberry-rose ice cream, 260
rice pudding cheesecake, 243–44
salsa dulce de tomatillo, 263
sweet raspberry-guajillo-
 chocolate-chip "salsa," 267
watermelon ice, 256–57
dill-avocado dressing, 158
dressings:
 avocado-dill, 158
 honey-lime, 147
 jalapeño, 145
 peanut-chipotle, grilled shrimp
  salad with, 150–51
 pomegranate and red onion, 61
drinks, 78–85
 blue margarita, 81
 mango torito, 84
 passion fruit margarita, 81
 passion fruit torito, 85
 sangrita de Jalisco, 85
 soursop torito, 84
 tequila, 83
 the traditional margarita, 78
duck breasts, seared, with
 pecan-prune mole, 172–74

ejotes al achiote, 235
elotes asados con chile, 227
empanadas de jaiba, 40–41
enchiladas, 110–28
 barbacoa for, 127
 beef, with ranchera sauce,
  121–22
 cooked green salsa for, 114
 crab, 116
 green salsa for the table, 114
 lamb, with tomatillo-pasilla sauce,
  123–24
 octopus, with roasted yellow
  tomato sauce, 118–19
 Rosa's pickled jalapeños for, 125
 softening and filling
  tortillas for, 115

spicy habanero escabeche for, 117
Swiss, 113
turkey-chorizo, with pecan-prune
    mole, 126–27
enchiladas, 110–28
    de borrego en salsa de pasilla,
        123–24
    de jaiba, 116
    de pavo y chorizo con mole
        de ciruelas, 126–27
    de pulpos, 118–19
    de puntas de res y salsa ranchera,
        121–22
    suizas, 113
ensaladas:
    de aguacate, tomate, y cebolla, 62
    de camarones con aderezo de
        cacahuate y chipotle, 150–51
    de la casa, 60
    de lentejas, manzanas,
        y platano, 229
    de nopales, 234
    de pollo estilo vendedor
        de frutas, 146
    de pollo rosa, 144
    mexicana Cobb, 157
ensaladilla de elote, 228
entradas. See appetizers
epazote, 15
    in beef tenderloin with wild
        mushrooms and
        tequila, 202–3
    broth, fresh corn in, 68
    in peach pico de gallo, 42
    in soupy black beans, 223
    in trout with wild mushrooms
        cooked in foil, 177–79
equipment, 9, 17–19
escabeche(s), 71
    mushrooms, with red bell
        peppers and chiles, 70
    spicy habanero, 116
escabeches:
    de hongos, 70
    picoso de habanero, 117
esquites, 68

filete de res con hongos al tequila,
    202–3
flan, cajeta and cream cheese, 252–53
flan de queso con cajeta, 252–53
flautas de pollo, 50–52
frijoles:
    bayos, 221
    charros, 221
    chinos, 224
    negros, 223
    refritos, 224–25
fruit(y):
    guacamole with, 74
    mole, salmon with, 175–76
    purees, 16

galletas de almendra
    y canela, 254
garlic(ky):
    in guajillo chile and
        pineapple adobo, 191
    in pozole, 196–97
    in red snapper Veracruz-style,
        180–82
    roasting techniques for, 22
    in Rosa's pickled jalapeños, 125
    in shredded flank steak
        salad, 153
    shrimp and mushrooms, 37
    in slow-braised boneless
        short ribs, 199–200
    in tomatillo-pasilla sauce, 124
    in Yucatán-style baby
        back ribs, 54–55
goat cheese, poblanos
    stuffed with
        spinach and, 165
guacamole:
    basic, 73–74
    with fruit, 74
    with seafood, 74
guacamole:
    con frutas, 74
    con mariscos, 74
guajillo(s), 7–8

and pineapple adobo, 191
-raspberry-chocolate-chip
    "salsa," sweet, 267
guisado de mariscos, 100

habaneros, 9
    spicy, escabeche, 116
halibut:
    peanut-crusted, 185
    pumpkin-seed-and-crab-crusted,
        184–85
    in roasted poblanos with
        seafood stuffing and
        black bean sauce, 192–93
    in roasted seafood-stuffed
        pineapple, 188–90
ham:
    in Rosa Mexicano's corn
        pudding, 226
    in Rosa's Mexican club
        sandwich, 137
    serrano, and cheese
        quesadilla, 131
haricots verts, slow-baked, 235
helados:
    de cacahuate con canela, 262
    de frambuesa con esencia
        de rosa, 260
hibiscus, mango, and berry trifle,
    245–46
hominy. *See* pozole
honey:
    in chicken salad fruit
        vendor-style, 146
    -lime dressing, 147
huachinango estilo veracruzano,
    180–82

ice, watermelon, 256–57
ice cream:
    peanut-cinnamon, 262
    raspberry-rose, 260
ingredients, 2–16
    mail-order sources for, 268

jalapeño(s), 9
    dressing, 145
    Rosa's pickled, 125
jalapeños en vinagre, 125

kitchen equipment, 9, 17–19

lamb:
    enchiladas with tomatillo-pasilla
        sauce, 123–24
    rack of, with pistachio, 210–11
langosta en adobillo, 106–7
lentil, apple, and banana salad, 229
lime juice:
    in basic ceviche, 29
    in coconut ceviche, 35
    -honey dressing, 147
    in margaritas, 78–81
    in peach pico de gallo, 42
    in pickled red onions, 101
    in pomegranate and red
        onion dressing, 61
    in red snapper Veracruz-style,
        180–82
    in shredded flank steak salad, 153
    in toritos, 84–85
    in watermelon ice, 256–57
lobster in "little adobo,"
    for tacos, 106–7

main courses, 162–211
    adobo-rubbed chicken steamed
        in parchment paper, 166–67
    ancho chiles stuffed with
        beef tenderloin, shiitakes,
        and cremini, 207
    beef and chorizo skewers, 204
    beef tenderloin with wild
        mushrooms and tequila, 202–3
    chicken and tortilla gratin,
        170–71
    cuitlacoche-"stuffed"
        chicken breast, 167

guajillo chile and pineapple
    adobo, 191
peanut-crusted halibut, 185
poblanos stuffed with spinach
    and goat cheese, 165
pork chops with cuitlacoche
    and Roquefort sauce, 208–9
pozole, 196–97
pumpkin-seed-and-crab-crusted
    halibut, 184–85
rack of lamb with pistachio,
    210–11
red snapper Veracruz-style,
    180–82
roasted poblanos with seafood
    stuffing and black bean
    sauce, 192–94
roasted seafood-stuffed
    pineapple, 188–90
roasted tomatillo-chipotle
    sauce, 201
salmon with fruity mole, 175–76
salsa mexicana, 183
seared duck breasts with
    pecan-prune mole, 172–74
shrimp skewers, 187
slow-braised boneless short ribs,
    199–200
trout with wild mushrooms cooked
    in foil, 177–79
Yucatán-style baby back
    ribs, 54–55
Manchego cheese, 13
    in Rosa Mexicano's corn
        pudding, 226
    for serrano ham and cheese
        quesadilla, 131
mango(es), 247
    hibiscus, and berry trifle,
        245–46
    red snapper ceviche with, 32
    torito, 84
margarita azul, 81
margaritas:
    blue, 81
    passion fruit, 81

salting glasses for, 78, 81
    the traditional, 78
Maria cookies, 244
masa roja, 41
meats:
    ancho chiles stuffed with
        beef tenderloin, shiitakes,
        and cremini, 207
    in "bald-headed ladies," 135
    beef and chorizo skewers, 204
    beef enchiladas with
        ranchera sauce, 121–22
    beef tenderloin with wild
        mushrooms and tequila, 202–3
    grilled chile-marinated
        skirt steak, for
        tacos, 94–95
    lamb enchiladas with tomatillo-
        pasilla sauce, 123–24
    pork chops with cuitlacoche
        and Roquefort sauce, 208–9
    in pozole, 196–97
    rack of lamb with pistachio,
        210–11
    serrano ham and cheese
        quesadilla, 131
    shredded flank steak salad, 153
    slow-braised boneless short ribs,
        199–200
    slow-cooked achiote-marinated
        pork, for tacos, 102–3
    Yucatán-style baby back ribs,
        54–55
    see also chorizo; ham
menus:
    cocktail party buffet for 8, 63
    grazing dinner for 6, 46
    land and sea for 6, 193
    patio party for 12, 69
    six if by sea, 182
    very vegetarian, 225
Mexican cooking, health
    benefits of, 152
molcajetes (grinding vessels),
    17–18, 75
moles. *See* sauces

mulato chiles, 8

mushrooms:
    and cuitlacoche, pork chops with
        Roquefort sauce and, 208–9
    "en escabeche" with red bell
        peppers and chiles, 70
    garlicky shrimp and, 37
    quesadillas, 46
    shiitakes and cremini, ancho
        chiles stuffed with
        beef tenderloin and, 207
    trout with wild, cooked in foil,
        177–79
    wild, beef tenderloin with tequila
        and, 202–3

natilla de canela, 264
nieve de chocolate, 257
nopales, 232

octopus enchiladas with
        roasted yellow
        tomato sauce, 118–19
onion(s):
    grilled spring, 95
    pickled red, 101
    pinto beans with bacon and, 221
    red, and pomegranate
        dressing, 61
    red, tomato, and avocado
        salad, 62
    roasting techniques for, 22

pasilla chiles, 8
pasilla de Oaxaca, 8
    tomatillo salsa, 53
    -tomatillo sauce, lamb
        enchiladas with, 123–24
passion fruit:
    margarita, 81
    torito, 85
pastel de arroz con leche, 243–44
peach pico de gallo, 42

peanut(s):
    chile, 77
    -chipotle dressing, grilled shrimp
        salad with, 150–51
    -cinnamon ice cream, 262
    -crusted halibut, 185
pecan-prune mole, seared duck
        breasts with, 172–74
*pechuga de pato con mole
    de ciruelas y nueces,* 172–74
pelonas, 135
peppers, bell:
    red, mushrooms "en escabeche"
        with chiles and, 70
    roasting techniques for, 21-22
*pescado en costra de pepita y
    cangrejo,* 184–85
pickles(ed):
    quick, poblano strips, 43
    red onions, 101
    Rosa's jalapeños, 125
pico de gallo, 57
    de Durazno, 42
    peach, 42
piloncillo sugar, 16
pimienta arabe, 190
piña rellena de mariscos, 188–90
pineapple:
    and guajillo chile adobo, 191
    roasted seafood-stuffed, 188–90
    in salmon with fruity mole,
        175–76
pistachio, rack of lamb with, 210–11
plantains, fried, 200
poblano(s), 11
    quesadillas with, 45
    quick pickled, strips, 43
    for rajas con crema, 195
    roasted, with seafood stuffing
        and black bean sauce,
        192–94
    stuffed with spinach and goat
        cheese, 165
pollo:
    adobado, 96, 133
    mixiote de, 166–67

pomegranate and red onion
        dressing, 61
pork:
    chops with cuitlacoche and
        Roquefort sauce, 208–9
    in pozole, 196–97
    serrano ham and cheese
        quesadilla, 131
    slow-cooked achiote-marinated,
        for tacos, 102–3
    Yucatán-style baby back ribs,
        54–55
potato and tuna salad, ancho chiles
        stuffed with, 154–55
poultry:
    seared duck breasts with pecan-
        prune mole, 172–74
    turkey-chorizo enchiladas with
        pecan-prune mole, 126–27
    see also chicken
pozole, 196–97
prickly pear:
    cactus-leaf salad, 234
    cactus leaves, 232
prune-pecan mole, seared duck
        breasts with, 172–74
pumpkin seed(s):
    -and-crab-crusted halibut,
        184–85
    in Rosa Mexicano house salad, 60
    toasting, 60

quesadillas, 130–33
    adobo-marinated chicken,
        131–33
    basic, 45
    how to cook, 130
    mushroom, 46
    with poblanos, 45
    pointers, 44
    serrano ham and cheese, 131
quesadillas:
    basica, 45
    con hongos, 46
    de pollo adobado, 131-33

queso Chihuahua, 13
    for adobo-marinated chicken
        quesadillas, 131-33
    in basic quesadillas, 45
    in chicken and tortilla gratin,
        170-71
    in mushroom quesadillas, 46
    in queso fundido, 56
    in Rosa's Mexican club
        sandwich, 137
    for serrano ham and cheese
        quesadilla, 131
    for Swiss enchiladas, 113
queso fresco, 13
    crispy chicken, and avocado
        sandwich, 138-39
    for fresh corn in epazote broth, 68
    in grilled corn street
        vendor-style, 227
    in shredded flank steak salad, 153
queso fundido, 56
queso Oaxaca, 13, 231
    Swiss chard with beets,
        raisins and, 230-31

raisins:
    in beef enchiladas with
        ranchera sauce, 121-22
    in chicken hash salad, 144
    in poblanos stuffed with
        spinach and goat cheese, 165
    Swiss chard with beets,
        queso Oaxaca and, 230-31
    in turkey-chorizo enchiladas
        with pecan-prune mole,
        126-27
rajas con crema, 195
raspado de sandia, 256-57
raspberry:
    -guajillo-chocolate-chip "salsa,"
        sweet, 267
    -rose ice cream, 260
red snapper:
    ceviche with mango, 32
    Veracruz-style, 180-82

refried beans, restaurant-style,
    224-25
relish, grilled corn, 228
rice, 214-20
    with achiote, 220
    green, 217
    pudding cheesecake, 243-44
    red, 219
    simple white, 216-17
    yellow, 218
Roquefort sauce, pork chops
    with cuitlacoche and, 208-9
rose-raspberry ice cream, 260

salads, 142-59
    ancho chiles stuffed with tuna
        and potato, 154-55
    cactus-leaf, 234
    chicken, fruit vendor-style, 146
    chicken hash, 144
    chile-spiced croutons for, 159
    grilled shrimp, with peanut-
        chipotle dressing, 150-51
    honey-lime dressing, 147
    jalapeño dressing, 145
    lentil, apple, and banana, 229
    Rosa Mexicano house, 60
    Rosa's Cobb, 157
    shredded flank steak, 153
    tomato, avocado, and
        red onion, 62
salmon con manchamanteles, 175-76
salmon with fruity mole, 175-76
salpicón de res, 153
salsas, 49
    cooked green, 114
    dulce de tomatillo, 263
    green, 47
    green, for the table, 114
    green, with avocado, 47
    mexicana, 183
    pasilla de Oaxaca tomatillo, 53
    peach pico de gallo, 42
    pico de gallo, 57
    red, "molcajete," 99

    sweet raspberry-guajillo-
        chocolate-chip, 267
    tomatillo and chile de árbol, 149
salsas:
    de cajeta, 266
    de frijoles negros, 194
    de pasilla de Oaxaca, 53
    de tomates amarillos, 119
    de tomatillos y chiles pasillas, 124
    de tomatillo y chile de árbol, 149
    de tomatillo y chipotle, 201
    dulce de frambuesas con chile
        guajillo, 267
    dulce de tomatillo, 263
    roja de molcajete, 99
    verde cocida, 114
    verde cruda, 47
sandwiches, 134-39
    "bald-headed ladies," 135
    crispy chicken, avocado, and
        queso fresco, 138-39
    Rosa's Mexican club, 137
sangrita de Jalisco, 85
sauces:
    adobos, 6
    black bean, roasted poblanos with
        seafood stuffing and, 192-94
    cilantro cream, shrimp with, 36
    cinnamon-custard, 264
    dulce de tomatillo, 263
    fruity mole, salmon with, 175-76
    guajillo chile and pineapple
        adobo, 191
    Mexican caramel, 266
    mole, 176
    pecan-prune mole, seared duck
        breasts with, 172-74
    pistachio pipian, rack of lamb
        with, 210-11
    poblano cream, for chicken
        and tortilla gratin, 170-71
    for pozole, 196-97
    ranchera, beef enchiladas with,
        121-22
    roasted tomatillo-chipotle,
        201

roasted yellow tomato, octopus
    enchiladas with, 118–19
Roquefort, pork chops with
    cuitlacoche and, 208–9
tomatillo-pasilla, lamb enchiladas
    with, 123–24
see also salsas
seafood:
    crab enchiladas, 116
    crab turnovers, 40–41
    garlicky shrimp and
        mushrooms, 37
    grilled shrimp salad with peanut-
        chipotle dressing, 150–51
    guacamole with, 74
    lobster in "little adobo," 106–7
    octopus enchiladas with roasted
        yellow tomato sauce, 118–19
    peanut-crusted halibut, 185
    pumpkin-seed-and-crab-crusted
        halibut, 184–85
    red snapper Veracruz-style,
        180–82
    salmon with fruity mole, 175–76
    shrimp skewers, 187
    shrimp with cilantro cream, 36
    stewed in tomato sauce,
        for tacos, 100
    -stuffed pineapple, roasted,
        188–90
    stuffing and black bean sauce,
        roasted poblanos with, 192–94
    for tacos, 107
    trout with wild mushrooms
        cooked in foil, 177–79
    tuna and potato salad, ancho
        chiles stuffed with, 154–55
    see also ceviche
serrano chiles, 11
serrano ham and cheese
    quesadilla, 131
shrimp:
    with cilantro cream, 36
    garlicky, and mushrooms, 37
    grilled, salad with peanut-chipotle
        dressing, 150–51

in roasted poblanos with
    seafood stuffing and black
    bean sauce, 192–93
in roasted seafood-stuffed
    pineapple, 188–90
in seafood stewed in tomato
    sauce, 100
skewers, 187
sincronizada de jamón
    serrano y manchego, 131
sopas:
    caliente de aguacate, 67
    de tortillas, 64
sorbet, chocolate, 257
soups, 64–69
    chicken broth, 66
    fresh corn en epazote broth, 68
    hot avocado, 67
    pozole, 196–97
    tortilla, 64
soursop torito, 84
spinach:
    in green rice, 217
    poblanos stuffed with
        goat cheese and, 165
Swiss chard with beets, queso
    Oaxaca, and raisins, 230–31
Swiss enchiladas, 113

tablones de res, 199–200
tacos, 88–107
    chicken in mole for, 127
    dinner party (taquiza), 91
    fresh corn tortillas for, 92
    grilled adobo-marinated
        chicken, 96
    grilled chile-marinated
        skirt steak, 94–95
    grilled spring onions for, 95
    lobster in "little adobo," 106–7
    making and warming
        tortillas for, 90–91
    pickled red onions for, 101
    red salsa "molcajete" for, 99
    at Rosa Mexicano, 97

seafood for, 107
seafood stewed in tomato
    sauce, 100
slow-cooked achiote-marinated
    pork, 102–3
tamales, 249
    brownie, 248–49
tamales de chocolate, 248–49
taquiza, la, 91
tequila, 83
    beef tenderloin with
        wild mushrooms and,
        202–3
    in margaritas, 78–81
tomatillos, 16
    and chile de árbol salsa, 149
    pasilla de Oaxaca salsa, 53
    -pasilla sauce, lamb enchiladas
        with, 123–24
    roasted, and chipotle sauce, 201
    roasting techniques for, 23
    salsa dulce de, 263
tomato(es):
    avocado, and red onion salad, 62
    for red snapper Veracruz-style,
        180–82
    roasting techniques for, 23
    in salsa mexicana, 183
    in tortilla soup, 64
tomatoes, roasted:
    in ranchero sauce, 122
    in red salsa "molcajete," 99
    in slow-baked haricots verts, 235
    in Swiss chard with beets, queso
        Oaxaca, and raisins, 230–31
    yellow, sauce, octopus
        enchiladas with, 118–19
toritos:
    mango, 84
    passion fruit, 85
    soursop, 84
toritos:
    de guanabana, 84
    de mango, 84
    de maracuya, 85
torta de elote, 226

tortas. *See* sandwiches
tortilla(s), 97
    for brownie tamales, 248–49
    and chicken gratin, 170–71
    chips, 76
    for crisp chicken flautas, 50–52
    for enchiladas, 113–27
    fresh corn, for tacos, 92
    making and warming, 90–91
    for quesadillas, 45–46, 130–31
    for queso fundido, 56
    softening and filling, for
        enchiladas, 115
    soup, 64
tortilla presses, 18
tostadas, 96
totopos, 76
tres leches citrico, 240–41
trifle, hibiscus, mango, and berry,
    245–46

trout with wild mushrooms cooked
    in foil, 177–79
trucha empapelada, 177–79
tuna and potato salad, ancho chiles
    stuffed with, 154–55
turkey-chorizo enchiladas with
    pecan-pruné mole, 126–27
turnovers, crab, 40–41

vegetables:
    cactus-leaf salad, 234
    fried plantains, 193
    grilled corn relish, 228
    grilled corn street
        vendor-style, 227
    grilled spring onions, 95
    mushrooms "en escabeche"
        with red bell peppers and
        chiles, 70

prickly pear cactus leaves, 232
roasting techniques for, 21-23
Rosa Mexicano's
    corn pudding, 226
slow-baked haricots verts, 235
Swiss chard with beets, queso
    Oaxaca, and raisins, 230–31
see also bean(s)

watercress:
    in crispy chicken, avocado, and
        queso fresco sandwich,
        138–39
    in Rosa's Cobb salad, 157
watermelon ice, 256–57

Yucatán-style baby back ribs,
    54–55